Sport Education in Physical Education

Sport Education is an exciting approach to teaching PE. *Sport Education in Physical Education: Research Based Practice* presents teachers with a sound framework for developing units of work that will provide their students with challenging and enjoyable sporting experiences and involve them in an array of roles. In Sport Education students are not only players, they also become skilled and knowledgeable as captains, coaches, managers, match reporters and more.

This book provides a complete guide to using the Sport Education model in PE and sport in schools. It includes:

- Key issues in PE such as inclusion, assessment, cross-curricular learning, citizenship and lifelong learning.
- Sport Education in the context of the National Curriculum for Physical Education.
- Real world examples of how Sport Education has been used in both primary and secondary PE.
- Sport Education in the context of games, gymnastics, athletics, swimming, outdoor and adventurous activities.

Sport Education in Physical Education is based upon original research and is the first collection of its kind. It will be an important resource for trainees, teachers and teacher educators looking to try Sport Education in their schools and training institutions.

Dawn Penney is Senior Lecturer at Edith Cowan University, Australia. **Gill Clarke** is Senior Lecturer at the Research and Graduate School of Education, University of Southampton, UK. **Mandy Quill** is a teacher of Physical Education and is Partnership Development Manager for The Hamble School Sport Partnership. **Gary D. Kinchin** is Senior Lecturer in Physical Education and Programme Director for the secondary PGCE course within the School of Education at the University of Southampton, UK.

Sport Education in Physical Education

Research Based Practice

Edited by Dawn Penney, Gill Clarke,
Mandy Quill and Gary D. Kinchin

Routledge
Taylor & Francis Group

LONDON AND NEW YORK

First published 2005 by Routledge
2 Park Square, Milton Park, Abingdon, Oxon, OX14 4RN

Simultaneously published in the USA and Canada
by Routledge
270 Madison Ave, New York, NY 10016

Routledge is an imprint of the Taylor & Francis Group

Transferred to Digital Printing 2005

© 2005 Dawn Penney, Gill Clarke, Mandy Quill and Gary D. Kinchin

Typeset in Goudy by RefineCatch Limited, Bungay, Suffolk

British Library Cataloguing in Publication Data
A catalogue record for this book is available from the British Library

Library of Congress Cataloging in Publication Data
A catalog record for this book has been requested

ISBN 0-415-28967-X (hbk)
ISBN 0-415-28968-8 (pbk)

Contents

Appendices and tables

Appendices

Tables

Preface

In writing this book we faced notable dilemmas regarding terminology, due to inconsistencies internationally. We therefore begin by drawing attention to decisions that we made in this regard. The decisions were not easy and we are aware that some readers will have to realign themselves to unfamiliar terms. We hope, however, that any discomfort will be short lived and that the read will be an enjoyable one. Specifically, we use the term *students* to refer to the children and young people in schools. 'Pupils' appears in some instances where we quote directly from other sources using that term. The terms *training teacher* and *beginning teacher* are used to refer to university or tertiary students currently undertaking an initial teacher education course.

The Editors

Acknowledgements

This book would not have been possible without the cooperation of the schools, teachers and students whose innovative work we report here. Thus, our thanks go to the staff and students at Mountbatten School and Language College; Hamble Community Sports College; Brookfield High School; and Mountfields Lodge Primary School for their commitment to Sport Education and to our writing project. Particular thanks go to the people who joined our writing team as co-authors for specific chapters, namely Valerie Kinchin, Ann MacPhail, David Kirk, Emily Scrivener and Barbara Wilkie. The scope of coverage of school years and activity contexts that is represented in the book would not have been achieved without their expertise and contributions. Finally, thanks also go to our families and friends who have shown patience and understanding for our efforts to complete this work.

Abbreviations

ACCAC	Awdurdod Cymwysterau Cwricwlwm Ac Asesu Cymru (Curriculum and Assessment Authority for Wales)
BAALPE	British Association of Advisers and Lecturers in Physical Education
BERA	British Educational Research Association
BPRS	Best Practice Research Scholarship scheme
BST	British Sports Trust
CSLA	Community Sports Leader Award
DCMS	Department of Culture, Media and Sport
DES	Department of Education and Science
DfEE	Department for Education and Employment
DfES	Department for Education and Skills
DofE	Duke of Edinburgh's Award scheme
GCSE	General Certificate of Secondary Education
HSLA	Higher Sports Leader Award
ICT	information and communications technology
IT	information technology
JSLA	Junior Sports Leader Award
NCPE	National Curriculum for Physical Education
OFSTED	Office for Standards in Education
PEAUK	Physical Education Association of the United Kingdom
PGCE	Postgraduate Certificate in Education
PSHE	personal, social and health education
QCA	Qualifications and Curriculum Authority
RYA	Royal Yachting Association
WO	Welsh Office
YST	Youth Sport Trust

Part 1
Introduction

1 What is Sport Education and why is it timely to explore it?

Dawn Penney, Gary D. Kinchin, Gill Clarke and Mandy Quill

Introduction

Sport Education is now a firmly established curriculum 'model' or 'approach' used within the physical education curriculum setting internationally. The work of Daryl Siedentop (1994) at Ohio State University in the United States of America (USA) has provided the impetus for the development of Sport Education in the USA, New Zealand and Australia particularly. By comparison many teachers and teacher educators in the United Kingdom (UK) are relatively unfamiliar with the term 'Sport Education' and the developments in physical education teaching that it is linked with. In some respects this is surprising. Invariably in recent years the talk (particularly amongst politicians and in government policy documents) has been of 'physical education and sport in schools'. While increasing linkages have long been sought between developments in education and those relating to efforts to enhance participation and achievements in sport, it is only recently that attention has turned to the specific potential of Sport Education to facilitate these linkages.

Developments in physical education are very openly of direct interest to policy makers within central government's education departments and curriculum agencies, and those departments and agencies concerned with the development of sport. In recent years there has been a clear push for 'joined up thinking' in government arenas and greater coherency in developments relating to physical education and sport for young people. Government statements have reaffirmed these concerns and also draw attention to the fact that interests in sport development and sport participation amongst young people are also tied in with interests relating to health and crime. In the foreword to the government's strategy for delivering its sport and physical activity objectives, aptly named the *Game Plan*, the then Secretary of State for Culture, Media and Sport, Tessa Jowell stated:

> The whole government knows the value of sport. Value in improving health and tackling obesity. Value in giving young people confidence and

purpose, to divert them from drugs and crime. And value in the lessons of life that sport teaches us.

(Jowell, in DCMS/Strategy Unit, 2002)

The strategy document confirmed clear *dual* government interests: in developing sport and in developing individuals, communities and society through sport. *Schools*, and their provision of physical education and sport for young people, are seen as the key to both developments.

This policy context in England is one in which it is very appropriate to look at the development of Sport Education as conceptualised and explored in this book. In making that statement we recognise that there are varying understandings of what Sport Education is and 'is about'. This chapter therefore provides some important background commentary on Sport Education, its history and development to date internationally and its potential for adoption in the UK. In relation to the latter point, our aim in this book is to particularly pursue the scope for Sport Education to be integral to:

- the implementation of the current National Curriculum Physical Education (NCPE) requirements in England and those in Wales;
- the fulfilment of National Curriculum requirements in other subject areas (particularly those of personal, social and health education, and citizenship) and for the curriculum as a whole (including established principles for inclusion); and
- work towards examination and other accredited courses in physical education.

The book focuses upon teachers working with the NCPE in England in innovative ways and draws directly upon their accounts of developing Sport Education amidst implementation of the NCPE. The experiences that we describe and the many issues that we raise in relation to the potential development of Sport Education are, however, not only of relevance to teachers and teacher educators in England. Physical educationalists throughout the UK and overseas should find many points of connection with the challenges, dilemmas and realities of curriculum developments that we address. The need for debate about matters such as assessment and inclusion in physical education, the role of the subject in contributing to development of citizenship and other cross-curricular learning, and its role in the development of lifelong learners, is certainly not unique to England. Nor is the need for practical examples of the ways in which teachers are exploring these various contributions and with what effects. Providing such examples has been a priority in producing this book.

In introducing the book it is appropriate to explain our stance towards Sport Education. It is our view that Sport Education offers exciting and timely potential for curriculum and pedagogical development in physical education in the UK and, more importantly, for the development of positive and enjoyable curriculum experiences that relate well to more children's learning needs and interests than may currently be the case. At the same time, however, we stress that in itself the label of 'Sport Education' guarantees nothing in relation to these aspirations. Sport Education is certainly not a magic answer to all or any of the shortcomings that we might see in current teaching and learning in physical education. It is but one model that can be utilised and developed within physical education and that may particularly aid progress towards specific learning outcomes. In looking to its potential development in the UK and, more specifically, within the context of implementation of the NCPE in England or in Wales, we urge critical reflection upon what *in particular* it is hoped will be achieved through the development of Sport Education in physical education. Furthermore, we reaffirm that Sport Education should not be seen as either the whole of or a replacement for physical education. Siedentop (1994: 6) categorically stated: 'I don't advocate that physical education should be totally transformed into sport education.' Undoubtedly Sport Education offers important development potential for teaching and learning, particularly in relation to interests in inclusion and lifelong learning. But realising that potential demands skilful, thoughtful teachers and teacher educators, able to read and respond creatively to the different contexts that they are working within. Indeed, throughout the book we stress that there is not one or right version of Sport Education. Quite deliberately we refer to it as a *framework* that can inform, structure and shape curriculum planning, teaching and learning across the full range of activities that are associated with physical education. Aesthetic activities and outdoor and adventurous activities are firmly embraced in our conceptualisation of physical education and sport and, therefore, Sport Education. The Sport Education framework presented here is one to work from and to develop in ways that are appropriate to each individual teaching and learning context. Thus, a major section of the book is devoted to illustrating the diverse ways in which it is possible but also appropriate to develop Sport Education in physical education, given particular school contexts, teaching and learning priorities, physical resources, staff expertise and group sizes and configurations. So what exactly are we talking about here?

What is Sport Education?

Sport Education originated as a curriculum and instruction model at Ohio State University in the USA. It was conceived by Daryl Siedentop with the objective that children be educated 'in the fullest sense', and to help develop 'competent, literate, and enthusiastic sportspeople' (Siedentop, 1994: 4). In many respects the development was a response to a concern that Siedentop had that the existing teaching of sport within physical education classes was 'decontextualised'. He believed that, 'too often, physical education teaches only isolated sport skills and less-than-meaningful games' (Siedentop, 1994: 8). Siedentop (1994: 7–8) explained that:

Skills are taught in isolation rather than as part of the natural context of executing strategy in game-like situations. The rituals, values and traditions of a sport that give it meaning are seldom even mentioned, let alone taught in ways that students can experience them. The affiliation with a team or group that provides the context for personal growth and responsibility in sport is noticeably absent in physical education. The ebb and flow of a sport season is seldom captured in a short-term sport instruction unit.

Siedentop's aim was to therefore present ways in which children could be offered more 'authentic' learning experiences in physical education. He identified six key characteristics relating to the focus of teaching and learning, its organisation and teacher and student roles, which may enhance the sporting authenticity of physical education. These characteristics of 'seasons'; 'affiliation'; 'formal competition'; 'culminating event'; 'keeping records' and 'festivity' have become identifying features of Sport Education. Below we introduce each characteristic and discuss a number of related issues relevant to the prospective development of Sport Education. Much of the rationale for the development of Sport Education in and through physical education will become apparent. But so too will some of the many questions and dilemmas that Sport Education poses for teachers and teacher educators. Reading about, for example, the use of teams as a grouping strategy and the provision of experiences of various roles raises questions such as 'who picks the teams?' and 'who decides who takes on what roles?' These and other questions are ones that we discuss in the chapters that follow. In Part 2 of the book we address the development of Sport Education in relation to a number of overarching concerns in curriculum planning and teaching in physical education. In Part 3 specific examples of Sport Education developments in a variety of schools, at different key stages[1] and in different activity contexts illustrate that there are no hard and fast answers to many of the questions arising. Rather, the appropriate answers will always be context dependent.

The key characteristics of Sport Education

The key characteristics, as developed from Siedentop (1994), are:

- Sport Education relates directly to a *season of play* and competition in an activity. The overall duration of the unit of activity and patterns of progression within it are designed to mirror the seasonal form and demands of the activity in its 'real world' setting. Units are therefore not confined to a short number of weeks that relate to a half or full term within school, but instead may run across terms and throughout a year. Within the unit, attention will shift from, for example, pre-competition skills and fitness development, to trial competitive games, to participation in a structured series of competitions (as in a league situation), with a view to a culminating competition or festival in the activity.

- Sport Education features a *culminating competition or festival* in a form that will provide for a celebration of the progress that *all* students have achieved through the season and that will recognise the extensive range of learning that has been developed in the season. This relates directly to the various roles and responsibilities that the students will have participated in as members of teams.

- In Sport Education *students are members of the same team* for the duration of the season. This arrangement is explicitly designed to promote cooperative learning and the development of inter-personal and social skills, and give all children a sense of membership and belonging. The team is thus both a supporting structure for learning and a means of prompting responsibility for learning. The team structure is central to a move towards students taking collective and individual responsibility for their learning and the parallel move to teachers progressively taking on a facilitation (rather than direct instruction) role, guiding and supporting students in extending their own and others' learning.

- Within a team *students will take on various roles* relevant to the activity and designed so that teaching and learning in Sport Education clearly extends beyond the role of player/performer in the activity. Activities and participation or performance are set in more of a real life context, with teaching and learning therefore addressing the various roles and responsibilities that may be taken on in that context, including team captain, manager, official, press/publicity officer, statistician and fitness coach. In addition Sport Education embraces roles and responsibilities that are designed to maximise linkages to 'wider learning' and encourage critical awareness of social issues and responsibilities. In Sport Education students will therefore be called upon to be equipment managers or 'the duty team' and to act as 'equity officers' ensuring fair play.

- Experience of *competition* in various formats is an integral part of Sport Education. Formats will vary according to the particular activity and stages of the 'season', and will be designed to facilitate and celebrate learning relating to all of the roles that students have been challenged to take on. Competitions will also always be structured with inclusion and cooperative learning in mind.

- Throughout a Sport Education season, detailed *records and statistics* are kept by teams in relation to various aspects of performance in the activity, with guidance and support from the teacher. The records play a key formative role in teaching and learning, with teams and individual students encouraged to reflect upon strengths and weaknesses in their performances and consider strategies to adopt for collective and individual improvement. Record keeping is designed to emphasise the breadth of issues relevant to performance. It will therefore include, for example, analysis of behavioural issues as well as levels of mastery of specific skills, tactical understanding and ability, and development of particular aspects of fitness relevant to the activity.

- Sport Education is fundamentally about *enjoyment and celebration of sport*. The notion of 'festivity' is a particular focus of attention in the culminating event to the season, but it is also promoted throughout the season and linked to the development of team identities. Teams therefore might be involved in designing their own uniforms (or team strips), deciding upon their team name and a logo and/or maintaining a team notice board.

These characteristics of Sport Education are key elements of the framework, but always need to be considered in relation to a number of *principles* that underpin them. Some of these are already explicit, such as the celebration of sport. But the celebration should be accompanied by a constant concern for inclusion and for experiences of Sport Education to therefore feature some notable contrasts to the 'real world' of sport. Siedentop (1994) was open in acknowledging that elite sport 'is too often tainted with problems that diminish the sport itself, and athletes are often used and abused for economic and political purposes' (p. 5). His emphasis was therefore that within Sport Education 'practices that might harm either individual participants or the sport itself should be reduced or eliminated' (p. 5). These practices include 'an over-emphasis on competition, a win-at-all-costs philosophy, that far too often is related to economic gains that have little to do with sport as sport, or the well-being of participants' (p. 13). He maintained the view (and it is one that we strongly endorse) that 'Junior sport policies and practices need serious examination, serious debate, and continual dialogue. They don't need competing mythologies and unexamined creeds' (Siedentop, 1995: 2) and that 'there is nothing inherently positive about the influence of sport on developing children and youths' (p. 3). His emphasis was 'that sport, properly conceived and conducted, can teach important qualities of character, but these qualities do not come automatically, and there are many negative qualities that poorly conducted sport also teaches' (p. 3). Siedentop was therefore very clear; the model 'is concerned with sport *education*, not merely sport activity' (p. 12, our emphasis). He stressed that Sport Education 'demands full participation at all points in the season by all students' (p. 12), with 'developmentally appropriate' formats of games and competition, and experience of various roles, key means of achieving this.

Sport Education is thus explicitly a model for education 'in, through and about' sport and physical activity (Arnold, 1979; Macfadyen and Bailey, 2001), for *all* children. It is informed by a holistic view of participation and performance in sport that embraces the full range of roles individuals play in sport, and similarly a holistic view of learning. It seeks to actively promote connections between what is so often still portrayed and/or experienced as 'different' learning within the school curriculum,[2] and thus achieve greater coherency in the curriculum. It also seeks linkages between learning in schools and learning and lives beyond them. With this in mind, there is a clear commitment to promoting greater self- and shared responsibility for learning. The intention is that students will be supported in developing the skills, knowledge and understanding to progress their own and others' learning, their participation in physical activity and sport, and their enjoyment of it, within and outside of the physical education curriculum. Finally, Sport Education endeavours to locate learning experiences and participation in physical activity and sport in the wider social, political and cultural context.

None of this is easy to achieve. Our discussion thus far has highlighted that, while it might be fairly straightforward to adopt some of the characteristics of Sport Education in a pragmatic sense, doing so in an informed and committed way is a very different (and demanding) challenge. It is only when the principles that reflect the underlying educational aims of Sport Education are intertwined with the key characteristics that we can legitimately claim to be adopting the Sport Education model or approach. From this perspective 'pedagogy is not only about the *"how"* of teaching, but also the *"what"* and *"why"* ' (Penney and Waring, 2000: 6, original emphasis). Developing Sport Education in physical education is thus not only about new curriculum content, or new curriculum organisation, or attempts to adopt a less directive role in teaching and promote 'child centred' learning and curriculum experiences. Rather, it is about *all* of these things and always with a concern for the individual and lifelong needs and interests of *all* children and young people.

So how has Sport Education been developed and what has been achieved to date?

As stated above, Sport Education's origins and much of its development to date have been overseas and particularly in the United States, Australia and New Zealand. In the main Sport Education has been developed in the context of games teaching in physical education. Yet, while games may seem the most obvious context in which the key characteristics that we have presented can be established, it is clearly not the only context within which Sport Education can be developed. There has been a growing recognition that other activity contexts, including gymnastic and dance activities, fitness activities, modified games and adventure activities, may all prove to be settings well suited to the adoption of the key characteristics of Sport Education and pursuit of its core aims (see Siedentop, 1994; MacPhail, Kinchin and Kirk, 2003). This book is intended to encourage further diversity in the ways that Sport Education is developed in physical education. Arguably the potential for Sport Education to provide a basis for very productive re-structuring and re-orientation of learning experiences in non-game settings, including athletics, swimming and outdoor and adventurous activities, remains under-explored.

In addition it is apparent that much of the development of Sport Education to date has been in a secondary or high school context. There is growing recognition that Sport Education may be equally suited to physical education in primary schools (MacPhail, Kinchin and Kirk, 2003). Sport Education may prove attractive to primary school teachers who are usually better placed than their secondary colleagues to develop the cross-curricular dimension of Sport Education and work towards a culminating event that is a truly 'whole school' occasion. The concern to be developing a range of learning in and through physical education, including social, inter-personal skills and cooperative skills, may also help to alleviate some primary teachers' feelings of inadequate expertise in sport specific skills (see Siedentop, 1994; Strikwerda-Brown and Taggart, 2001; Taggart et al., 1995). In Chapters 8 and 9 we see that, although some may question the extent to which primary age students can take responsibility for either their own or others' learning, the students themselves dispel such scepticism.

Internationally, Sport Education has been used in physical education in mixed and single sex settings, and with pupils of all abilities. Some of the strongest arguments for its development relate to claims that it will have particular benefits for learning and enjoyment amongst those students who may frequently feel marginalised in physical education and/or show limited interest or progress in the subject. There have been some very encouraging reports of Sport Education transforming the physical education experiences of less able children (Carlson, 1995) and similarly succeeding, at least to some degree, in providing enjoyable and interesting experiences for girls who had previously showed little affinity to the subject (Curnow and Macdonald, 1995; Hastie, 1998). In other instances Sport Education has been directed towards students identified as 'at risk' of underachievement in their education and lives, and of developing notably negative social attitudes and behaviours. Further, Sport Education's success in generating renewed interest and involvement amongst these students has been highlighted (Hastie and Sharpe, 1999).

The varying foci in these examples – on those children deemed 'less able', girls and 'at-risk rural adolescent boys' (Hastie and Sharpe, 1999) – draw attention to the need to take a closer look at 'who can learn what' in Sport Education seasons, and whether and how it can provide for the learning needs and interests of all pupils. In 1995 Siedentop highlighted findings of students' particular enjoyment of being on a team and experiencing the benefits of membership and affiliation, of taking responsibility for the non-playing roles, learning from each other, being more supportive of one another, and believing physical education to be more important. But these celebrations of Sport Education need to be accompanied by acknowledgement that some professionals have questioned its ability to effectively support advancement in motor-skill development (particularly amongst higher skilled students) and by a recognition that Sport Education has its own inherent dangers of marginalisation of some learners. Increasing the extent to which students take responsibility for their own learning, positioning them within teams and introducing new roles does not mean that learning experiences will necessarily be any more equitable than those in more traditional physical education lessons. Chapter 4 pursues these issues and highlights some of the complexities of teaching and learning in Sport Education settings.

These references to particular groups of learners also illustrate that both the main reasons behind the development and the manner in which Sport Education has been developed have varied. We therefore now return to the notion of Sport Education being a 'flexible framework', that has been taken and developed in different ways to suit particular curriculum, social, cultural and institutional contexts and the teaching and learning priorities within these. So called 'hybrid' versions of Sport Education have emerged, as developers have seen benefits in combining elements of Sport Education with other pedagogical and curriculum frameworks or models. Two such examples are Hastie and Buchanen's (2001) development of a model termed *'Empowering Sport'*, and Ennis's (1999) development of *'Sport for Peace'*.

Empowering Sport

Hastie and Buchanen's (2000) work combined features of Hellison's (1995) 'teaching of personal and social responsibility' (TPSR) programme with the Sport Education model, to develop a focus on the notion of empowerment in learning and amongst learners. Hastie and Buchanen (2000) explained that TPSR was designed to provide 'a series of learning experiences in which the challenge is to move through a series of goal-levels, which begin with irresponsible behavior and move to caring, giving support, showing support, and helping others' (p. 26). Importantly, the individual (and their responsibility) is at the centre of TPSR, with learning experiences informed by and always directed towards personal behaviour. Hastie and Buchanen saw this as a contrast to the 'sport' focus of Sport Education. Secondly, they identified that TSPR does not have the same formal structure in terms of the games that are included within a lesson, and in relation to the seasonal format of Sport Education. TPSR uses modified and *explicitly* cooperative games, rather than established and 'full' forms of competitive forms of sport, in order to maintain a clear focus on responsibility for one's own behaviour and on caring and support for others. The 'Empowering Sport' hybrid version of Sport Education was therefore designed to explore whether a Sport Education season emphasising 'fairness and appropriate competition' when combined with TPSR's focus on 'self-control and respect' could provide a context in which some of the dangers of producing instances of antisocial behaviour and barriers to encouraging pro-social behaviour, associated with competitive sport, would be overcome (Hastie and Buchanen, 2000).

The season was a 26 lesson season of modified Australian Rules Football and featured the basic phases of skill practice, pre-season and formal competition. Each lesson adopted TPSR procedures to focus on awareness of responsibility issues (and goals) and reflection about achievement of the goals at the end of the session. Team based problem-solving tasks were also developed with some of these specifically addressing TPSR issues. During the pre-season, a playing contract system was established in which teams playing against one another negotiated over some of the arrangements and rules of the game (such as whether the teacher would act as a referee and how many points would be awarded for a goal) and also signed a written agreement to the terms established. Within the formal competition phase, students could self-select to enter a 'time-out' area to recompose themselves if they recognised that they were losing control and moving down in their level of self-responsibility. Hastie and Buchanen were positive about the integration of TPSR and Sport Education that they achieved via new arrangements such as these that brought personal responsibility into focus, but also prompted the students themselves to be taking responsibility in and for their own and others' learning. They concluded that 'the personal well being aspects of TPSR served to improve the quality of the Sport Education season' (Hastie and Buchanen, 2000: 34).

Sport for Peace

While Hastie and Buchanen's study was targeted towards boys, Ennis's (1999) work was directed specifically at disengaged girls. Ennis drew upon peace education theory and Sport Education to develop what she termed the 'Sport for Peace' curriculum. This utilised the basic Sport Education curriculum framework but extended it 'to include a focus on negotiation, care and concern for others, and self and social responsibility' (Ennis, 1999: 36). Teaching and learning directly addressed 'use of negotiation, conciliation, mediation, arbitration . . . ways of analysing conflict, words that lead to conflict, and ways to improve communication, manage anger, and build consensus' and the concepts of care and concern for others (p. 36). Notably, student responsibility (see Chapter 6) extended to the responsibility 'for creating an emotionally safe environment for team-mates and opponents' (p. 36).

Extending the application of Sport Education

In promoting equity and inclusion in physical education, in sport and in children and young people's lives beyond schools we need to acknowledge that there are seemingly all too few examples of the development of Sport Education being extended to extra-curricular (or 'out-of-hours learning') and community based sport settings. This is disappointing given the length of time that Sport Education has been in place within the physical education curriculum in parts of the USA and Australia in particular. Extending the development of Sport Education to extra-curricular and junior community sport contexts seems crucial if its influence is to be anything more than short-lived for many students. Previously we have highlighted that, without this extension, there is a need to be cautious in making claims about the 'authenticity' of experiences provided in curriculum based Sport Education. For many students the Sport Education curriculum experiences may be a stark and harsh contrast to those available to them beyond the curriculum (Penney, Clarke and Kinchin, 2002).

Another area of potential and arguably much needed development for Sport Education is within initial teacher education (ITE) programmes. One of our concerns in relation to the development of Sport Education in England is that the extent of knowledge and experience of Sport Education amongst newly qualified teachers continues to be very varied. Currently there is no guarantee that Sport Education will be incorporated into the university based component of training programmes, or feature in the school based component. If the development of Sport Education is to be success-ful, widespread and sustained, we need to be providing beginning teachers with a sound introduction to relevant pedagogical skills and knowledge. Further we need to be providing structured opportunities for them to try teaching using the Sport Education model. Potentially, some units of work within university based training could mirror the organisational, progression and pedagogical features of Sport Education in schools. Beginning teachers could thereby gain experience of the ways in which the model can be applied in practice and insights into the challenges posed for teachers and students experiencing Sport Education for the first time. In incorporating Sport Education in initial teacher education, opportunities may also be provided to explore 'alternative' modes of assessment in physical education, including journals (see Kinchin, 2000, 2001; see Chapter 4). As interest in and experi-ence of Sport Education grow we will hopefully see the development of more examples of university based Sport Education linked to school based experience of teaching Sport Education (see Chapter 15).

Sport Education in the UK: prospects and potential

Earlier we highlighted our interests in the scope for Sport Education to be integral to teachers' implementation of the National Curriculum Physical Education (NCPE) requirements; accompanying National Curriculum requirements for other subject areas and the whole curriculum; and thirdly, examination and other accredited course provision in physical education. Here we begin to explore that scope, by discussing some of the detail of the National Curriculum and the other courses currently being followed in schools in the UK. We aim to draw attention to a number of points of clear connection between National Curriculum aims and requirements that are being addressed in physical education, and the learning priorities and learn-ing experiences that are central to Sport Education. Thus, our intention is to demonstrate the compatibility of Sport Education and current curric-ulum aims and requirements, and therefore the considerable scope for the development of Sport Education within schools and ITE in England and Wales.

Reforming the curriculum; transforming teaching; transforming learning

In 1999 at the time of the last revision of the National Curriculum in England and Wales, the then Secretary of State for Education emphasised the government's ambition to 'create a nation capable of meeting the challenges of the next millennium', 'raise the level of educational achievement for all young people, enabling them to fulfil their potential and to make a full contribution to their communities' and ensure that young people would become 'healthy, lively and enquiring individuals capable of rational thought and discussion and positive participation in our ethnically diverse and technologically complex society' (Blunkett, 1999). Since then, the government has been pushing forward with structural reforms to the education system in England and further curriculum changes. More and more secondary schools have been designated as 'specialist schools', with a clearly established focus for their 'identity', 'ethos' and development activities within and beyond the curriculum (see DfES, 2002). These schools have been positioned as hubs of new local networks that it is hoped will support and spread innovation in curriculum development and provision for young people that is orientated towards learning as a lifelong activity, not confined to school boundaries or school years. In launching its 14–19 strategy entitled *Opportunity and Excellence* the government restated its vision: 'We want to transform the learning experience for young people, so that they have a commitment to continued learning, whether in school, college or the workplace' (DfES, 2003a: 3). We might add 'leisure time' to this list and, in so doing, highlight that physical education and school sport are arguably key contexts in which the foundations for lifelong learning may be laid. Indeed, throughout this book we explore how experiences of physical education and sport in schools might be 'transformed' through the development of Sport Education, so as to achieve that aim.

Physical education in the National Curriculum

The revised National Curriculum for Physical Education in England sought to clarify the 'importance' of physical education as a curriculum subject. It was explained that:

> Physical education develops pupils' physical competence and confidence, and their ability to use these to perform in a range of activities. It promotes physical skilfulness, physical development and a knowledge of the body in action. Physical education provides opportunities for pupils to be creative, competitive and to face up to different challenges as individuals and in groups and teams. It promotes positive attitudes towards active and healthy lifestyles.

Pupils learn how to think in different ways to suit a wide variety of creative, competitive and challenging activities. They learn how to plan, perform and evaluate actions, ideas and performances to improve their quality and effectiveness. Through this process pupils discover their aptitudes, abilities and preferences, and make choices about how to get involved in lifelong physical activity.

(DfEE/QCA, 1999a: 15)

The new NCPE went on to identify four aspects of skills, knowledge and understanding as the focus for teaching and learning in the subject throughout each of the four 'key stages' of the National Curriculum. The four aspects established were:

- acquiring and developing skills;
- selecting and applying skills, tactics and compositional ideas;
- evaluating and improving performance; and
- knowledge and understanding of fitness and health.

(DfEE/QCA, 1999a: 6)

The NCPE stipulated that these aspects be addressed through a statutory range of activities (the 'breadth of study') set for each key stage. This framework is central to our discussion of the development of Sport Education in schools in England. It is necessarily a key point of reference for teachers considering the compatibility and potential value of adopting Sport Education in their implementation of the NCPE. Although the framework is not the same within the NCPE for Wales, there are some clear points of commonality in the focus established for teaching and learning in the two documents. Rather than aspects, the NCPE for Wales featured statements introducing requirements for each of the key stages and clarifying the focus to be retained across various activities. For example, it is stated that at key stage 3:

Activities should build on previous experiences, extend skills and challenge pupils to refine and apply them in new situations. Pupils should be taught how to analyse their own and others' performance in order to improve effectiveness and quality. They should be placed in problem-solving situations and taught how to plan, make appropriate decisions and evaluate outcomes. They should be taught the rules of activities and how to apply them. Their growing awareness of others' strengths and limitations of performance should be used constructively when working together and in competition. Pupils should be taught to exercise safely and appreciate the value of regular exercise.

(Qualifications, Curriculum and Assessment Authority for Wales (ACCAC), 2000: 10)

Like the NCPE in England, the NCPE in Wales also has a required breadth of study. However, there are variations in both the categorisation of activities and required breadth of study in the two countries. For key stage 1 the requirement in England is that children will be taught the knowledge, skills and understanding (relating to the four aspects) through dance activities, games activities and gymnastic activities. In key stage 2, teaching must *additionally* feature two activities from swimming activities and water safety; athletic activities; and outdoor and adventurous activities. Swimming activities and water safety must be included unless the key stage 2 requirements have been completed in advance through development of this area of activity in key stage 1. In key stage 3 the required breadth of study is four areas of activity, comprising games activities and three areas from dance activities, gymnastic activities, swimming activities and water safety, athletic activities, and outdoor and adventurous activities, with at least one of the three chosen being either dance activities or gymnastic activities. Finally, at key stage 4, the required breadth of study is any two of the six areas of activity (DfEE/QCA, 1999a).

One of the notable contrasts in Wales is that specific requirements have been established for 'health-related exercise' in addition to areas of activity that are broadly comparable to those in England. At key stage 1 in Wales children should therefore be taught health related exercise and three areas of activity: games, gymnastic activities and dance. The option to begin to fulfil key stage 2 requirements for swimming is also highlighted. At key stage 2 the requirement is health related exercise and five areas: games, gymnastic activities, dance, swimming and either athletic activities or outdoor and adventurous activities. In key stage 3 the requirements in Wales mirror those in England in singling out games as a compulsory area. This should be accompanied by health related exercise, plus *either* gymnastic activities or dance and, *in addition*, one of swimming, athletic activities or outdoor and adventurous activities. At key stage 4 requirements in Wales clearly deviate from those in England. Health related exercise is retained but now must be accompanied by two activities from one or more of four 'areas of experience', comprising 'sport' (defined as having a competitive focus); 'dance' (defined as having an artistic and aesthetic focus); 'adventure activities'; and 'exercise activities' (defined as being 'non-competitive forms of exercise') (ACCAC, 2000).

Returning to the four aspects within the NCPE in England, an important point to highlight in relation to our interest in Sport Education is the way in which, particularly at key stage 4, it is emphasised that teaching and learning should not be confined to pupils' personal development as performers. The following extracts from the requirements for key stage 4 are arguably closely aligned with characteristics and goals of Sport Education:

- Selecting and applying skills, tactics and compositional ideas: Pupils should be taught to:
    - use advanced strategic and/or choreographic and organisational concepts and principles;

- apply rules and conventions for different activities;
- Evaluating and improving performance: Pupils should be taught to:
    - make informed choices about what role they want to take in each activity;
    - judge how good performance is and decide how to improve it;
    - prioritise and carry out these decisions to improve their own and others' performances;
    - develop leadership skills;
- Knowledge and understanding of fitness and health: Pupils should be taught:
    - how preparation, training and fitness relate to and affect performance;
    - how to design and carry out activity and training programmes that have specific purposes.

(DfEE/QCA, 1999a: 23)

These requirements signalled an important extension of the breadth of learning addressed within the NCPE in England. They also provided very clear connections between the NCPE and an expanding range of accredited courses for physical education and newly established National Curriculum requirements for citizenship. Accredited courses in physical education now include General Certificate of Secondary Education (GCSE) examination courses for physical education and dance, and courses directed towards leadership and/or volunteering and coaching roles. Many secondary schools now provide opportunities for students to gain the British Sport Trust Junior Sports Leader Awards (JSLA) and/or the Duke of Edinburgh's (DofE) awards that focus on community based volunteer work, and the organisation of and participation in an outdoor expedition (see chapter 7). In Part 3 of this book we expand upon particular National Curriculum requirements and accredited course requirements with which linkages are being made in specific developments of Sport Education. In Chapter 6 we particularly explore linkages between physical education and citizenship education. At this point, we reaffirm the relevance of Sport Education to interests in fulfilling National Curriculum, examination and accredited course requirements by highlighting that in Sport Education it is intended that students will:

- Develop skills and fitness specific to particular sports.
- Appreciate and be able to execute strategic play in sports.
- Participate at a level appropriate to their stage of development.
- Share in the planning and administration of sport experiences.
- Provide responsible leadership.
- Work effectively within a group towards common goals.
- Appreciate the rituals and conventions that give particular sports their unique meanings.
- Develop the capacity to make reasoned decisions about sport issues.

- Develop and apply knowledge about umpiring, refereeing and training.
- Decide voluntarily to become involved in after-school sport.

(Siedentop, 1994: 4–5)

Throughout the book we stress a need to be looking beyond the immediacy of subject. We note that the NCPE requirements and framework discussed above were set alongside a number of other, broader commitments and interests, running throughout the curriculum and for all subjects to address. Introducing the new National Curriculum, the Secretary of State for Education and Chair of the Qualifications and Curriculum Authority (QCA) stated that the focus of this National Curriculum, together with the wider school curriculum, was:

- to ensure that pupils develop from an early age the essential literacy and numeracy skills they need to learn;
- to provide them with a guaranteed, full and rounded entitlement to learning;
- to foster their creativity; and
- to give teachers discretion to find the best ways to inspire in pupils a joy and commitment to learning that will last a lifetime.

(Blunkett and Stubbs in DfEE/QCA, 1999a: 3)

These interests were specifically reinforced through prompts for all subjects to address as follows:

- their contribution to pupils' 'spiritual, moral, social and cultural development';
- their provision of clear opportunities for pupils to develop a number of identified 'key skills': communication, application of number, information technology, working with others, improving own learning and performance, and problem solving;
- their provision of opportunities for pupils to develop thinking skills, 'financial capability' and 'enterprise and entrepreneurial skills', to experience work related learning and develop their knowledge and understanding of 'education for sustainable development';
- their contribution to teaching and learning relating to the use of language and information and communication technology; and
- the new statutory requirement to apply three 'principles of inclusion': 'setting suitable learning challenges'; 'responding to pupils' diverse learning needs'; and 'overcoming potential barriers to learning and assessment for individuals and groups of pupils'.

(see DfEE/QCA, 1999a, 1999b)

As we have indicated above, these wider interests have since been reiterated in the government's outline of its '14–19 strategy'. This stressed that 'the curriculum and assessment arrangements must emphasise and promote competence in analysis, problem-solving and thinking, so that young people have the confidence to explain and defend their conclusions' (DfES, 2003a: 3). It also highlighted the government's interest in strengthening the cross-curricular dimension of teaching and learning and specifically mentioned both physical education and citizenship as areas for development in this regard. Interests in 'lifelong engagement' with learning were reaffirmed. The government stated its concern that, during the 14–19 years, all students will 'continue to learn to be responsible and healthy adults' (DfES, 2003b: 6), and that they 'should be involved in wider activities and experience beyond the curriculum, including volunteering, which can enrich learning, whilst developing and expressing creative and practical skills and interests' (p. 22). The government made clear that its desire is to see 'students whose potential has been developed through a broader education with the skills, experience and personal development to play a full part in society and to contribute to a productive economy' (DfES, 2003b: 15), with far greater coherence in education provision, experiences and learning through the 14–19 years and across different sites of learning.

Conclusion

The chapters that follow represent a timely, critical and reflective investigation of the extent to which physical education can justifiably claim to be engaging with educational (and individual) needs and interests that go across the curriculum and run throughout lives. As stressed above, we are not presenting Sport Education as an alternative to physical education. We are investigating whether and in what ways and in what contexts it may help to advance and strengthen teaching and learning for *all* in physical education, amidst continuing observations of, for example:

- an over-riding focus on highly specific motor-skill development and comparable lack of attention to other aspects of learning that physical education claims/aims to address – and is required to address in the context of the NCPE and accredited courses (such as GCSE and JSLA);[3]
- a dominance of directed teaching approaches with relatively few opportunities provided for children to take responsibility in learning (and to be supported in developing this ability);[4]
- physical education failing to engage some children (with girls and students with lower motor-skill ability frequently identified) and many young people disengaging with physical activity and sport either during or immediately after their school years;[5]
- learning experiences within physical education and across the curriculum being recognised as notably 'divided' and lacking in coherency from the learner's perspective (see Note 2).

Again, it is important to counter notions of easy answers to all the short-comings of physical education. As we will see, Sport Education has its own potential shortcomings and pitfalls. We are as concerned to address and illustrate those 'in practice' as we are to demonstrate its positive potential. Furthermore we are interested in pushing the boundaries of thinking and practice in Sport Education and physical education. At several points we discuss ideas that we have not yet had the opportunity to explore in practice, but that we hope will be taken up by readers. With these hopes and challenges in mind, the following chapter turns attention to issues involved in developing research based practice that integrates research and curriculum and pedagogical innovation, and in supporting both teachers and young people as researchers in schools.

Notes

1 The requirements within the National Curriculum and expectations regarding attainment are presented in relation to four key stages that relate to the compulsory years of education. Key stage 1 covers education to age 7 years, key stage 2 age 7–11 years, key stage 3 age 11–14 years and key stage 4 age 14–16 years.
2 Griffith (2000) has provided case studies of the fragmented nature of children's curriculum experiences in key stages 3 and 4. Arguably, fragmentation within physical education is as much a concern as that in the secondary curriculum as a whole. Harland et al.'s (2002) longitudinal study of learning through the key stage 3 curriculum in Northern Ireland highlighted that 'Lesson-to-lesson pupils generally felt that their subjects followed on, though least "follow-on" was observed in several practical subjects, especially PE and music' (p. iv).
3 See Laker (2000) and OFSTED (2002a, 2000b) for further discussion of this point.
4 The 2000/01 physical education subject inspection report for the secondary years stated that 'in some lessons, particularly at key stage 3, there is too much teacher direction and control. As a result the pace of learning is modest and pupils do not always have a clear idea of the objectives for the lesson and what they were aiming to achieve' (OFSTED, 2002b: 2).
5 See, for example, Bedward and Williams (2000), Penney and Harris (1997), Bass and Cale (1999), Roberts (1996).

References

Awdurdod Cymwysterau Cwricwlwm Ac Asesu Cymru (ACCAC) (2000). *Physical Education in the National Curriculum in Wales*, Cardiff: ACCAC.
Arnold, P. J. (1979). *Meaning in Movement: Sport and Physical Education*, London: Heinemann.
Bass, D. and Cale, L. (1999). Promoting Physical Activity through the Extra-curricular Programme, *European Journal of Physical Education*, 4, pp. 45–64.
Bedward, J. and Williams, A. (2000). Girls' Experience of Physical Education: Voting with their Feet?, in A. Williams (ed.), *Primary School Physical Education: Research into Practice*, London: Routledge Falmer Press.
Blunkett, D. (1999). Letter of introduction in QCA (1999) *The Review of the National Curriculum in England: The Secretary of State's Proposals*, London: QCA.

Carlson, T. (1995). 'Now I Think I Can': The Reaction of Year Eight Low-skilled Students to Sport Education, *Australian Council for Health, Physical Education and Recreation (ACHPER) Healthy Lifestyles Journal*, 42, 4, pp. 6–8.

Curnow, J. and Macdonald, D. (1995). Can Sport Education Be Gender Inclusive? A Case Study in an Upper Primary School, *Australian Council for Health, Physical Education and Recreation (ACHPER) Healthy Lifestyles Journal*, 42, 4, pp. 9–11.

Department of Culture, Media and Sport (DCMS)/Strategy Unit (2002). *Game Plan: A Strategy for Delivering Government's Sport and Physical Activity Objectives*, London: Strategy Unit.

Department for Education and Employment (DfEE)/Qualifications and Curriculum Authority (QCA) (1999a). *Physical Education: The National Curriculum for England*, London: DfEE.

Department for Education and Employment (DfEE)/Qualifications and Curriculum Authority (QCA) (1999b). *Citizenship: The National Curriculum for England*, London: DfEE.

Department for Education and Skills (DfES) (2002). *Education and Skills: Investment for Reform*, London: DfES.

Department for Education and Skills (2003a). *14–19: Opportunity and Excellence: Summary*, London: DfES.

Department for Education and Skills (2003b). *14–19: Opportunity and Excellence*, London: DfES.

Ennis, C. (1999) Creating a Culturally Relevant Curriculum for Disengaged Girls, *Sport, Education and Society*, 4, 1, pp. 31–49.

Griffith, R. (2000). *National Curriculum: National Disaster? Education and Citizenship*, London: Routledge.

Harland, J., Moor, H., Kinder, K. and Ashworth, M. (2002). *Is the Curriculum Working? The Key Stage 3 Northern Ireland Curriculum Cohort Study*, Slough, UK: National Foundation for Educational Research.

Hastie, P. (1998). The Participation and Perception of Girls within a Unit of Sport Education, *Journal of Teaching Physical Education*, 17, pp. 157–71.

Hastie, P. and Buchanen, A. M. (2000). Teaching Responsibility through Sport Education: Prospects of a Coalition, *Research Quarterly for Exercise and Sport*, 71, 1, pp. 25–35.

Hastie, P. and Sharpe, T. (1999). Effects of a Sport Education Curriculum on the Positive Social Behaviour of At-Risk Rural Adolescent Boys, *Journal of Education for Students Placed at Risk*, 4, 4, pp. 417–30.

Hellison, D. (1995). *Teaching Responsibility through Physical Activity*, Champaign, Illinois: Human Kinetics.

Kinchin, G. D. (2000). Tackling Social Issues in Physical Education Class: What about Journal Writing?, *Strategies*, May/June, pp. 22–5.

Kinchin, G. D. (2001). Using Team Portfolios during a Sport Education Volleyball Season, *Journal of Physical Education, Recreation, and Dance*, 72, 2, pp. 41–4.

Laker, A. (2000). *Beyond the Boundaries of Physical Education: Educating Young People for Citizenship and Social Responsibility*, London: Routledge Falmer Press.

Macfadyen, T. and Bailey, R. (2001). Physical Education: Make or Break in a New Century? A Consideration of Some of the Key Issues Surrounding Secondary Physical Education, *British Association of Advisers and Lecturers in Physical Education (BAALPE) Bulletin of Physical Education*, 37, 3, pp. 205–32.

MacPhail, A., Kinchin, G. and Kirk, D. (2003). Students' conceptions of sport and Sport Education, *European Physical Education Review*, 9, 3, pp. 285–300.

Office for Standards in Education (OFSTED) (2002a). *Primary Subject Reports 2000/01: Physical Education* (HMI 365), London: OFSTED.

Office for Standards in Education (OFSTED) (2002b). *Secondary Subject Reports 2000/01: Physical Education* (HMI 381), London: OFSTED.

Penney, D. and Harris, J. (1997). Extra-curricular Physical Education: More of the Same for the More Able? *Sport, Education and Society*, 2, 1, pp. 41–54.

Penney, D. and Waring, M. (2000). The Absent Agenda: Pedagogy and Physical Education, *Journal of Sport Pedagogy*, 6, 1, pp. 4–37.

Penney, D., Clarke, G. and Kinchin, G. (2002). Developing Physical Education as a 'Connective Specialism' (Young, 1998): Is Sport Education the Answer?, *Sport, Education and Society*, 7, 1, pp. 55–64.

Roberts, K. (1996). Young People, Schools, Sport and Government Policy, *Sport, Education and Society*, 1, 1, pp. 47–57.

Siedentop, D. (1994). *Sport Education: Quality PE through Positive Sport Experiences*, Champaign, Illinois: Human Kinetics.

Siedentop, D. (1995). Junior Sport and the Evolution of Sport Cultures, Paper presented to the Junior Sport Forum, Auckland, New Zealand, November 1995.

Strikwerda-Brown, J. and Taggart, A. (2001). No Longer Voiceless and Exhausted: Sport Education and the Primary Generalist Teacher, *Australian Council for Health, Physical Education and Recreation (ACHPER) Healthy Lifestyles Journal*, 48, 3–4, pp. 14–17.

Taggart, A., Medland, A. and Alexander, K. (1995). 'Goodbye Superteacher!' Teaching Sport Education in the Primary School, *Australian Council for Health, Physical Education and Recreation (ACHPER) Healthy Lifestyles Journal*, 42, 4, pp. 16–18.

2   Researching Sport Education

Partnerships in action

*Dawn Penney, Gill Clarke and
Mandy Quill*

Introduction

> Contributing to research-based knowledge is not an aspiration which all
> educational institutions, teachers and learners will share. On the other
> hand, if research is to be seen as useful for learning and teaching, then a
> basic aspiration of researchers in this field must be that the learning
> teacher, the learning learner and especially the learning school will be
> learning from, among other things, research.
>
> (McIntyre and McIntyre, 2002: 4)

In this chapter we discuss the process of developing physical education
through school based research. Significantly this has been the basis for the
work reported in this book. Our intention is to encourage critical reflection
and much needed debate about how we view research, what we understand it to be, when it can occur and who can undertake it. It is our contention that establishing teacher-led research in schools, developing 'teachers
as researchers' and thus embedding research in teaching and curriculum
development demand that we challenge many commonly held perceptions
of research. Here we therefore describe the respective roles of university
based researchers, teachers and students in research that, as a research team,
we were agreed should be undertaken as a *collaborative endeavour*. The intention was never to do research 'on' Sport Education in schools, or 'on'
teachers, or 'on' students. Rather, the hope was to develop a set of relations
and roles that would involve university researchers working *with* teachers,
and teachers and in some instances university researchers working *with* students in developing Sport Education as a research based innovation in
schools.

Such an approach is not easy or straightforward. In a review of teaching
and learning research capacity in the UK, this type of research was identified as 'the most difficult sub-field to conceptualise and in which to see a
clear way forward' (McIntyre and McIntyre, 2002: 4). Such research cannot
be rigidly structured or neatly sequenced. Research undertaken from this
collaborative stance and as an integral rather than separate element of

curriculum development is necessarily highly flexible and responsive to many emerging issues. For everyone involved the Sport Education experience has been a learning process that is ongoing and continues to be challenging but one that is also rewarding.

Much of the impetus and support for our research has come from a government initiative specifically designed to offer teachers the opportunity to undertake research within schools with support from university based researchers. As McNamara (2002) observed, the DfES Best Practice Research Scholarships[1] 'were seen as promising models of evidence-based practice grounded securely in practice-based evidence' (p. 25). In Part 3 particularly, readers will be able to judge for themselves whether the scholarships awarded to Mandy Quill to work with Gill Clarke at the University of Southampton have fulfilled this promise.

Collaboration and partnerships in research

We have already indicated the need to closely investigate the nature of collaboration and partnerships within research. It is naïve and unrealistic to think of collaborators as 'equal partners'. As Stronach and McNamara (2002) explain: 'As with most things in education, the notion [of partnership] is both complicated and contradictory' (p. 155). ' "Partnership" is not really about consensus. Rather, it is a paradox – more like a managed difference or productive dissonance. And that becomes a problem only when partnership is portrayed as unproblematic, because hidden in the pretence is a power-play' (p. 156). Here it is acknowledged that the various partners will have different interests in and hopes for the research. They may have different motivations for becoming involved, different priorities for what to focus upon, different views in relation to how quickly or otherwise projects should progress, the investment of time and resources that is justified and/or the form that 'findings' and reporting need to take. This may seem to present a situation in which research will be a non-starter, but quite the opposite is true. If collaboration is to be positive for all involved, then addressing the differing perspectives, circumstances and expertise of all the partners is a critical first step. It is the only sound basis upon which to advance. It demands that, when we talk of research being 'collaborative', we need to question 'on what and whose terms?' and 'with what and whose agendas in mind?'

From the outset and throughout our research we have tried to be open about these matters and to foster a climate in which, without hesitancy, we can voice concerns or make suggestions. As in any relationship, trust and mutual respect have to be at the heart of the research relationship. In this chapter we explain some of what that has demanded from us. We are certainly not implying that we have achieved the ideal. We continue to build our relationships and reflect critically upon a number of key aspects of involvement and ownership in research including:

- the agendas or issues that are addressed;
- the methods that may be used;
- who plays what roles and has what responsibilities at various points in the research; and
- the ways in which the findings arising can actively inform ongoing curriculum development while also reaching wider professional and academic audiences.

Rethinking research and rethinking roles

> . . . an emphasis on teachers and schools as the agents of research, and of specific institutions or local contexts as the primary beneficiaries, implies some merging or at least some redefinition of the roles of schools and of academic researchers. It does not imply any diminution in the need for rigour in research on teaching and learning, but it does suggest the critical importance of partnerships between researching schools and academic research institutions. Capacity both for such research and for its use must depend on how the work of these partnerships becomes part of a redefinition of the work of each of the collaborating institutions.
>
> (McIntyre and McIntyre, 2002: 4)

Universities: facilitating, guiding and supporting school based teacher-research

From the university researchers' perspective, committing to and fulfilling a 'guiding and supporting' role is not without problems. The pressures to progress projects rapidly and then generate outputs in the form of articles submitted to academic journals, over and above professional publications, presentations or other form of collaborative dissemination and learning (such as joint in-service workshops), are all too real. Involvement in research with schools and teachers that is fundamentally concerned with curriculum and pedagogical development in those schools and the professional development of the teachers involved is therefore potentially fraught with tensions for university staff. We have strong commitments to actively encourage, prompt and directly support the development of practices in physical education that challenge and at the same time build upon established practice, specifically with interests in equity and inclusion in mind. But those commitments are necessarily accompanied (and to a degree always compromised) by parallel concerns to pursue the same agendas in very different arenas and via different means. Producing this book is a part of the balancing act that we try to play between professional commitments and expectations of us as university academics.[2] At times the context that we work in seems notably unsupportive of collaborative endeavours and of moves to deconstruct divisions between university academics and teachers.

More practically, adopting a 'guiding and supporting' role has involved something of a retreat from more familiar ones of directing, leading and 'doing' research. It has required us to take a step back and be willing to do so – and thus have faith in teachers 'as researchers'. It has meant acknowledging that, if we are serious in our interests to embed research in practice, it will not and cannot follow neat and clinical patterns of development. It has to be adaptive to the ever changing and always unpredictable contexts of schools and schooling. Adaptation and responsiveness thus become essential characteristics of school based research, not things that will deem the research invalid or as having failed. In stressing adaptation and responsiveness we are not, however, advocating 'no structure' or an absence of planning. The development of school based teacher-research demands much prior thought and planning. Furthermore it requires that we reconsider issues of 'what is data', of how, when and by whom it can be collected, of who can be researchers, and of the forms in which 'findings' can and should be shared with others. This takes nothing away from the fact that an essential characteristic of research is rigour. Clear, detailed forward planning, albeit with an essential element of in-built flexibility, is essential for successful research and arguably particularly so in collaborative research. Prompting and supporting this planning process is a key role for university staff supporting teacher-research. It is also one of the most difficult roles. Time for any sort of planning in schools, let alone 'research planning', is scarce. In addition, teachers (like many other researchers) may feel a need to be 'getting on with the research' and not see thorough planning as part of that progress. Further, within a school year the opportunities for data collection and for advances to be made in curriculum developments are clearly limited. There are dangers that data collection will start before the focus of the research project has been adequately discussed or a number of other key issues addressed. Clarifying the focus of investigations (and therefore reaching agreement on this within schools and with partners) is essential if appropriate decisions are to be made about when, where and how data is collected, from whom and by whom. Equally there is the prospect that data will be collected before anyone has really thought through what will be done with it and whether anyone will be able to transfer the data into easily accessible findings that can actively feed into curriculum development processes and forums. University staff may be able to take on some of the collation and analysis of data. However, if the aim is to support the development of research in schools and the integration of research with practice, then there are important arguments for ensuring that data stays firmly within the school, organised and analysed by teachers, support staff and potentially also students.

Needless to say, time returns as our major concern: time for teachers to work with university staff to develop the skills, knowledge and understanding to do this, and then time 'as researchers' in their schools to be doing it. But on a more positive note, schools are now contexts in which an enormous amount of information gathering, data management and analysis is going on, often using well organised computer based systems. Much data and considerable expertise relevant to research exists in schools. A key role and challenge for university staff is how to work with teachers to make more of the research potential within schools and in particular to look at ways in which existing recording and assessment systems can be accessed, adapted and extended for research projects. It is critical that as many connections as possible are made between the 'research process' and good curriculum development and teaching practices within schools. If research remains perceived as something quite separate from and additional to teachers' work, it is destined to not only have problems in development but also, and more importantly, have a limited impact on practice.

Before moving on to look more closely at research from the school and teacher perspective, it is worth commenting further about understandings of what research 'is'. If we are to move towards achieving the integration of research and curriculum development and of collaboration that we have referred to, then 'process' is an important notion to stress and discuss with teachers. Specifically, the emphasis needs to be that there are important links and overlap between the activities of designing research, data collection, analysis and reporting or dissemination of the findings, and that this process is always going to be somewhat problematic in terms of trying to 'ring fence' any one of these activities. Indeed, to do so draws false and unhelpful boundaries and fails to recognise that, for example, data collection involves elements of informal and ongoing analysis. Furthermore, it overlooks the fact that the times and forums that are seen as sites of data collection (lessons, staff meetings, focus or discussion groups with students) are likely to also be key opportunities for reflective analysis and for dissemination that *is* directly linked into development of practice (Penney, 2003).

Teachers as researchers

So what is it to be a 'teacher-researcher' trying to embed research in practice? We have already highlighted the likely tensions in terms of time for what will inevitably be perceived by some as a new and additional activity and role. Quality time remains probably the most fundamental key to the success of research developments in schools. Provision of time and support to undertake research but also to develop one's own and others' knowledge of research and skills as a researcher are key. McIntyre and McIntyre (2002) reported that teachers engaging in research 'rarely had the time nor the training that was needed, nor the necessary infrastructure to support them' (p. vi). With these issues in mind, it is appropriate to return to issues of ownership and partnership. A situation in which a partnership is established only with *an individual* teacher is likely to prove little more productive than a situation in which university staff are seen to be very much 'doing' the research ('on' the school). Within the school and key departments, there has to be a collective commitment to what the research project and partnership is trying to achieve. Colleagues need to be involved, to understand what it is about and to acknowledge the relevance of the activities for their own practice. Achieving this collective commitment and support in the research is one of the challenges that we raise for teacher-researchers. As with any new development, reactions will vary and the process becomes one of trying to make the most of those open in their support, while trying to counter resistance.

Beyond this general concern for support, what are the pragmatic support roles that teacher-researchers need to seek out from colleagues? In many projects it will be instantly evident that one person cannot do everything and that issues of staffing, timetabling and groupings mean that teaching colleagues need to become fellow 'teacher-researchers'. The teacher leading the project from a school perspective thus needs to be able to build their own 'team' atmosphere, negotiate the roles that others can take and support them in that undertaking. This can involve, for example, talking through an observation or interview schedule with another teacher who will be acting as the researcher with their teaching group, or working with administrative staff or teachers in another department to develop systems for managing, recording and working with the data collected.

So far we have talked of support in relation to teaching colleagues and other staff within schools. But we also need to consider students. In any research, support from participants is crucial to success and school based research is no exception. We therefore now turn attention to how we can foster students' active involvement and interest in research, with a view to them being not merely participants in the research, but fellow collaborators and members of the research team.

Teachers: supporting students as co-researchers

Many teachers may have criticisms of research that they feel has been done upon them, with little consideration of their interests or priorities for investigative studies and with limited opportunities for any 'real' involvement in projects. But perhaps more frequently, children would be justified in feeling that they are positioned as the subjects of research and curriculum development activities, that it is claimed are being undertaken for and in their interests, yet with little consultation with them. An important element of our ongoing work is therefore towards the more active involvement of students in school based research and ways in which teachers working in partnership with university staff can support their development as researchers. Research thus becomes viewed not only as integral to curriculum development and teaching, but also as integral to learning. Collaborative teacher–student research can be a very positive and rewarding learning experience in which important skills, knowledge and understanding are developed amongst the students involved. This is an area in which we are continuing to 'experiment' and learn. New roles and relationships cannot be instantly established. Rather they need to be developed progressively, over time, with patience and planning. The introduction of Sport Education itself involves roles and relationships that may be new to both teachers and learners, quite apart from the added complications of also becoming researchers! We point out, however, that the types of teaching and learning relationships and responsibilities that Sport Education seeks to develop are ones that lend themselves to the parallel development of teachers and students as researchers. Furthermore, many activities that both teachers and students are already involved in can be relatively easily adapted and positioned within research. For example, peer and self-evaluation are an integral element of many learning experiences. They can equally be integral to research. In Part 3 we see many instances in which research–teaching–learning boundaries are blurred, as indeed they arguably should be more often than is currently the case.

Thus we would encourage teachers to involve students in the research process and to listen to what they have to say about their experiences of Sport Education. Their thoughts and reflections can be telling, and may call into question our interpretations of their learning experiences and some of our assumptions about the form of experiences that will best promote progress, enjoyment and inclusion in learning. The student focus group interviews at Mountbatten School and Language College (see Chapters 10, 11 and 12 and appendices to this chapter) drew attention to the fact that some students will not welcome opportunities or requirements for them to take up some of the roles identified within Sport Education, particularly if they do not feel that they have the skills or knowledge required for the role. One student explained that 'it [a role other than being a team member] would have been too much to handle'. Another acknowledged 'I don't like taking charge' and a third recognised that they lacked qualities that were needed for some of the Sport Education roles: 'I'm not orgenised [sic]' (Clarke and Quill, 2003). In Chapter 4 we highlight the need for sensitivity in the processes of allocating roles and introducing children to new roles. An approach that is designed to ensure that all students experience a particular role will not necessarily assist in promoting enjoyment and inclusion in physical education.

Many of the same points are relevant if we consider the potential roles of students in research and as researchers. Dyson and Meagher (2001) have stressed that 'there is no "one size fits all" model of participatory research' (p. 59). They outlined the range of research activities that we can consider in relation to the prospective nature and extent of students' participation in research:

- young people as respondents (providing data);
- young people as field researchers (directly involved in the collection of data);
- young people as advisers (on any or all aspects of the research, including design, methods, analysis and dissemination);
- young people as analysts and interpreters;

- young people as disseminators;
- young people as research designers.

(adapted from Dyson and Meagher, 2001: 60)

Clearly, our expectations in relation to students' research roles and responsibilities need to be sensitive to different maturities, experience, abilities and interests. The provision of opportunities to participate in various ways needs to be well supported and progressive in terms of their demands. But several features of Sport Education lend themselves to developing those opportunities. Research can become part of a team's activities, with individual members of the team having various research roles and responsibilities. There is also the scope to make direct links between the skills, knowledge and understanding developed in certain Sport Education roles and potentially parallel research roles. For example, the Sport Education statistician may play a lead role in data analysis or the match reporter may become an interviewer in research. Appendix B shows 'tips' produced to guide students taking on the interviewer role.

Thus, although as we have indicated that the process of involving students in the designing and conducting of research takes time, training, careful planning, support and maybe risks, we are positive about what may be gained through that process. Our experiences to date have suggested that it can be an empowering and beneficial experience for those involved and lead to students being more actively engaged in decision-making processes that relate to their learning and lives. Recent research conducted by Fitzgerald *et al.* (2003) has reaffirmed this potential and the scope to pursue it in physical education settings. Dyson and Meagher (2001) rightly highlight, however, a need to be cautious in any generalisations and to remain reflective throughout the process of involving children in research. They point out that, if involvement in the research process demands resources (skills, knowledge and understanding) which particular students do not possess, then the process will provide 'a further instance of their marginalisation and disempowerment' (p. 66). They warn that:

> Attempts to involve young people which do not recognise this reality and are unprepared for its impact run the risk of doubly disenfranchising marginalised groups. If involving young people simply means involving those who are already most like professional researchers, then marginalised young people will effectively be excluded even from processes which are ostensibly designed to empower them.

(Dyson and Meagher, 2001: 66)

Changing roles and blurring boundaries: ethical issues

As university researchers we routinely have to address ethical issues in research and adhere to formal procedures established by our institutions designed to ensure that research projects are undertaken with due consideration to ethical issues. The British Educational Research Association (BERA) Ethical Guidelines have provided a further important reference point for educational researchers. One of the points within the BERA guidelines reaffirmed a matter that we have already stressed, namely that 'Honesty and openness should characterise the relationship between researchers, participants and institutional representatives.' A related point is that 'Participants in a research study have the right to be informed about the aims, purposes and likely publication of findings involved in the research and of potential consequences for participants, and to give their informed consent before participating in research' (BERA, 1992).

When we are faced with concerns to openly blur the boundaries between research and teaching practices and to explicitly embed research in those practices, ethical issues and dilemmas inevitably arise. For example, while aware of the need for 'informed consent' to participation in research, we can debate how formally this needs to be addressed if we are talking about participation in research based teaching and learning. Further, where should and can we draw the boundaries between when teachers are acting as teachers and as teacher-researchers and when, therefore, students are participating in lessons and/or in research? These and other dilemmas are not easily resolved. Arguably we need to come back to the underpinning issues of openness and honesty. If a research based development is being undertaken, with data being collected above and beyond normal assessment and recording activities and/or if that 'normal' data is now being used for new purposes, then from a research perspective everyone has a right to know that, and agree voluntarily to participate (or not). But even if we establish that much, we then face dilemmas of how and, particularly, how formally we should, and realistically can, seek such agreement.

In the current educational and social climate it is perhaps not surprising that we place great importance upon ethical issues and, particularly, informed consent being addressed in projects. Gaining agreement from parents or carers may seem an added administrative burden, but equally we can view this action as a move to positively involve them in innovation within schools and to enhance their involvement in their children's learning. There are benefits to be gained from informing parents of research based curriculum developments, explaining the nature of projects and their children's involvement in them, and giving them clear points of contact to raise any queries or concerns that they may have. Equally, we can point to the benefits of children being aware of what projects are directed towards, what is involved and how their own learning may benefit.

Alongside informed consent, there are a number of other ethical issues to consider that are by no means new to schools and teachers: of confidentiality, anonymity in research, and data protection. In many instances existing procedures relating to student records will be appropriate for fulfilling these concerns in research. But systems and records assume a certainty and formality in terms of both 'what is data' and when research (or data collection) is happening. In interactions with students and with teaching colleagues there will be instances in which there is no such certainty. If we are seeking to promote teacher-research, then 'when I am a researcher' and 'when I am a teacher' are not distinctions that we should be looking for. Rather, the lack of distinction should reinforce the need for openness in what is being undertaken. It arguably presents a case for clarifying agreement to 'extended use' of data that may arise from teaching activities and other inter-actions that are all part of normal professional practice – but that are now also more than that.

Similarly, ethical issues arise in relation to the active involvement of children 'as researchers', gathering, analysing and potentially reporting on data from peers. The key point here would seem to be that this involvement must ensure that confidentiality and trustworthiness in the research process are not compromised (Dyson and Meagher, 2001).

All of these are issues that we continue to engage and grapple with. We do not pretend to have found all or simple answers to the dilemmas posed. We have become progressively more aware of ethical dilemmas and of responses that we might make. Those dilemmas extend to reporting and writing research. The BERA Ethical Guidelines (1992) stated that 'Educational researchers should communicate their findings and the practical significance of their research in clear, straightforward, and appropriate language to relevant research populations, institutional representatives, and other stakeholders.' This directly addresses our shared responsibilities to ensure that the research that we undertake is useful to those who have contributed to it, and that it is effectively communicated to a range of audiences. We have already discussed some of the tensions and seemingly conflicting priorities in relation to whom we should be seeking to communicate with and in what forms. Reaching multiple audiences with diverse interests and expectations is not easy. In the course of our research we have worked together in undertaking to produce materials for presentations to teachers, for professional journals to reach more teachers, teacher educators and other organisations with interests in physical education and sport and for academic audiences and journals. This book is designed to complement those activities and in some respects 'cross boundaries'. We hope that it will be read by many teachers, but also by teacher educators, university researchers, beginning teachers and by other individuals working in physical education and sport policy, curriculum and professional development arenas. In undertaking writing collaboratively, we have sought to further strengthen our partnership and also openly and explicitly evidence that partnership as such (see McIntyre and McIntyre, 2002: xi). Moreover it is not insignificant that in producing this book we moved from a position of having three university based editors at the outset of writing, to the position now represented in print, which acknowledges the invaluable contribution that Mandy, the most experienced of the teacher-researchers involved in our work, made to the production process. We recognise further challenges for ourselves and others to pursue, relating particularly to students presenting their findings and reflections on their Sport Education learning and research experiences.

Looking to the future: principles for positive partnerships

Taking a philosophical stance, Stronach and McNamara (2002) draw on Bratman's (1992) work to identify three aspects of 'cooperative activity': '*mutual responsiveness; commitment to joint activity; commitment to mutual support*' (p. 159). Although these were not explicit reference points in our own moves to establish positive collaborative research relations, they provide a useful framework for such developments.

Mutual responsiveness is concerned with each party responding to 'the intentions and actions of the other, knowing the other will behave similarly' (p. 160). Trust thus again emerges as key to positive research relations.

Commitment to joint activity is that 'the participants should share an appropriate commitment to joint activity, but not necessarily for the same reasons, and their mutual responsiveness should support this commitment' (p. 160). They identify two aspects to this. Firstly,

> An 'appropriate' commitment may mean that each intends to carry out the joint action, but perhaps for different reasons. In which case, there must be meshing sub-plans. That is, sub-plans may be different so long as they are not mutually exclusive, and each party must be committed to the fulfillment of the other's sub-plans as well as the joint activity. It is also a condition that there is common knowledge of these joint intentions.
>
> (Stronach and McNamara, 2002: 160)

Stronach and McNamara highlight that an important feature of sub-plans is the multiple agendas that they reflect and address. This is a useful reminder that research can never be viewed in isolation, from any partner's perspective. It is always part of a bigger picture and relates to various development priorities and demands upon people's time. Furthermore, the bigger picture is not static. Research occurs in changing rather than fixed circumstances. Thus, Stronach and McNamara recognise that, even if an initial 'mesh' is achieved between respective sub-plans, changing contexts may cause tensions; 'sub-plans may change' and terms of collaboration may only become clear, and in some respects problematic, as they are 'enacted'. In their experience this meant that ' "implementation" of the project was always a matter of negotiation and compromise, not only with the outcome of actually "meshing sub-plans" so much as minimising "clashing sub-plans" and creating a spirit of creative compromise' (p. 161). But alongside the need to be prepared to make compromises, we can reflect that changing contexts can also provide positive (and perhaps unexpected) boosts to collaborative research potential.

The changing infrastructure of education and, in particular, physical education and school sport in England is a case in point. With an increasing focus upon establishing coherent inter-linked structures capable of supporting and promoting lifelong learning and lifelong participation in physical activity and sport (see Chapter 7, DfES, 2003; DCMS/Strategy Unit, 2002), we may see renewed potential for the development of collaborative research that spans various phases of education and that encompasses school and community based learning/participation contexts.

Secondly, Stronach and McNamara identify that 'Partnership must mean the *free agency of each party* and the *absence of coercion and manipulation*' (p. 161). They highlight this as something that was lacking in their project experiences and draw attention to not only unequal power-relations between 'partners' but also factors that played a role in determining those relations – including gender and professional hierarchies. We have been fortunate in that we have known each other for many years and, over that time, have recognised and come to be more open about the respective strengths that we each bring to various situations and our views about how best to therefore advance the research. We have sought to be sensitive to situations in which data collection may be seen as threatening for teachers trying new practices for the first time, and therefore considered in particular who is best placed to undertake data collection. Sometimes it will be an experienced teaching colleague, but perhaps not always or for everyone. Similarly, there is not one arrangement that we can deem as appropriate for focus group interviews with students. There will be advantages and disadvantages to a familiar teacher, an unfamiliar adult researcher, a well known or relatively unknown peer acting as the interviewer. The point here, however, is that in 'partnership based research' we need to be able to talk about and negotiate these strategies.

In the course of developing our research we have also been aware and become increasingly explicit about the professional, institutional and academic hierarchies that we work within and at times have firm desires to challenge. We have thus endeavoured to enact Stronach and McNamara's final principle of a '*commitment to mutual support*', whereby 'each partner supports the efforts of each other in the joint activity, and so makes possible a successful performance' (p. 162). This is identified as having three elements:

- Each agent must look out for and support the goals of the other, as well as their own.
- Such support must not be restricted to 'pre-packaged' cooperation at the beginning of the joint activity. That is, not only must there be 'mutual responsiveness of intention' but support must include 'mutual responsiveness in action'. It must be an ongoing concern.
- Support cannot mean cooperation at one level and competition at another.

(Stronach and McNamara, 2002: 162–3)

In relation to these points we have had to be aware of and sympathetic to the changing work pressures and demands that we have all faced through the research and work as a team to adapt accordingly in order to maintain our collective progress. We have also always retained a view that we should actively resist systemic and institutional pressures for more individualistic and competitive actions in research.

Conclusion

McIntyre and McIntyre (2002) have provided a different but certainly complementary set of principles to address in considering research partnerships: *expertise, motivation* and *opportunity* to be involved in research. In this chapter we have highlighted that formation of a partnership needs to address each of these issues in the context of the partnership. It demands that we ask questions such as what respective expertise the partners bring to the partnership, what their respective motivations for involvement are and what opportunities they each have to play particular roles, take on particular responsibilities and give time to the research. Underpinning all of this is the key commitment: to the partnership itself with a shared belief in the value of collaborative research between universities and schools as a major factor in raising standards of teaching and learning for all, complex and challenging as that is.

Notes

1   Best Practice Research Scholarships (BPRS) was a government initiative providing small-scale research projects undertaken in partnership by teachers in schools and supporting tutors, usually in a higher education institution. Awards were for a 15 month period, with a brief report required by the Department for Education and Skills at the end of the research. BPRS reports can be accessed via the teachernet website: http://www.teachernet.gov.uk/Professional_Development/opportunities/bprs/

2   Part of the balancing act referred to has, for Dawn Penney, involved dealing with an international move and change of jobs at a point when the book was close to completion. Dawn has greatly appreciated the support and understanding of her co-editors and the publishers, amidst the delay in completion.

References

British Educational Research Association (BERA) (1992). *British Educational Research Association Ethical Guidelines*, BERA (see http://www.bera.ac.uk).

Clarke, G. and Quill, A. (2003). Researching Sport Education in Action: A Case Study, *European Physical Education Review*, 9, 3, pp. 253–66.

Department of Culture, Media and Sport (DCMS)/Strategy Unit (2002). *Game Plan: A Strategy for Delivering Government's Sport and Physical Activity Objectives*, London: Strategy Unit.

Department for Education and Skills (DfES) (2003). *A New Specialist System: Transforming Secondary Education*, London: DfES.

Dyson, A. and Meagher, N. (2001). Reflections on the Case Studies: Towards a Rationale for Participation, in J. Clark, A. Dyson, N. Meagher, E. Robson and M. Wooten (eds), *Young People as Researchers: Possibilities, Problems and Politics*, Leicester: Youth Work Press.

Fitzgerald, H., Jobling, A. and Kirk, D. (2003). Valuing the Voices of Young Disabled People: Exploring Experience of Physical Education and Sport, *European Journal of Physical Education*, 8, pp. 175–200.

McIntyre, D. and McIntyre, A. (2002). *Economic and Social Research Council (ESRC) Teaching and Learning Programme: Capacity for Research into Teaching and Learning. Final Report*, Cambridge: University of Cambridge (see http://www.tlrp.org/).

McNamara, O. (2002). Evidence-Based Practice through Practice-Based Evidence, in O. McNamara (ed.) (2002) *Becoming an Evidence-Based Practitioner: A Framework for Teacher-Researchers*, London: Routledge.

Penney, D. (2003). Countering Control: Challenging Conceptualisations of Educational Research, *Curriculum Perspectives*, 23, 1, pp. 60–4.

Stronach, I. and McNamara, O. (2002). Working Together: The Long Spoons and Short Straws of Collaboration, in O. McNamara (ed.) (2002) *Becoming an Evidence-Based Practitioner: A Framework for Teacher-Researchers*, London: Routledge.

Appendix A: Pupil interview questions

University
of Southampton

Year 8 Gymnastics-Sports Acrobatics ~ Pupil interviews

This year you have experienced a different way of working within PE. You have been in the same team for all the sports acrobatics lessons and some of you have taken on different roles. The interview questions are designed to find out how you felt about this. There are no right or wrong answers.

Interview Questions

1) What team were you in?
2) Are you male or female?
3) Did you have a role?
4) If 'yes' what was it? - *Then ask questions 5 to 8.*
   If the answer is 'no' go to question 9.
5) Did you like having a role?
6) How did it make you feel?
7) What qualities are needed to do your role?
8) Do you think some roles are more important than others?
Can you explain your answer? - *Now go to question 11.*
9) Would you have liked a role? Can you give reasons for your answer?
10) Do you think some roles are more important than others? Can you explain your answer?
11) Has the performance made you work harder?
12) Have you found any of the work difficult?
   Please explain your answer.

Being a brill interviewer
Top tips!

⇒Firstly, be confident and reassure your interviewee, make them feel at ease, it is not a test, nor anything too personal!

⇒You can read the first bit to remind them about the sports acro course.

⇒What we are interested in is _what they really think_ about the course. We want to make sports acro lessons as good as possible for them. When they answer we don't even need their name just whether they are a boy or girl.

⇒Ask the questions clearly and one at a time, be interested in what they are saying - smile, make eye contact.

⇒Give them time to think and to answer the question.

Don't interrupt them.

⇒Listen carefully to what they are saying - is their answer clear, do you need to know more?

If so, ask them to explain their answer further.

⇒Thank them for taking part and tell them that later we will let them know what we found out.

And finally ... can you tell us how you felt about doing the interview. You can record this on the tape or write it down. Have you any suggestions to improve the interview? Thanks a lot.

Dr Gill Clarke and Mandy Quill

Part 2

Issues for physical education and Sport Education

Editors' note

> Sport education is not a throw-out-the-ball model where you abdicate your professional responsibilities.
>
> (Siedentop, 1994: 15)

In Sport Education the intention is that progressively students take greater responsibility for their learning experiences and many aspects of the Sport Education season. But as Siedentop emphasised, teachers remain very clearly 'the architects of the educational environment and the persons who are ultimately responsible for its efficiency and vitality' (Siedentop, 1994: 15) and, we would add, equity.

The chapters in this section reaffirm the centrality of teachers in Sport Education and the many challenges that they are likely to face in taking some of its defining principles and characteristics forward in practice. Significantly the chapters address matters of ongoing debate in relation to curriculum development and teaching within physical education as a whole, not only in Sport Education. They focus respectively upon inclusion; assessment; cross-curricular links; citizenship and leadership; and lifelong learning.

Individually and collectively the chapters aim to extend the understanding of Sport Education as a pedagogical model or framework, which has inherent flexibility and presents many possibilities to teachers. The emphasis is that there is not one way of doing things and that, depending upon how it is developed, Sport Education may have positive or negative effects upon the quality and equity of teaching and learning in physical education. It is a framework with much potential but one that also raises many issues and challenges that teachers and teacher educators seeking to realise the potential need to address. Each chapter therefore takes a particular focus in prompting reflection about the prospective role of Sport Education in the ongoing development of physical education as a curriculum subject and as a profession. Discussion links the development of Sport Education in physical education with broader educational debates, including how we may ensure that every teacher is equipped 'to inspire a desire to learn' and able to 'make subjects come alive' (DfES, 2003: 45). The chosen foci for the chapters also connect with the 'core principles' for teaching and learning that the government presented in its plans for the continued transformation of secondary education in England. Those principles were to:

- *Ensure every child succeeds:* provide an inclusive education within a culture of high expectations.
- *Build on what learners already know:* structure and pace teaching so that students know what is to be learnt and how.
- *Make learning vivid and real:* develop understanding through enquiry, e-learning and group problem-solving.
- *Make learning an enjoyable and challenging experience:* stimulate learning through matching teaching techniques and strategies to a range of learning styles.
- *Enrich the learning experience:* infuse learning skills across the curriculum.
- *Promote assessment for learning:* make children partners in their learning.

(DfES, 2003: 44)

References

Department for Education and Skills (DfES) (2003). *A New Specialist System: Transforming Secondary Education*, London: DfES.

Siedentop, D. (1994). *Sport Education: Quality PE through Positive Sport Experiences*, Champaign, Illinois: Human Kinetics.

3 Inclusion in Sport Education

Dawn Penney and Gill Clarke

Introduction

The Education Reform Act of 1988 established a 'broad and balanced' National Curriculum as a statutory entitlement for all pupils in all state schools in England and Wales. Yet, it was always acknowledged that, in practice, the National Curriculum would not be the same in all schools. Important aspects of curriculum design, planning and crucially approaches adopted in teaching remained matters that, quite appropriately, individual schools and the teachers within them would make decisions about. We are arguably no more able to make generalisations about the quality or appropriateness of individual learning experiences within schools across England and Wales than we were prior to 1988. The requirements of the National Curriculum for Physical Education (DES/WO, 1992) were ultimately such that students could still experience a differing range of activities within their physical education, and could be grouped in various ways, taught using more or less directive approaches and assessed by differing means. Thus, the development of a National Curriculum and specifically NCPE left issues of equity and inclusion as needing to be positively engaged with by individual teachers (see for example Barton, 1993; Talbot, 1993).

The revised National Curriculum requirements for England that came into effect in 2000 were consequently notable in including an *explicit* commitment to inclusion. The then Secretary of State for Education, David Blunkett, made clear the shift in emphasis from an entitlement *provision* to an entitlement *to learning*:

> An entitlement to learning must be an entitlement for all pupils. This National Curriculum includes for the first time a detailed, overarching statement on inclusion which makes clear the principles schools must follow in their teaching right across the curriculum, to ensure that all pupils have the chance to succeed, whatever their individual needs and the potential barriers to their learning may be.
>
> (Blunkett, 1999, in DfEE/QCA, 1999: 3)

Teachers in all subject areas were required to plan and teach the 'new' National Curriculum with 'due regard' to the principles of:

- setting suitable learning challenges;
- responding to pupils' diverse learning needs; and
- overcoming barriers to learning and assessment for individuals and groups of pupils.

(DfEE/QCA, 1999: 28)

Regrettably, with schools and teachers within them being judged very publicly via published league tables of examination results, there seem real dangers that reflections about educational provision and the needs of students are increasingly focusing on narrow performance measures over and above educational processes. Debates continue regarding the performance of girls as compared to boys in Standard Assessment Tests (SATs) and public examinations. Meanwhile in 2000 the Office for Standards in Education (OFSTED) reported that African-Caribbean, Pakistani and Bangladeshi pupils were less likely to gain five higher grade GCSE passes[1] than White or Indian children and drew attention to a widening of these attainment gaps. Persistent and growing inequalities in the apparent likelihood of success in formal tests and examinations are important to acknowledge. But a focus on those measures tells us little about the myriad of factors that have played a part in producing differential patterns of achievement. Further, the narrow focus fails to ask important questions about the relevance of the curriculum and its associated tests for those young people who are deemed to be failing or underachieving.

In this chapter we look at Sport Education in relation to concerns that we should seek to provide meaningful, appropriate learning opportunities and experiences for all students. We therefore explore the need to anticipate, recognise and counter factors that limit the quality of students' experiences, their learning progress and realisation of their learning potential. As we indicated in Chapter 1, as a framework for curriculum and pedagogy, Sport Education guarantees little. Rather, it articulates organisational and pedagogical strategies that can be adopted and adapted in order to promote equity and inclusion in physical education. The various characteristics of Sport Education (such as grouping pupils in teams, and introducing new roles) can help teachers meet the individual learning needs and interests of *all* students. But for this to be achieved it is essential to be aware of potential pitfalls and accept that positive outcomes in relation to equity and inclusion will only arise from sustained work that is firmly focused on achievement of those outcomes.

Inequalities and inequity in physical education: longstanding and *outstanding* issues

Before looking specifically at Sport Education, it is worth reflecting upon the issues of equity and inclusion in relation to physical education more broadly. Many people reading this book will be fortunate in having enjoyed physical education at school and have felt a sense of achievement in it and perhaps have been encouraged to pursue particular sporting activities outside of school. That encouragement may have enabled entry into a sporting and social community and led to a sense of 'real' belonging. In recent years in the UK, representatives of government and physical education professional communities have made much of the individual and social benefits of participation in physical education and school sport, including the personal qualities that are developed through it (see Chapter 1, Conway, 2003; Gilroy and Clarke, 1997; Penney and Evans, 1999; Penney and Chandler, 2000). No-one fortunate enough to experience some of the potential benefits would deny them. The experience of physical education and sport is not, however, positive for all children. While some may feel affinity with its various activities, others may feel out of place. While some enjoy a sense of achievement others feel only a sense of disillusion, inadequacy and failure. Accordingly, while some see endless opportunities arising from continuing to participate in sport, others see no place for them in adult sport (Boorman, 1998).

For many years researchers in physical education have highlighted some of these concerns. Variously, they have drawn attention to issues of marginalisation and exclusion as they relate to particular groups of children, thereby highlighting that aspects of individual identity – including gender, ability and ethnicity – place some children in a position of notable disadvantage in comparison to others (see Evans, 1993; Penney, 2002). Yet, for all the findings and observations, physical education and sport in schools remain arenas in which there is much work to do in relation to a whole host of issues relating to equity and inclusion. Some of the issues continue to be all too familiar: the provision for and participation of girls, children deemed to be 'low ability', children from ethnic minority groups. Some issues, such as provision for 'gifted and talented' children, have been flagged as development priorities in recent government policies. Meanwhile other issues fail to be adequately acknowledged as issues at all. These include recognising that:

- Many boys as well as girls are marginalised by the dominant activities, values and behaviours that continue to be reinforced in physical education and sport settings (Bramham, 2003).
- Many physical education and sport settings fail to challenge homophobia and heterosexism and fail to promote any broadening of understandings of conceptions of masculinity and femininity (Clarke, 2002).
- Many physical education policies and practices have yet to embrace a view of individual learners that acknowledges their *multiple* identities

(relating to one's age, gender, ethnicity, sexuality, ability, social class, cultural beliefs . . .). Assumptions about learning needs and interests are often still based upon simplistic categorisations of learners.

● We have yet to move from a 'deficit' view of differences between children to one that celebrates these differences as a valuable resource (Evans and Davies, 1993).

Recent comments from Flintoff and Scraton (2001) illustrate some of these points. They highlighted that in many recent studies focusing on girls in physical education and sport:

> girls continue to be viewed as a 'problem' for not engaging positively in PE, and the reasons cited by the girls remain remarkably similar to those from yesteryear – the wearing of PE uniform; the no-jewellery rules; compulsory showers; and having to play games outside in the cold.
>
> (Flintoff and Scraton, 2001: 5)

Their study revealed young women struggling to see a sense of purpose in their physical education. 'At best it was seen as a break from academic work; at worse, an unnecessary imposition impacting negatively on their academic studies, and one in which they rarely learned new skills useful for their out of school lives' (Flintoff and Scraton, 2001: 11). Flintoff and Scraton pointed to other research which revealed physical education failing to provide young women with 'either the experiences or resources to help them develop physical identities as other than the antithesis of men – less able, less strong and less competitive' (p. 8). They reported that, seemingly *despite* rather than *because* of experiences in physical education and school sport, 'it seems that more women than ever before are taking part in physical activity in out of school contexts' (p. 5). But at the same time they stressed that 'there remain significant differences between groups of women in their physical activity involvement, and there are few studies which acknowledge the ways in which particular women, for example, South Asian women, experience or are marginalised within sport' (pp. 5–6). Bramham (2003) has similarly highlighted the ways in which expressions of masculinity in physical education are 'grounded in shared ethnicity' and the dominant masculinity is embedded with racism and sexism. Bramham (2003) also stressed, however, the need to recognise gender relations and identities as negotiated and not universally determined by class and race identities.

Research has also highlighted that if we are to better understand students' 'lived experiences' of physical education and sport we need to acknowledge the extent to which the very public experience of physical education is influenced by their perceptions of their own bodies (see Evans *et al.*, 2004). Undoubtedly, physical education and sport in schools shape those perceptions and self-identities in powerful and sometimes limiting and damaging ways. Often entrenched, stereotypical views of the particular shapes and sizes that can and should be seen to be active are either reinforced or remain unquestioned.

There are, therefore, many outstanding challenges for physical education and physical education teachers. It is then important to consider whether we can view Sport Education as a pedagogical development with the potential to provide what has so often been seen to be lacking in physical education for many students, namely, a sense of personal relevance and purpose; a sense of belonging; feelings of enjoyment; a sense of achievement; a desire to continue participation, to continue personal improvement – and a belief that the opportunities for them to do so really exist. Can Sport Education provide a positive learning experience for *all* students and perhaps, in particular, for those girls and boys who are not amongst the potential elite performers, and for those who see little appeal or cultural relevance in physical activity and/or the sports that dominate provision and publicity (often soccer in the UK)? Further, can Sport Education contribute to a real shift in thinking in terms of how teachers and the children and young people in their classes think about differences, and in particular physical differences?

In a recent study focusing upon boys' school culture, Swain (2002) highlighted that divisions are constantly drawn that identify children as either 'one of us' or 'one of them', with not merely differences but perceived *deficiencies* at the heart of these judgements. Meanwhile Cockburn and Clarke (2002) have emphasised the continued tension that those girls who have an interest in being actively involved in competitive sport face, since they are frequently positioned by their peers as *either* 'sporty' *or* 'feminine'. The two identities are polarised, such that they cannot be held simultaneously:

> A girl can identify herself as a masculinised 'doer' of PE (a 'tomboy'), or a feminised ('girlie') 'non-doer' of sport and physical activity. It is highly unlikely that girls can achieve being both physically active *and* (heterosexually) desirable, so they are often obliged to choose *between* these images. The result is a paradox, a double standard to which teenage girls and young women are subjected. The girls in this study described theirs as a 'no win' situation.
>
> (Cockburn and Clarke, 2002: 661)

As Cockburn and Clarke stress, there is a need not only for these girls but also for many boys and young men 'to be offered multiple and fluid identities that are not positioned as the inferior "other"; and sporting identities that are not socially condemned and costly to their sense of security and belonging' (p. 663). Flintoff and Scraton (2001) have similarly stated that 'Challenging the destructive, macho behaviour of some boys within PE remains a key issue for the profession. This will not only benefit girls but also many boys too' (p. 18). Certainly, issues of inclusion, belonging, identity and relevance do not relate *only* to girls, nor should they be seen as uniformly applicable to *all* girls. Throughout all key stages of physical education (see Chapter 1) we need to move to a situation in which we clearly recognise individuals, individual learning needs and interests, and avoid simplistic generalisations.

Sport Education: positive potential

Traditionally Sport Education has been presented as a model that will bring benefits in relation to more equitable and inclusive practices, particularly in relation to gender and ability. Many of its characteristics are firmly associated with efforts to include students who may be marginalised in other physical education and sport contexts. The emphasis is that everyone is important within a team. In introducing roles other than player, 'other' learning and therefore more learners are recognised. Moreover, the formats of games and competitions are such that everyone has a chance to 'fully participate'. Siedentop (1994) recognised that 'Many physical educators have been concerned that students who are less skilled or less socially accepted by peers are typically left out of opportunity and camaraderie when sports are taught and played in physical education' (p. 1). He explained that Sport Education 'solves that concern because it gives all students the chance to know and love the sport and the opportunity to have a good educational and social experience as part of a team' (pp. 1–2). He also stated that, in Sport Education, 'students quickly become members of teams and maintain that affiliation through the season. Team membership allows for role differentiation and individual responsibility relative to the group, which in turn, creates the potential for self-growth' (pp. 10–11). Siedentop also believed that 'Sport education presents developmentally appropriate competition to all students regardless of skill level, gender, or disability' (p. 13).

Clearly this sounds very positive and in many respects we *should* maintain a positive outlook. Research in several countries has lent support to the view that Sport Education can succeed where other strategies or approaches have failed, for instance in engaging girls and children lacking in motor-skill development, and in fostering the development of cooperative behaviours amongst girls and boys of all abilities (see for example Carlson, 1995). But as we have indicated, none of this is achieved without skilled, knowledgeable and caring teachers. Success is achieved *because of them* and by virtue of their abilities and professionalism. In the remainder of this chapter we try to 'unpack' some of what teachers need to know and do if they are to succeed in promoting equity and inclusion in and through Sport Education. Many of the issues that we discuss are ones that have emerged from our ongoing research with teachers developing Sport Education in schools. The reports of those developments in Part 3 and the insights that they provide of Sport Education 'in practice in schools' therefore continue our commentary from a 'context specific' perspective.

Sport Education: down to the detail

As a framework and model for curriculum and pedagogical development in physical education, Sport Education needs to be treated as any other model or initiative. Interest and optimism need to be accompanied by close and critical questioning. It is a model that requires us to pose the following challenging questions in relation to inclusion and equity:

- Who has what learning opportunities in Sport Education?
- Whose and what learning is *really* valued in Sport Education, and beyond it?
- What activities, in what formats, played to what rules, are most likely to create inclusive learning opportunities and experiences?
- Whose current and prospective future identities are really represented in a 'team identity'?

These are not questions that we have definitive answers to. Rather, we raise them as questions that we continue to engage with as we work with teachers and students involved in Sport Education, with a view to better informing future practice. Nor are they questions that there can be definitive answers to. As we have explained, there are no hard and fast rules for:

- the size or make-up of teams;
- how teams are chosen;
- the range of roles that will be addressed in units;
- how decisions will be made about allocation of roles; or
- what form competitions and the final festival will take.

The chapters within Part 3 illustrate that decisions about all of these matters will necessarily be context specific. Nevertheless, the decisions will have important implications for inclusion and pose some difficult dilemmas for teachers. They will directly influence the degree to which claimed learning opportunities are a reality – and for which students.

Teams: membership, structure, individual and collective identities

It has often been assumed that Sport Education demands mixed ability and mixed sex grouping strategies. Neither is true and, as others have emphasised, nor should these strategies be seen as automatically creating more equitable or inclusive learning environments (see Evans, 1993). Teams in Sport Education can be determined by the teacher, by students, or by both in a process of negotiation. Teams are typically smaller than in adult sport settings and frequently designed to achieve like ability in terms of the playing performance of teams. Although this is the most frequent grouping arrangement, it is not the only way to structure teams. It is important to recognise that this arrangement will not necessarily result in greater equity and inclusion. In some instances and in some activities students who are at the lower end of the ability spectrum (when judged in terms of their competence as players) may feel more marginalised in a mixed ability setting than when working within ability based groups. Even if the mixed ability team is highly supportive, these students may remain acutely aware of where they stand in a performance based hierarchy. This may be particularly so if there is also something of a compensatory attitude towards the other roles they take up in the Sport Education setting and the other skills, knowledge and understanding that they demonstrate in those roles. By this we mean that there is a danger that 'other' roles and 'other' learning are very obviously identified as of low status.

There also remains a need to consider how more competent performers are positioned in mixed ability settings and the learning opportunities that are available to them in those settings. Sport Education settings have been cited as challenging these students in 'different ways', specifically to take on a coaching or leadership role and to develop the social and inter-personal skills that underpin positive collaborative learning (Kinchin, 2001). The greatest challenge for some very able students will undoubtedly be to learn to value and view difference in positive rather than deficit terms. Yet, the opportunities for these students to advance their own skill proficiency or improve their abilities to select and apply skills in complex game situations may well be restricted by virtue of a mixed ability group or team arrangement.

Ultimately, there will be a need to critically review the learning outcomes that it is hoped will arise from a Sport Education unit (for various learners). We cannot expect every aspect of learning to be successfully addressed in Sport Education. Rather, teaching and learning priorities need to be established and discussed with the students themselves. Only when these priorities are clear and accompanied by a better understanding of the particular context of developing Sport Education can we really consider what the most appropriate arrangements will be for team composition. Flintoff and Scraton (2001) recently reported clear preferences amongst some young women for single sex grouping at key stage 4 and also criticisms of experiences in mixed settings and particularly in games such as basketball and soccer, where boys dominated play. But Flintoff and Scraton also pointed to young women's awareness of an important downside to single sex grouping, namely that 'this did little to challenge the sexism of boys' (p. 15). 'It was only through playing alongside the boys that some felt the boys would accept them as players in their own right' (p. 16).

It is clear that decisions about team membership and roles within teams need to be made with a recognition of their likely implications in terms of the 'label' that students will feel that they have been given and whether or not they will feel that they 'belong', or want to belong. Perhaps one of the most important realisations is of the need for flexibility and variety in grouping arrangements in particular years and in different activity contexts. The examples of Sport Education in Part 3 demonstrate that, with particular students in particular activity settings, there will be arguments for and against mixed ability and/or mixed sex teams.

Maintaining the same teams throughout units of work that may well be longer than usual means that there is more time and opportunity for the social dimensions of learning to be addressed and advanced. At Mountbatten School and Language College (see Chapters 10, 11 and 12) positive social learning outcomes have been evident in some of the students' reflections about their Sport Education experiences. For example, one of the girls involved in a season of netball commented 'I prefer being in the same team each week because you get to know people's ability.' One of her peers explained that 'better players began to understand others' difficulties' and another highlighted that 'we learned to be patient and listen' (see Chapter 10 and Clarke and Quill, 2003). But it is important to recognise that advancements in inter-personal and cooperative skills are not an assured outcome. They have to be planned for and clearly explained as something that is being pursued in the Sport Education unit.

As we have explained (see Chapter 1), the experience of new roles and the opportunity that this provides to extend the range of skills, knowledge and understanding being addressed in physical education are a further important dimension of Sport Education. This dimension also links directly with claims that Sport Education can actively engage more students in enjoyable and positive learning experiences. Later chapters demonstrate that to a degree the case for celebration is well justified. Learning and learning opportunities are being extended in Sport Education settings (see Clarke and Quill, 2003). Students acting as captains or coaches are developing the skills, knowledge and understanding to plan, lead and evaluate their team's skill practices, develop programmes that will enhance their team's strengths and address weaknesses, and provide individual support to team-mates. Statisticians are becoming skilled and knowledgeable in the collection and analysis of performance data and are coming to understand the ways in which it can inform planning for future practices and eventually competitions. Commentators and publicity managers are developing creative writing and communication skills. But with inclusion in mind we need to also reflect upon *which children* are being provided with these various learning opportunities and how decisions relating to the experience of particular roles might best be made. It is inevitable that decisions will position learners and learning in a hierarchical manner. Hence, key questions to address are whether we are willing and able to anticipate and actively seek to counter established learning/learner hierarchies, in relation particularly to gender, ability and ethnicity in physical education and sport, but also to culturally specific norms and values. For example:

- Are we willing to work through the reactions that selection of a girl as the captain or coach within a mixed basketball or soccer team may give rise to?
- Can we even encourage girls to volunteer themselves for, and see themselves as legitimately holding, such roles?
- Are there some boys and girls within the class for whom the specific activity has little cultural relevance and who may therefore be struggling from the outset to identify with a role and/or their team? If so, how should we respond?

Interestingly in her description of the 'Sport for Peace' modification of Sport Education, Ennis (1999) explains efforts to establish more democratic and inclusive decision-making structures amongst the class, stating that 'Authority was dispersed horizontally throughout the class rather than vertically through a few influential students' (p. 38). The impression is that collective decision making was strongly encouraged. Indeed, she pointed out that:

> Students were given responsibility for many decisions they considered important such as how players rotate through positions, how disagreements would be solved and conflict negotiated, and what adjustments would be made in player personnel and team strategies to increase opportunities for success against particular opponents.
>
> (Ennis, 1999: 38)

Yet, there remained instances in which traditional hierarchies between learners, relating to both ability and gender, re-emerged. Notably, Ennis reported that 'Highly skilled players, both girls and boys, were elevated to the position of coach ... Other skillful players were given a central role by the coach assisting lower skilled participants' (p. 43), while 'Low-skilled participants also were given responsibilities. Some of these showcased their competence and organizational ability in off-the-court supportive roles' (p. 43). Ability in relation to specific motor skills returns as the key basis upon which many children are positioned and identities given to them. Roles relating most directly to performance carry the highest status and are associated with the most visibly able players. Other roles are portrayed as exactly that: 'other', of inherently less value and something of a compensation for an inability to perform as a player. Hence, it is incumbent upon us to be proactive in countering these likely value judgements.

> If you control what is defined as knowledgeable, you therefore control who is defined as knowledgeable, and thus legitimate the function of bureaucracies and the social reproduction of the class system.
>
> (Harris, 2003: 54)

In Chapter 4 we discuss the significance of assessment in this regard.

Activity choice, playing formats, rules and rewards

The activity or sport chosen for a Sport Education unit is another decision that students may participate in, but it is also a matter that needs to be recognised as having important implications for equity and inclusion. We cannot divorce activities from their specific historical and cultural significance. Different activities carry different messages and meanings. Thus, activity selection will be key to Sport Education either successfully connecting with or seeming abstracted from students' real and future lives. But with apparently enhanced 'connections' may come complications in relation to concerns for greater equity and inclusion in physical education and sport. Some of the activities that many students may be most able to identify with (such as soccer in a UK context) will also be activities that very strongly (and differentially) position students, by virtue of gender, ability, ethnicity, body shape, size, social class or religion. There are therefore arguments for choosing activities that are 'new' to the students. This may then give rise to fewer pre-conceptions about who should be participating in what roles and may also mean that there is less variation in skill levels within a class.

Irrespective of the particular activity, Sport Education and the 'Sport for Peace' curriculum referred to above emphasise the need to create 'authentic cooperative environments', such that all students will feel affiliation with their team and its success, and take responsibility for enhancing the inclusion and improvement of fellow team members. Instilling the values of caring for and supporting others is a challenging task for teachers involved in Sport Education. Nevertheless it is one that needs to be worked at with students and openly acknowledged as a process that will take time to develop. This will involve negotiations with students and between them in their teams. It will likely be a learning experience for all involved.

Some of the potential benefits of Sport Education are evident in a number of reflections made by Ennis. She reports girls explaining that the Sport for Peace curriculum 'reduced the pressure to "be like the boys" and "always do it perfectly the first time" to be accepted; instead, providing a positive, yet challenging atmosphere for them to focus on participating, while improving their skills and playing ability' (Ennis, 1999: 40). Meanwhile a requirement for all students to be given roughly equal playing time 'motivated the skilled players to teach and nurture the low-skilled girls as an instrumental component of the teams' success' (p. 40) and saw higher skilled players recognising the need for patient and supportive approaches in coaching roles.

The equal playing time requirement highlights ways in which modification of game rules and formats can serve to promote inclusion within Sport Education. As explained in Chapter 1, one of the underlying concerns in Sport Education is to ensure the provision of 'developmentally appropriate' learning experiences. Small-sided, shorter duration games with modified rules and equipment can help achieve this and encourage more equal involvement of all students within activities. Siedentop (1994) points out that 'smaller balls, softer balls, shorter equipment, nearer or lower targets, and larger goals all create a more friendly game for students and increase their chances of success without altering the basic nature of the sport' (p. 21). Ennis (1999) illustrates the value (for inclusion) of other intervention strategies in reporting that:

> Most boys quickly learned the value of passing the ball to girls on strategic plays. In a few situations, in which boys did not play cooperatively, teacher manipulation of the curriculum structures, game rules, and class policies required boys to make these changes.
>
> (Ennis, 1999: 42)

She explained that 'policies were created that required all players to receive a pass before a shot could be taken, changed the game format from three-player to two-player co-educational teams, and provided bonus points for total team participation' (Ennis, 1999: 42). In Ennis's view the effect of these strategies was 'to create a different, more educationally and socially positive environment, for all students in physical education' (p. 42).

Competition formats will also have a direct impact upon the atmosphere created within Sport Education. 'Round-robin' and league arrangements that give teams opportunities to play each other on several occasions will encourage the valuing of experiences as educational opportunities for improvement in individual and team performances. They will help avoid a 'win at all costs' atmosphere and encourage students to see the positive aspects of all competitive experiences, irrespective of match results or outcomes judged only by criteria that are applied in formalised adult sport. In these respects assessment can play a key role in shaping experiences and attitudes. If assessment remains narrowly focused upon playing performance judged in 'traditional' sporting terms, then arguably much of the work to promote a broader range of skills, knowledge and understanding and include more students will be undermined. Clear messages will immediately go out that, ultimately, only certain skills, knowledge and understanding really matter. Everything else is an aside. Alternatively, innovation in units in relation to the types of assessment tasks developed and methods of assessment used can mean that very different messages are sent out. If we are serious about wanting students to develop positive cooperative behaviours, take greater responsibility for their own and others' learning, or actively pursue cross-curricular dimensions of learning in Sport Education, then we need to have ways of recognising and rewarding those things. We discuss these issues further in the next chapter.

Conclusion

In this chapter we have raised many questions about equity and inclusion in and through Sport Education. We have certainly placed the development of

Sport Education very firmly in the hands of teachers. In considering all or any of the decisions to be made, we might usefully keep in mind a few things that may help children to feel that they have a place and are valued in physical education or sporting activities and so develop a desire to continue their involvement. Interestingly, Siedentop (1995) identified the following as things that children want from junior sport experiences:

- to participate – and specifically play on a losing team rather than be a sidelined member of a winning team;
- to improve their performance, thus enjoying a growing sense of competence;
- to be among friends; and
- to have fun.

Note

1   This refers to attainment of five or more A*–C grades in General Certificate of Secondary Education examination courses.

References

Barton, L. (1993). Disability, Empowerment and Physical Education, in J. Evans (ed.), *Equality, Education and Physical Education*, London: Falmer Press.

Boorman, D. (1998). The Physical: A New Millennium, a New Beginning?, in G. Edwards and A. V. Kelly (eds), *Experience and Education: Towards an Alternative National Curriculum*, London: Paul Chapman Publishing.

Bramham, P. (2003). Boys, Masculinities and PE, *Sport, Education and Society*, 8, 1, pp. 57–71.

Carlson, T. (1995). 'Now I Think I Can': The Reaction of Year Eight Low-skilled Students to Sport Education, *ACHPER Healthy Lifestyles Journal*, 42, 4, pp. 6–8.

Clarke, G. (2002). Difference Matters: Sexuality and Physical Education, in D. Penney. (ed.), *Gender and Physical Education: Contemporary Issues and Future Directions*, London: Routledge.

Clarke, G. and Quill, A. (2003). Researching Sport Education in Action: A Case Study, *European Physical Education Review*, 9, 3, pp. 253–66.

Cockburn, C. and Clarke, C. (2002). 'Everybody's looking at you!': Girls negotiating the 'femininity deficit' they incur in physical education, *Women's Studies International Forum*, 25, 6, pp. 651–65.

Conway, M. (2003). A National Strategy for PE, School Sport and Club Links, *British Journal of Teaching Physical Education*, 34, 2, pp. 6–7.

Department of Education and Science (DES)/Welsh Office (WO) (1992). *Physical Education in the National Curriculum*, London: DES.

Department for Education and Employment (DfEE)/Qualifications and Curriculum Authority (QCA) (1999). *Physical Education: The National Curriculum for England*, London: DfEE.

Ennis, C. (1999) Creating a Culturally Relevant Curriculum for Disengaged Girls, *Sport, Education and Society*, 4, 1, pp. 31–49.

Evans, J. (ed.) (1993). *Equality, Education and Physical Education*, London: Falmer Press.

Evans, J. and Davies, B. (1993). Equality, Equity and Physical Education, in J. Evans (ed.), *Equality, Education and Physical Education*, London: Falmer Press.

Evans, J., Davies, B. and Wright, J. (eds), (2004). *Body, Knowledge and Control*, London: Routledge.

Flintoff, A. and Scraton, S. (2001). Stepping into Active Leisure? Young Women's Perceptions of Active Lifestyles and their Experiences of School Physical Education, *Sport, Education and Society*, 6, 1, pp. 5–22.

Gilroy, S. and Clarke, G. (1997). 'Raising the Game': Deconstructing the Sporting Text – from Major to Blair, *Pedagogy in Practice*, 2, pp. 19–37.

Harris, C. (2003). Syllabus Development in New South Wales: Curriculum Control and its Impact on Teachers, *Curriculum Perspectives*, 23, 1, pp. 50–5.

Kinchin, G. (2001). A High-skilled Pupil's Experiences with Sport Education, *ACH-PER Healthy Lifestyles Journal*, 48, 3–4, pp. 5–9.

Office for Standards in Education (OFSTED) (2000). *Educational Inequality: Mapping Race, Class and Gender*, (HMI 232), London: OFSTED.

Penney, D. (ed.) (2002). *Gender and Physical Education: Contemporary Issues and Future Directions*, London: Routledge.

Penney, D. and Evans, J. (1999). *Politics, Policy and Practice in Physical Education*, London: Routledge.

Penney, D. and Chandler, T. (2000). Physical Education: What Future(s)?, *Sport, Education and Society*, 5, 1, pp. 71–87.

Siedentop, D. (1994). *Sport Education: Quality PE through Positive Sport Experiences*, Champaign, Illinois: Human Kinetics.

Siedentop, D. (1995). Junior Sport and the Evolution of Sport Cultures, Paper presented to the Junior Sport Forum, Auckland, New Zealand, November 1995.

Swain, J. (2002). The Resources and Strategies Boys Use to Establish Status in a Junior School without Competitive Sport, *Discourse: Studies in the Cultural Politics of Education*, 23, 1, pp. 91–107.

Talbot, M. (1993). A Gendered Physical Education: Equality and Sexism, in J. Evans (ed.), *Equality, Education and Physical Education*, London: Falmer Press.

4 Assessment and Sport Education

Dawn Penney, Gary D. Kinchin and Mandy Quill

Introduction

> In physical education we typically see teachers assessing students on fitness tests, isolating skills in contrived settings, or awarding points subjectively for effort, dress, and participation. The recent focus on assessment that authenticates student achievement demands that teachers be able to show what students are learning in physical education. This goes beyond identifying the content covered in class and requires that we be able to demonstrate what students have learned, what they can do, how they have changed, how they can share their knowledge and skills, what real-life applications they can implement, and how their physical activity choices reflect their status as independent learners.
>
> (Siedentop and Tannehill, 2000: 180)

Assessment remains a key issue for debate and development in physical education in England and internationally. From many teachers' perspectives, the development of a National Curriculum for Physical Education (NCPE) has provided all too little guidance on assessment. The government's line has repeatedly been that it is for individual schools and teachers to decide upon the forms and focus of assessment that will be capable of informing ongoing teaching and learning, and enable progress in learning in physical education to be reported at the end of key stages (see Chapter 1).

The most recent revision of the NCPE provided teachers in England with a more detailed frame of reference for monitoring and reporting progress in learning, in the form of eight level descriptions of 'the types and range of performance that pupils working at that level should characteristically demonstrate' (DFEE/QCA, 1999: 42). However, teachers were still left with many dilemmas in relation to assessment and reporting systems. Learning in physical education was now described in relation to four aspects of skills, knowledge and understanding (see Chapter 1) and teachers were required to address these in a range of activity contexts at each key stage. Exactly how teachers should reach a level judgement about a student's learning was unclear. Guidance produced by the Physical Education Association of the United Kingdom (PEAUK) (2000) confirmed that:

- summative judgements in relation to level descriptions are at the professional discretion of teachers;
- aspects of different level descriptions are met through taking part in a variety of activities;
- pupils may be more advanced in one aspect of physical education than another;
- teachers are not expected to find an exact fit on all aspects.

(PEAUK, 2000: 7)

The guidance also stated that activities should not be 'levelled', in so far as 'language such as Level 2 games, Level 4 gymnastics, Level 6 dance should not be used' (PEAUK, 2000: 7).

These statements raised important issues in relation to the specific learning that assessment in physical education should focus upon. Here is not the place, however, to get bogged down in debates about how aspects and areas of activity should respectively feature in assessment and reporting. Rather, we see a need to engage with broader issues in relation to assessment in physical education and, more specifically, focus upon what 'assessment *for teaching and learning*' can really look like in the subject. In 2002, a report from the Office for Standards in Education (OFSTED) (2002a) entitled *Good Teaching, Effective Departments* noted that:

> In successful subject departments significant assessments are built into the scheme of work and become part of the general teaching approach. These assessments are standardised and build up a profile of pupils' progress. They can be managed within the time available and allow for better tracking and monitoring of pupils whose strengths and weaknesses are identified at an early stage so that additional support or challenge can be initiated.
>
> (OFSTED, 2002a: 68)

The report also stated that, in those subjects (including physical education) in which there are no statutory tests,

> it is particularly important that departments have procedures to promote consistent, high-quality assessment to ensure the accuracy of end-of-key-stage assessment against National Curriculum level descriptions. In good departments this is now systematic, so that every teacher operates in the same way and shares the same standards.
>
> (OFSTED, 2002a: 68)

Turning attention specifically to physical education it was noted that:

In general, assessment in Key Stages 3 and 4 is less well developed in PE than in other subjects. There is a tendency for teachers to make judgements about pupils' effort and behaviour rather than their knowledge, understanding and skills. Only a minority of PE departments have well-structured assessment criteria linked closely to learning objectives and units of work.

(OFSTED, 2002a: 44)

Meanwhile, OFSTED's 2002 subject reports for physical education also made some important observations on current assessment practice. The report addressing physical education in the primary sector (key stages 1 and 2) stated that:

As was reported last year, assessment remains one of the weakest aspects of teaching PE . . . The use of assessment to guide curricular planning is less than satisfactory in a third of all schools. Often there are no whole school assessment systems to help teachers plan lessons more effectively based on information of what pupils already know and can do . . .

Where assessment is good, teachers record end-of-key-stage judgements about the attainment of pupils and this provides an effective means by which progress can be tracked and curriculum opportunities adjusted to meet pupils' differing needs. However, few schools have good procedures in place to ensure that teachers' assessments are consistent.

(OFSTED, 2002b: 2)

The accompanying report for physical education in the secondary years (key stages 3 and 4) (OFSTED, 2002c) painted a similar picture:

- 'The quality and use of assessment remain an area of weakness' (p. 1).
- 'There is a need to identify more explicitly how all the required aspects of the National Curriculum will be taught and assessed systematically through different areas of activity, particularly in Key Stage 3' (p. 3).
- 'The majority of departments have not revised their systems to use the new levels introduced as part of the National Curriculum 2000. Where assessment is good, departments use assessment information effectively to influence practice' (p. 5).
- '. . . often assessment of non-examination pupils is neglected' (p. 5).
- 'Pupils' skills of observation and evaluation remain relatively weak because pupils are not always given opportunities to develop these aspects. Often these skills are not identified in schemes of work, and there is no provision for their assessment' (p. 4).

Many of the above observations and the challenges that they pose are far from unique to physical education. The 2003 OFSTED report *Good*

Assessment in Secondary Schools highlighted that 'A consistent message of OFSTED reports over several years has been the indifferent quality of assessment compared with other aspects of teaching in secondary schools' (p. 1). More specifically, it was stated that teachers were 'often giving insufficient guidance to pupils about how to improve their work and providing few opportunities for pupils to reflect on comments' (p. 1).

Assessment: An authentic, individualised and active process

Although the above observations are important, they perhaps obscure some key points. Namely, are we clear about the purposes of the assessment being embarked upon and; therefore, the types of assessment that will be appropriate and effective? Williams *et al.* (1999) point out that:

> The rhetoric of post-war schooling in western technological societies, particularly in the last three decades, has been one of maximising the potential of individuals and of preparing responsible citizens for effective participation in democratic societies . . .
>
> Yet, in what can be claimed to be the most significant and influential aspect of schooling – assessment – most students have been deprived of opportunities to maximise and demonstrate their individual potential. Instead they have been subjected to assessment practices which, on the whole, have been controlled by people other than their teachers, limited in their scope and relevance, and focused on describing student learning within frameworks of standardised indicators.
>
> (Williams *et al.*, 1999: 146)

In Williams *et al.*'s view 'these practices have had much to do with the reproduction of social inequality, the perpetuation of exclusive interpretations of what is worth knowing and exposure to disenfranchising methods of demonstrating learning' (p. 146). To counter such trends, they set out to explore 'the possibilities of assessment contributing to *empowerment in learning*' (p. 147, our emphasis), focusing attention on three positions along a continuum of assessment practices. Citing Niebet (1994) they explain the continuum in terms of 'an ideological divide between those who hope to raise standards by more extensive testing and those who hope to improve the quality of learning by using different methods of assessment' (Williams *et al.*, 1999: 147). The three positions that Williams *et al.* identify are:

- 'standardised testing in its many forms';
- a so called 'middle-ground', comprising 'other conventional forms of assessment' that 'typically allow for some teacher involvement in decision-making about content, learning approaches and assessment activities. Some allow for various forms of student involvement . . .'; and finally,

- 'those assessment practices to which the term "authentic" is attached', inherent in which is 'the commitment to individuals being empowered in their personal growth through education, including decisions about content, teaching and learning methods and methods of demonstrating development and achievement'.

(p. 147)

'Authenticity' is one of the fundamental aims and claims of Sport Education, but so too is a commitment to inclusion and to the greater active involvement of students in curriculum development and learning processes (i.e. students having greater responsibility for their own and others' learning). In this chapter we explore some of the ways in which these aims/claims may be reflected in assessment practices in Sport Education. Throughout the chapter and through the practical examples of the development of Sport Education in Part 3, we prompt reflection upon some of the implications of these commitments for a range of inter-related issues relating to assessment, namely:

- the particular skills, knowledge and understanding that we are assessing (the *'what'* of assessment);
- *how* we undertake assessment;
- *when* we do so; and
- *who* is involved, in what ways, in assessment processes.

In exploring these issues we also highlight a need to reflect critically upon the compatibility of the various aims and claims of Sport Education. For example, if we define 'authentic assessment' as characterised by a focus upon 'real world' contexts, problems and life situations can we simultaneously promote equity and inclusion, or do we face an inherent contradiction? In developing assessment tasks and methods that consciously seek to extend the range of skills, knowledge and understanding that are recognised in physical education, we may well be presenting very obvious contrasts to some of the realities of the 'real worlds' beyond schools. However, if we have a commitment to do more in schools than merely mirror established social worlds and their inherent inequities, then there are very strong arguments for practices that present exactly such contrasts. The concern is then clearly not only with real lives and societies as they currently stand, but also and arguably more importantly with real lives and societies *as they might be*. Teaching and learning addresses 'preferred futures' and prompts exploration of whether they can become 'possible futures' for the students involved (see Chapter 7).

Notions of authenticity are arguably closely linked to a need for greater *individualisation* of learning and assessment. Having structures and strategies that are designed to better address individual learning needs and interests is a key government concern for education in England (DfES, 2003a). Specifically the government has plans to extend the development of Individual Learning Plans (DfES, 2003b) and to revisit the balance between examination, continuous and 'portfolio' assessment, and similarly look at 'the role of formative assessment . . . and how it helps young people identify their future learning and development needs, as well as recording and accrediting previous progress' (DfES, 2003b: 45). In 2003 the government also stated its desire for schools 'to use Information and Communications Technology (ICT) in their development of more individualised learning and assessment programmes for every child' (DfES, 2003a: 47). With moves toward more individualisation come a shift in learning relations, to again involve the learner far more actively in the learning (and assessment) process. Self- and peer assessment, both of which frequently feature in Sport Education, emerge as fundamental to the development of assessment 'for learning'.

'Assessment for learning' has been described by OFSTED (2003) as a process concerned with learners and teachers seeking, interpreting and using evidence to establish a learner's current position, the next steps in their learning and how those steps can best be taken. Progressing learning is a shared responsibility and how progress is to be achieved is a matter of negotiation. As a whole, assessment 'must be manageable for students and teachers, and must accommodate recognition of a wide range of learning and achievement' (DfES, 2003c: 8). These are worthy intentions, but how can we advance things in practice, in schools and, specifically, in Sport Education in physical education?

Assessment: principles into practices

Researchers in Australia have identified a number of principles to encourage engagement in assessment, that Sport Education seems well positioned to take up. Drawing on Meyers and Nulty's work (2002) we therefore identify a number of key points to be addressed in developing assessment in Sport Education.

Firstly, we highlight the need to state the rationale for the unit of work, but also for specific assessment tasks within it, in 'real world terms', making the 'real life' relevance explicit for the children or young people involved (Meyers and Nulty, 2002).

Sport Education units are concerned to make connections with the real world of sport in society. This poses important challenges for teachers in relation to their assessment of learning. It prompts negotiation of assessment tasks with students in order to ensure that, from their perspective, there is a 'real life' relevance to the assessment, and that they understand the skills, knowledge and understanding being addressed via particular assessment tasks and methods. Our experiences have highlighted that we should not assume that the relevance of assessment tasks will be apparent to *all* students. Clarke and Quill (2003; see also Chapter 10) have drawn attention to the impact that the public profile of particular activities will inevitably have in relation to their perceived relevance. They have also illustrated the ways in which relevance will be shaped by the gendered and culturally specific dimensions of activities and the social and professional arenas that they relate to. Thus, in the context of soccer:

> Sport Education tapped into an already existing and pervasive culture. Male footballers appear regularly in the media for pupils to aspire and relate to as role models; pupils see the England team wearing their team strip, warming up on the pitch with their trainer; they hear the match commentary on the radio and television and read match reports in local and national newspapers.
>
> (Clarke and Quill, 2003: 259–60)

In the UK, neither women's soccer nor many other sports enjoy this sort of visibility. Clear, meaningful reference points and role models for participation and performance in many activity contexts may well be notably lacking. Thus, we can reflect that, while in schools in the UK it may be relatively easy to convey the 'real life relevance' of the task of producing a match report for a Sport Education soccer lesson, this may be harder to achieve in the context of netball (see Chapter 10). Clearly we need to recognise that students will not all see the same relevance in particular tasks. Issues of age, gender, ability, ethnicity, class and culture all potentially shape the extent to which individual learners will see the 'real life' connection that an assessment task is intended to make. We need to consider, for example, whether, amidst the male dominance inherent in soccer publicity in the UK, girls will see personal relevance in either writing a match report or planning to lead a skill-practice session. Furthermore, will they or boys for whom the game has little appeal or cultural relevance be able to position themselves in the role of reporter or coach?

It is increasingly apparent that assessment in Sport Education presents teachers with opportunities to challenge longstanding and often stereotypical perceptions about the roles and activity contexts that students regard as having real life relevance for them. There is important scope to be openly debating with students whether they can aspire to particular roles in various activity settings, and the ways in which their perceptions link with issues of gender, ability and ethnicity. Indeed, using innovative assessment methods this kind of reflection and debate can be the focus of an assessment task within the Sport Education season. Journals (or personal learning logs) have been used in Sport Education to engage children with social, political, ethical and cultural issues relating to the activity that they are experiencing in their season (see Kinchin, 2000). Drug-taking and testing, body image, media coverage, or sponsorship deals are issues that students could be required to research and on which they would then provide a written commentary or visual, verbal or computer based presentation, either individually or as part of a team task. Personal reflection on one's own views, beliefs and behaviours in sport can also be an integral part of such a task (see Kinchin and O'Sullivan, 2003). as we discuss further in Chapters 5 and 6, the potential links to be made between learning and assessment in Sport Education and that being planned within citizenship, english, ICT or other subject areas are very clear.

We have already alluded to the scope for assessment tasks in Sport Education to take a wide variety of forms. The form and/or method of assessment will clearly have implications for 'real life relevance' (or 'authenticity') from students' perspectives. For example, being asked to produce a match commentary in only a written form may not have comparable meaning for students as a requirement to produce an audiotaped commentary. Similarly, in relation to the role of the coach, the requirement to *practically* lead a warm-up, skill-practice or fitness session with one's team (having first been required to produce a plan for the session) sets learning in the real life context. We might also reflect that in the real world of sport coached sessions are frequently video-recorded to provide a focus for individual and group evaluation of performance. Self- and peer evaluation using a video-recording could be a further group assessment task within the Sport Education season.

There are thus many ways in which the 'real life relevance' of assessment can be enhanced in Sport Education. Yet it is important to recognise that amidst the opportunities to making 'real life connections' some notable dilemmas can also arise. In Chapter 1 we explained that Sport Education does not seek to merely mirror or replicate all of the conditions, beliefs and attitudes that are seen in sport and societies. Rather, there is an interest in critical questioning and in pursuing ways in which students can be encouraged to challenge inequities in sport and society. If we are serious about promoting the development of skills, knowledge and understanding that will enable students to become more critically aware and act in socially just ways, then assessment during the Sport Education season will need to explore that dimension of learning. As indicated above, this can be through specific tasks or projects built into journal or portfolio based work. Equitable and inclusive attitudes and behaviours can also be monitored and promoted on an ongoing basis through point reward systems that run through the Sport Education season. Such systems, do, however, give rise to some tension in relation to notions of 'authenticity' and 'real life relevance'. Systems that reward teams for incidents of 'fair play' are clearly at odds with many of the sporting contexts which students will be able to relate to. This prompts the need to be even more explicit about the rationale for the system and to recognise that in Sport Education it is intended that students have experiences that help them develop visions of changes that they may wish to see in sport and wider society. As we discuss in Chapters 6 and 7, there are important issues of empowerment of learners to consider here.

The point system developed in the netball season at Mountbatten School and Language College (see Chapter 10) provides another example of tension between practices in Sport Education and those in real life contexts. In matches that teams played against each other through the season, points were awarded for winning but also for having scored more than half of the goals gained by the winning team. This arrangement is unlikely to be seen in junior or adult netball leagues outside of school. This leads to questions about the rationale and furthermore the relevance of the arrangement for the teams involved. The arrangement at Mountbatten School and Language College (see Chapter 10) had an important role to play in maintaining enthusiasm, interest and effort throughout individual matches and the season as a whole. Even if a team was losing a match, or was not at the top of the league, there was a clear incentive to continue to play to the best of their ability and score as many goals as possible. In relation to 'real life relevance', the importance of not giving up and continuing to support each other in a collective effort was made explicit. So too was the notion of progress and consistency in a team's performance through a season. Each team could review their improvement in terms of the goals that they were scoring and conceding, rather than only using wins or losses as their reference point in reflection and analysis.

The next of Meyers and Nulty's (2002) principles relates to a further dimension of relevance. This time the focus is upon the connections that students see between the learning that they are developing in physical education and that being developed in other areas of the curriculum and elsewhere in their lives outside of school. Meyers and Nulty (2002) specifically stress the need to be developing assessment tasks that require students to develop their 'learning resources', but also develop a broader view of their 'learning resources'.

The team structure, the maintenance of the same teams through the season and the introduction of various roles, all seem characteristics that are well suited to support efforts to broaden children's views and understanding of both their own and others' 'learning resources'. Everyone within a team can be seen to bring different learning resources to a task and to have different strengths and weaknesses in learning (relating for example to the four aspects within the NCPE, the various roles within Sport Education and/or cross-curricular knowledge and skills). The challenge for the team will be how to use their collective resources to best effect and, in so doing, support each other's further development. The team, with guidance and support from the teacher, can identify the contributions that each member can and should make to a group assessment task given the need to consider both the team performance and individual learning progress. This may provide important opportunities for students to reflect upon their own and others' learning targets and the experiences and support needed to progress towards the targets. This may mean negotiating priorities in relation to individual and group learning goals.

Planning a series of assessment tasks that, over time, foreground different aspects of learning will reinforce an appreciation of the breadth of learning that Sport Education is concerned to develop, and challenge all students to extend the breadth of their personal learning resources. Well structured journals or team portfolios (see Kinchin, 2001) can achieve this, incorporating, for example, tasks that require students to:

- record a team logo and/or team kit or uniform;
- document the key responsibilities associated with their own role and subsequently the role of one of their team-mates (this may be linked to a shadowing or mentoring experience);
- identify one strength and one weakness in relation to their personal playing performance, and identify ways in which they can extend the strength and address the weakness;
- identify a key strength in their team's performance and an area for further development, and identify practices and tactics or strategies that will enable the team to improve its performance;
- record warm-up routines used by the team and at some point in the season take responsibility for designing and leading the warm-up or a part of it;
- develop and record training programmes that are directed towards specific elements of fitness and/or the requirements of specific playing positions;
- outline a new strategy or tactic used by the team and produce an evaluation of its effectiveness;
- routinely gather data relating to identified aspects of individual and team performances. Summarise and critically reflect upon the data gathered in relation to achievement of a range of desired learning outcomes (including skill and performance outcomes, collaborative learning outcomes and outcomes relating to cross-curricular learning).

Journals and portfolios are clearly not the only means via which these or other learning and assessment tasks can be built into a Sport Education season. An ongoing point reward system (that is frequently linked to a league table of teams) can incorporate points being awarded for many aspects of learning and for achievements in all of the roles included in the Sport Education unit. A requirement for each team to maintain a section of a Sport Education notice board is another way of challenging learners to utilise skills and knowledge that they may well associate with other subject areas, in the context of physical education. The assessment tasks and methods used in Sport Education can play a vital role in encouraging students to develop more holistic views of learning, rather than seeing it as rigidly subject based and, furthermore, confined to schools. Once again, there is tremendous potential for creativity in assessment and also collaborative planning of assessment with teachers from other subject areas so that the Sport

Education unit is formally recognised as a context in which there is an aim and expectation that 'other learning' will be advanced. In Chapters 5, 6 and 7, we discuss the opportunities that Sport Education presents to link learning across subjects and to encourage students to see learning as ongoing in their lives outside of schools.

The third point that we draw from Meyers and Nulty (2002) is the need to set assessment tasks that are *realistic, inter-linked and cumulative in effect*. The seasonal structure of Sport Education and the retention of membership of a team throughout the season both help to facilitate inter-linked and cumulative assessment and, as indicated above, there are various means via which the links can be reinforced. Point systems and league tables running throughout the season and/or requirements to maintain a journal, portfolio or weekly postings to a team board can all prompt an appreciation of links between different activities through the season and provide means of charting cumulative learning. Tasks can be included that specifically focus upon cumulative progress in individual learning or as a team. Other tasks might challenge students to review the effect over time of improvements in, for example, their ability to execute a particular skill or in a specific element of their fitness, upon their performance.

Time and experience will be critical in getting to know the assessment tasks and methods that students of a particular age, with a certain level of past experience of Sport Education, and with various strengths and weaknesses in their learning, can successfully take on. Learning experiences and teaching practices in other subject areas will be important to consider in relation to the level and types of assessment task that are built into seasons and the extent of guidance or structuring that will be needed. For example, students may or may not have used journals in other subject areas. With journals, portfolios or team boards the nature and extent of guidance required will vary according to the age group involved, the level of learning in relation to physical education and a number of other subject areas, the extent of experience of Sport Education and familiarity with these types of assessment methods. As students become more familiar with the ways of working within a Sport Education unit and the expectations of them as learners within Sport Education, they will be able to take the ideas that are presented to them further. In many of the chapters in Part 3 it is evident that Sport Education can inspire students to be creative in their responses to assessment tasks.

We are aware, however, that some of the ideas that we have alluded to, such as production of a match commentary, may appear overly ambitious or unrealistic suggestions in some school contexts. With all of the ideas there is a need to consider adaptations that will mean that expectations and demands can be graduated to suit learners' abilities. For example, it is clearly not realistic to expect the newly appointed 'reporter' to commentate 'live' into a dictaphone during their first Sport Education session and to come up with an articulate, coherent commentary. Rather, this might be the final task in this role, carried out during the season's culminating festival and following a series of structured progressive commentary tasks during the season. One of those tasks may well be something that the whole class undertakes, with students having to listen to an extract from either a radio or television commentary and identify key characteristics of 'good commentating' for that medium and in the context of the particular sport. Links could be established with work in English to reinforce the development of skills, knowledge and understanding relating to communication. In time, the challenge might be to undertake a comparative analysis of a radio and television commentary for the same event, or analyse differences in the styles and skills needed in two different activity settings (for example, a sprint and long-distance race incorporated within a Sport Education athletics season, or rhythmic and Olympic gymnastics within a Sport Education gymnastics season). Using video extracts with sound dubbed out could also be a way of building progression into the development of the skills of commentating. Students can watch the video and rehearse their commentary, re-run the tape and record (into an audiotape recorder) their commentary, repeating the process until they feel that they have a recording that they are happy with. Evaluating their commentary could then be a team task, with the focus upon providing pointers for the student commentator to improve their skills during the remainder of the season. In this way, learning and responsibility for learning are shared.

Finally, in relation to the concern for assessment to be inter-linked and cumulative, it is appropriate to highlight the strength and significance of ongoing formative assessment practices in Sport Education. Many assessment tasks within Sport Education may not be formally identified as such, because they will be totally integral to group and individual learning experiences that continuously promote self-evaluation and ongoing review of progress in learning. Assessment does not always involve a written task. As we have illustrated, the use of innovative assessment tasks and methods can help to establish assessment as very firmly embedded in learning activities.

Finally we draw attention to Meyers and Nulty's (2002) emphasis of the need to *make explicit the inter-connections between the different elements of the unit that will produce the desired learning outcomes.* To some extent the points that we previously made have already addressed this principle. We have drawn attention to various ways in which Sport Education can create opportunities for children to consolidate and extend their learning in a structured way towards specific outcomes. Nevertheless, the task of promoting inter-connections between various learning experiences over the duration of a Sport Education season will remain challenging. Furthermore, we should acknowledge that achieving such inter-connections is vital if Sport Education is to succeed in the raising of standards in learning within NCPE, GCSE and other accredited course contexts. The OFSTED assessment report stressed that 'Being specific with pupils about what they need to do to reach the next level is essential' (OFSTED, 2003: 31).

The breadth of learning outcomes being pursued in Sport Education units arguably makes it all the more important that students have a clear vision of the intended outcomes for the unit (season), and the various key steps towards them that will feature at points in the season. It is also important to ensure awareness and understanding of the longer-term learning goals that progress in a particular unit is directed towards. Revisiting skills, knowledge and understanding that has been a focus early in the season in subsequent (and more challenging) learning and assessment situations will help children to see both linkages and progress in their learning. Point reward systems can address some of these linkages. For example, there is no reason why, within a particular lesson, bonus points could not be awarded for the successful application of a previously practised skill or a set team-play within the now more demanding open learning context. This might be the successful execution of lay-ups in a basketball game situation, or incorporating a specific gymnastic movement into a linked sequence.

Similar efforts need to be made to promote inter-connections that relate to progress towards the other learning outcomes desired in Sport Education. Early on in a season, attention may well focus on becoming familiar with rules and expectations relating to fair play in an activity. Subsequent rewards for good sporting conduct or penalty points for unfair, abusive or selfish behaviour can then be used to promote the outcome of students valuing and displaying responsible conduct in sport settings, and in their everyday interactions with their peers and adults.

Siedentop (1994) highlighted the ways in which point systems could engage with the broad scope of the learning outcomes desired in Sport Education, in saying that 'Teams win points not only by winning contests, but also by passing tests, doing extra practices, doing warm-ups appropriately, playing fairly, turning in booklets, completing publicity assignments and the like' (p. 33). We clearly need to recognise that a points system should not be viewed as the sole or most important means via which we facilitate students' awareness of progressive steps towards desired learning outcomes. Particularly during first experiences of Sport Education, many of the outcomes may well be unfamiliar and contrast sharply with students' expectations regarding learning in physical education. A combination of strategies is likely to be necessary in order to develop their understanding of the outcomes and the new learning framework that they are being challenged to work within.

Building trust and ensuring fun in new learning relationships

In this and the opening chapter we have discussed the new learning roles and relationships that are central to Sport Education. A number of factors will influence the degree to which, within the new learning relationships, new forms of assessment can be successfully developed. Alexander (2001) identified the following as 'critical factors' for effective self-assessment, but they seem equally applicable to peer-assessment tasks. Furthermore they are relevant to both individual and group tasks in Sport Education. The four factors are:

1   a relationship of trust between teacher and pupils;
2   the ability of pupils to set (or negotiate) their own objectives and criteria;
3   the value given to pupils' own assessment of themselves; and
4   fun: the activity is enjoyable.

(Alexander, 2001: 80)

Undoubtedly, for trust to be established and maintained, much will rest on the second and third points, that is, the extent to which students feel that they have any real say in shaping assessment tasks and then whether they see their own assessment being valued and truly 'counting' in overall judgements about their progress. If self- and peer assessment remain merely additional extras to what is deemed the 'real' judgements of a teacher, then the trust and engagement will be lost.

Furthermore, if assessment is to be seen by students as something genuinely and positively directed towards informing provision to progress learning, then there is another dimension of trust that is needed. This is a trust that means that students will have the confidence to be creative in their learning and feel that they are able to 'take risks' in some of their responses to assessment tasks. Indeed, the 2003 OFSTED assessment report pointed to the need to provide 'opportunities for divergent thinking in an atmosphere that ensures pupils do not feel bad if they make a mistake' (OFSTED, 2003: 10). A key element of such an atmosphere is captured in Alexander's fourth point above. *Fun* is key to learning and assessment in all its forms, not only the effectiveness of self-assessment. The seasonal structure, the team membership and identity, the experiences of different roles, the greater independence and ownership of learning are all meant to ensure that learning in Sport Education is fun, for everyone involved. Being involved in new forms of assessment, being able to work with others on tasks and being challenged to demonstrate skills, knowledge and understanding through a mix of practical, oral and written modes are potentially an important dimension of a fun learning environment. Fun repeatedly comes through as a characteristic of learning in the Sport Education experiences that are described in Part 3 of this book. It has also been clearly evidenced in the quality of work produced by many of the students involved.

Conclusion

In many respects the results achieved in assessment will be deemed the measure of the success or shortcomings of a new curriculum framework and pedagogical initiative. But many of the ideas that we have discussed in this chapter offer means via which success can be celebrated throughout a Sport Education season. Methods such as the use of journals and portfolios offer important opportunities for sharing progress with parents and guardians and involving them more in their children's learning. Team boards make learning in physical education notably visible to all staff, to students throughout the school and to visitors to the school. With developments such as these in mind we also point to a further challenge, that 'Teachers who develop authentic teaching, learning and assessment must also find authentic alternatives to traditional methods of recording and reporting student achievements' (Williams *et al.*: 156). In relation to the latter point, schools that we have worked with have utilised an increasing range of forums and formats for reporting student progress and achievements (see Part 3).

In Chapter 1 we stressed the need to view Sport Education as a flexible framework. It is appropriate to conclude this chapter by adding that it should also be seen as dynamic, that is, something that should be adapted, extended or sometimes scaled down in the light of how students are responding to it, and the progress that is being made by different students in relation to various aspects of their learning. It is good practice for data from assessment to be used 'to challenge departments to consider in detail the effectiveness of their teaching and other matters, such as grouping arrangements and examination entry policy' (OFSTED, 2003: 8). In the chapters in Part 3 we provide examples of teachers adopting this critically reflective stance in the context of their development of Sport Education. The examples of Sport Education 'in action' give 'real meaning' to the notion of 'assessment for teaching and learning' that we highlighted in opening this chapter.

References

Alexander, T. (2001). *Citizenship Schools: A Practical Guide to Education for Citizenship and Personal Development*, London: Campaign for Learning.

Clarke, G. and Quill, A. (2003). Researching Sport Education in Action: A Case Study, *European Physical Education Review*, 9, 3, pp. 253–66.

Department for Education and Employment (DfEE)/Qualifications and Curriculum Authority (QCA) (1999). *Physical Education: The National Curriculum for England*, London: DfEE.

Department for Education and Skills (DfES) (2003a). *A New Specialist System: Transforming Secondary Education*, London: DfES.

Department for Education and Skills (DfES) (2003b). *14–19: Opportunity and Excellence*, London: DfES.

Department for Education and Skills (DfES) (2003c). *14–19: Opportunity and Excellence: Summary*, London: DfES.

Kinchin, G. D. (2000). Tackling Social Issues in Physical Education Class: What about Journal Writing? *Strategies*, 13, 5, pp. 22–5.

Kinchin, G. D. (2001). Using Team Portfolios in a Sport Education Season, *Journal of Physical Education Recreation and Dance*, 72, 2, pp. 41–4.

Kinchin, G. D. and O'Sullivan, M. (2003). Incidences of Student Support for and Resistance to a Curricular Innovation in High School Physical Education, *Journal of Teaching in Physical Education*, 22, pp. 245–60.

Meyers, N. M. and Nulty, D. (2002). Assessment and Student Engagement: Some Principles, Paper presented at the Learning Communities and Assessment Cultures Conference, University of Northumbria, August 2002.

Office for Standards in Education (OFSTED) (2002a). *Good Teaching, Effective Departments: Findings from a HMI Survey of Subject Teaching in Secondary Schools, 2000/01*, London: OFSTED.

Office for Standards in Education (OFSTED) (2002b). *Primary Subject Reports 2000/01: Physical Education* (HMI 365), London: OFSTED.

Office for Standards in Education (OFSTED) (2002c). *Secondary Subject Reports 2000/01: Physical Education* (HMI 381), London: OFSTED.

Office for Standards in Education (OFSTED) (2003). *Good Assessment in Secondary Schools*, London: OFSTED.

Physical Education Association of the United Kingdom (PEAUK) (2000) *Physical Education: Assessment, Recording and Reporting at Key Stages 1 to 4*, Reading, UK: PEAUK.

Siedentop, D. (1994). *Sport Education: Quality PE through Positive Sport Experiences*, Champaign, Illinois: Human Kinetics.

Siedentop, D. and Tannehill, D. (2000). *Developing Teaching Skills in Physical Education* (4th edn), Mountain View, California: Mayfield.

Williams, D., Johnson, B. and Peters, J. with Cormack, P. (1999). Assessment: From Standardised to Authentic Approaches, in B. Johnson and A. Reid (eds), *Contesting the Curriculum*, Australia: Social Science Press.

5 Sport Education and cross-curricular learning

Dawn Penney and Mandy Quill

Introduction

As is the case with all curricula, the National Curriculum in England and Wales is intended to be more than the sum of its parts. It is hoped that the collective fulfilment of subject based requirements will mean that a number of overlying aims relating to the curriculum 'as a whole' are addressed and 'added value' in relation to learning thereby achieved. The latest revision of the National Curriculum for Physical Education in England (DfEE/QCA, 1999a) stressed that teachers in all subject areas should be aware of and actively seek to advance:

- children's spiritual, moral, social and cultural development;
- the development of identified 'key skills' of: 'communication'; 'application of number'; 'IT' (information technology); 'working with others'; 'improving one's own learning and performance'; and 'problem solving'; and
- learning relating to 'other aspects of the curriculum', specifically: 'thinking skills'; 'work-related learning' and 'education for sustainable development'.

(DfEE/QCA, 1999a: 8–9)

In addition, explicit requirements were established for all subjects to address the use of language and the use of information and communication technology across the curriculum.[1]

Similarly, the revised National Curriculum for Physical Education in Wales (ACCAC, 2000) highlighted that teachers should be providing opportunities for children to develop and apply the following 'common requirements':

- *Curriculum Cymreig*: 'knowledge and understanding of the cultural, economic, environmental, historical and linguistic characteristics of Wales';
- *Communication skills*: 'of speaking, listening, reading, writing and expressing ideas through a variety of media';

- *Mathematical skills:* 'of number, shape, space, measures and handling data';
- *Information technology skills:* 'to obtain, prepare, process and present information and communicating ideas with increasing independence';
- *Problem-solving skills:* 'of asking appropriate questions, making predictions and coming to informed decisions';
- *Creative skills:* 'the development and expression of ideas and imagination';
- *Personal and social education:* 'the attitudes, values, skills, knowledge and understanding relating to Personal and Social Education'.

(ACCAC, 2000: 5)

Undoubtedly, making connections between teaching and learning that occurs in the context of different subjects and thus developing coherency in learning across the curriculum remain important challenges for teachers in all subject areas. Research by Harland *et al.* (2002) in Northern Ireland and by Griffith (2000) in relation to the National Curriculum in England reaffirms that, regrettably, the curriculum experience is worryingly fragmented from the student perspective. The challenge to establish coherency is one for individual subjects, not just the whole curriculum. In government arenas there are very clear expectations that physical education will advance a broad range of learning. Interests in physical education and school sport clearly go well beyond the development of physical skills. As Cutforth (2003) has highlighted, the government 'is putting its faith in the profession to contribute significantly to the wider educational policy agenda – citizenship, health, behaviour, self-esteem, social responsibility, attainment – to name but a few' (p. 6). Thus, while physical education and school sport in England may be enjoying unprecedented levels of government investment, 'this investment also represents a huge challenge for the physical education profession – with increased investment comes increased responsibility and accountability to deliver results' (Cutforth, 2003: 6).

It is appropriate, however, to also acknowledge that the results expected from this government investment should not come as a surprise to the professional community. Indeed, they have featured prominently in claims that professional associations have made about learning in physical education. In 1999 a 'World Summit on Physical Education' issued a statement that 'quality physical education' helped to 'ensure integrated and rounded development of mind, body and spirit' and enhance children's social development. These sentiments were echoed by the Physical Education Association of the United Kingdom (PEAUK) in its statement that physical education:

- provides opportunities to promote spiritual, moral, social and cultural development and develops personal qualities such as self-esteem, independence, citizenship, tolerance and empathy;

- provides opportunities to promote key skills such as communication (verbal and non-verbal), application of number, IT, working with others, improving own learning and performance and problem solving;
- makes a strong contribution to the development of pupils' language through the extensive use of speaking and listening skills.

(PEAUK, 2001)

In our view Sport Education offers a robust framework for developing the cross-curricular potential of physical education in ways that will help to engage all students in the subject and in learning more broadly. Further, we contend that establishing such a framework may prove vital for the future prosperity of physical education in England. If current levels of investment are to be maintained or extended, the contribution of physical education and school sport to developing children's skills, knowledge and understanding in relation to personal, social and health education (PSHE), citizenship, literacy, numeracy and ICT will need to be evidenced. This and the following chapter therefore focus upon what may often be labelled as the 'other learning' that can be developed in and through physical education and sport in schools. We explore a number of ways in which Sport Education can be used to advance learning across the school curriculum. Again the ideas and examples that we provide have arisen from collaborative school based research and curriculum development (see Chapter 2) and are presented as ideas to be adapted and extended as appropriate in individual school contexts.

Sport Education: a prompt and structure for engaging with 'other learning'

As we explained in Chapter 1, Sport Education was developed with the explicit objective that children be educated 'in the fullest sense' (Siedentop, 1994: 4) and be provided with learning opportunities that extend beyond a sole focus on the role of player/performer. A number of the roles that typically feature in Sport Education, including press or publicity officer and team statistician, point directly to potential cross-curricular linkages. So too do some of the individual and collective responsibilities that are usually incorporated within a Sport Education season. These include, for example, designing a team logo or producing match reports, team photographs or other items for a team notice board or team portfolio (see Chapter 4). Thus, both the content and pedagogy of Sport Education encourage and enable connections to be established between learning in physical education and learning in other subject areas. Before focusing upon specific linkages, it is worth noting a number of general points in relation to the development of cross-curricular learning in Sport Education.

Inclusion

As indicated above, particular roles within Sport Education can be seen to link directly with learning in one or more other subject areas. The role of publicity officer or reporter can be linked with literacy and, more specifically, with the development of a range of writing and communication skills. The tasks required of the reporter/publicity officer will shape the nature and extent of Sport Education's contribution to the development of these skills. Potentially, this is also a role in which ICT skills, knowledge and understanding may be advanced, with different media (print, involving written and photographic materials; audio; video) used in the production and presentation of reports. An additional link could be made with music, with students exploring compilations that are appropriate to 'introduce' and provide background to sport commentary in particular activity settings.

The learning that can be associated with the role of reporter/publicity officer is therefore substantial. Other roles, such as coach or statistician, present similarly extensive possibilities for cross-curricular developments. However, if these various linkages are to be pursued then we need to consider ways to ensure that the learning opportunities associated with a particular role are enjoyed by more than a select few students. Important challenges arise in relation to the need to ensure that learning opportunities developed will be accessible to students with very different learning capabilities and needs. On some occasions it may be appropriate and beneficial for the whole class to undertake a task that is associated with one of the roles. Ideally learning experiences in Sport Education will be recognised and used to reinforce specific skills, knowledge or understanding which are also a current focus in another subject area. Hence, depending upon the learning priorities within mathematics, various statistical tasks could be set at particular points in the season for completion by everyone in the class rather than only the statistician. Similarly, at some point in the season and to link with ongoing work within English, all of the class might be required to write a match report that focused on the use of a particular genre.

While it is important to recognise possibilities for cross-curricular tasks that could usefully be undertaken by a whole class, it is clearly inappropriate to envisage that the potential learning links will be pursued with all learners, or to the same extent. Decisions about role allocations and provision of opportunities for students to shadow a classmate in a role, or at some point in the season undertake a specific task relating to a role, should be made with individual cross-curricular learning needs in mind. As far as possible, Sport Education should seek to provide learning experiences that will enable all students to extend existing learning strengths, and help them to address areas of learning that have been identified as in need of development. Arrangements to share roles, work within a peer-mentoring framework or rotation of roles are all relevant to this aim. The challenge will be to promote an atmosphere and understanding within teams in which there is a shared commitment to celebrating different strengths in learning and supporting each other in working on areas in which progress is felt to be limited and/or difficult. This will not always be easy. For example, a teacher may be well aware that a particular student could benefit greatly from the additional focus on literacy that involvement in the role of team reporter would provide. Yet there is clearly the likelihood that the student will be hesitant about the prospect of taking on this role and all too aware of the limitations of their current skills, knowledge and understanding in relation to the demands of the role. Inevitably, it will only be in time and probably after several experiences of working within the Sport Education framework that students will readily seek out opportunities to focus upon areas of learning in which they lack confidence or expertise.

Progressive development

In considering cross-curricular learning in Sport Education it will not be possible to attempt to develop every possible linkage at once or in the context of any single Sport Education unit. Nor would it be appropriate. The approach should be selective and reflect the learning needs of the particular students involved, the curriculum activities being undertaken in potential 'link subjects' and the practicalities of developing prospective links. The complexity of cross-curricular experiences will need to suit different learning capabilities and grow over time to reflect advances in learning. Starting with cross-curricular learning activities that are relatively straightforward is advisable. Time for planning and meeting with other staff is undoubtedly an important consideration. Particularly in early days of development it will be important to be sensitive to the time required to develop cross-curricular activities and to avoid placing excessive demands upon either physical education or other subject staff. Hopefully after the first experiences of incorporating a cross-curricular link within a Sport Education season, the interests of all staff involved will have been stimulated. The development process should then focus on joint reflection, review, refinement and, possibly, expansion of the link activities.

Structured development

The above emphasis of the need to be selective and to adopt a clearly phased approach to development relates to concern that the intended learning outcomes of a Sport Education unit should be made explicit and then be pursued in a structured way. There is an obvious danger that Sport Education is promoted as making numerous connections to learning in other curriculum areas and to the development of several 'key skills', but then fails to direct adequate attention to many of the claimed connections. If Sport Education is to be an effective vehicle via which progress in learning any one

of PSHE, citizenship, literacy, numeracy, ICT or other area is advanced, relevant, clearly focused and well structured learning opportunities need to be
planned. Whatever cross-curricular link we are considering, progressions
in learning experiences should be clear for both teachers and learners and
tasks embedded in the experience that can inform planning for progression
(see Chapter 4).

Collaborative development

Needless to say, the effectiveness of any developments that are directed
towards strengthening linkages across the curriculum will be greatly
enhanced if they are undertaken collaboratively, with roles and responsibilities shared amongst staff with various subject expertise. Discussions
about the joint learning activities that it is best to incorporate within a season
will be vital in establishing shared vision and ownership. These discussions
may highlight opportunities for learning experiences to be developed in the
Sport Education season that:

- consciously revisit and seek to extend particular skills, knowledge and
  understanding that has *recently been addressed* in another subject area;
- directly link with learning experiences that are occurring *simultaneously*
  in another area of the curriculum, such that over a number of weeks
  there is an ongoing 'dynamic' between teaching in Sport Education and
  that in one or more other subject areas; and/or
- anticipate and seek to *prepare a foundation* for learning experiences in
  another subject area that will come after the Sport Education season has
  been completed.

There will then be a need to clarify whether there is joint interest in pursuing
the opportunities identified and to consider the practicalities of the prospective developments for all involved. Everyone involved will need to feel
that there is value in advancing the new ideas, that the prospective developments are realistic, and also be confident that there are structures in place for
dialogue and shared reflection as developments progress. Roles and
responsibilities in the development process need to be clear, agreed and part
of an infrastructure to support the process (Hickey and Dinan-Thompson,
2003).
    In secondary schools it seems inevitable that a lack of time for collabora-
tive curriculum planning activities and limited awareness amongst staff of
the recent, ongoing and planned future learning activities in other subject
areas will be cited as barriers to this well grounded joint development of
cross-curricular learning. Yet, we are hopeful that over time, and particularly
as more staff become familiar with what Sport Education involves and seeks
to achieve, interest and enthusiasm for joint work will grow, and teaching and
learning in Sport Education will permeate longstanding subject boundaries.

But at the same time we are positive about the cross-curricular developments that may arise in the context of Sport Education in primary schools. Certainly we expect that many teachers within primary schools will relate well to the broader perspective on learning that is embedded in Sport Education and, furthermore, may have opportunities to make notable advances in cross-curricular work.

Assessment

Having stressed the need for cross-curricular learning to be well structured, progressive, linked with identified individual learning needs and valued by teachers and learners, assessment emerges as a key consideration in developments. In Chapter 4 we discussed at some length the notion of 'assessment for learning'. The point to reaffirm here is that if we are genuinely concerned that Sport Education should advance a range of learning then we must devote considerable attention to establishing assessment for that range. Only then will we be able to state with confidence that Sport Education is engaging with learners' needs in their 'full sense' as Siedentop (1994) intended.

Sport Education: many points of potential connection in teaching and learning across the curriculum

The constraints of space prevent us from addressing at length the numerous cross-curricular developments that can be inspired and advanced through Sport Education. We necessarily provide only a 'broad brush' view of the potential and thus centre attention upon three areas of prospective development: English, literacy and communication skills; mathematics and numeracy; and thirdly, information and communications technology (ICT). For each area we indicate potential learning experiences. We point to opportunities for links to extend to further curriculum subjects. Chapter 6 then specifically considers links between Sport Education, PSHE, citizenship and leadership. The points below are not intended to be exhaustive. Rather, teachers developing Sport Education will come up with ideas of their own and will also recognise the ideas that it will be appropriate to try out with particular groups of students.

English, literacy and communication skills

- Writing match reports. The required length and issues relating to genre/ style can be specified and vary throughout the season or as students progress from one Sport Education unit to another, to link with the sequence of learning in English and potentially drama. Teams might be required to produce a script of a team performance or write one of their match reports as a poem. The reporter or team can also be required to produce suitable photographs to accompany written reports. Guidance might address specific words or phrases to be used in reports (see Appendix A).

- Reviewing and analysing the content and style of reports published in newspapers and specialist sports magazines for various sports and special events such as the Olympics or Commonwealth Games. Tasks can be developed that link with learning in media studies, geography, history or modern foreign languages. Analytical tasks focusing on sports reporting and publicity materials can also be used to extend awareness and understanding of inclusion (see Chapter 3). For example, attention could be directed to the gendered language evident in students' own work as well as in media coverage of sport.

- Writing player profiles, possibly also featuring use of photography and/ or involving students interviewing a classmate to gather information for the profile. A basic interview schedule can be provided or the design of the schedule can be a further team or individual task. Recording skills can link with work in ICT. Again, profiles produced can also prompt further investigation of inclusion issues including particularly the ways in which prejudices and stereotyping may be seen in some of the profiles produced.

- Producing an audio commentary, for either a set video sequence of play or for a 'live' game or performance. The demands of commentary tasks can be graduated towards live commentary during the end of season festival.

- Producing an outline for a warm-up routine or skill practice to be undertaken with the team. Attention can focus on key terminology and the style and structure needed to ensure that the outline is an effective guide for the leader/coach. The effectiveness of the outline can be evaluated after it has been used in a practical setting.

- Leading a warm-up routine or skill practice. Attention will be upon both verbal and non-verbal communication skills required to organise and go through the practice effectively and the skills needed to respond to issues that may arise during a practice, such as uncertainty amongst some team members about what is required.

- Producing and compiling materials for a personal journal, team board, team portfolio or a special display for a school parents' evening or an induction day for students about to join the school. Links can be made with skills, knowledge and understanding being addressed within art and ICT. Examples of team logos developed by students at Mountbatten School and Language College together with portfolio materials appear in Chapters 10, 11 and 12.

- Planning a group presentation for a school assembly or parents' evening, undertaking a specific element of the presentation and evaluating the presentation from an individual and group perspective.

- Officiating during a team practice session, formal competition or performance and, if required, submitting written reports relating to behavioural incidents within matches.

- Developing verbal and non-verbal communication within a team to establish a shared understanding of tactics and strategies to be used within a game setting or points of transition within a dance or gymnastic performance.
- Producing a programme for the end of season festival, incorporating links to learning in art and ICT (with the use of scanned photographs or images and/or development of a web based version of the programme).
- Developing lyrics for a team chant or song, linking with learning activities in music.
- Negotiating and producing formal 'contracts' for all team members and/ or those members in specific roles (detailing the responsibilities that it is agreed will be fulfilled in the role).
- Negotiating within a team the allocation of roles and responsibilities within many of the above learning activities. Team talk sessions can be planned and structured to prompt students to explore, from an equity perspective, assumptions that underpin their views about the capabilities of others and who should take on particular roles or responsibilities. Recording a team talk can enable the group to critically evaluate ways in which stereotypical assumptions relating to, for example, gender, sexuality, ethnicity, body shape and physical abilities are reflected in their own language, and verbal and non-verbal inter-actions with each another (linking with PSHE and citizenship, see Chapter 6).
- Negotiating with other teams the penalties that should be enforced if rules or playing agreements are broken and, similarly, awards that should be made to individual players or teams for outstanding contributions to their team and/or the Sport Education experience. So called 'champagne moments' at Mountbatten School and Language College (see Chapters 10–12) were developed to prompt students to identify instances in which play or behaviour within Sport Education was considered exceptional. These included moments that featured students acting in notably cooperative and inclusive ways towards team-mates or an opposing team. Other 'moments' related to exceptional performances by players (with 'exceptional' understood to be relative to playing ability) and to performance in one of the Sport Education roles. Thus, a referee may be recognised for their success in calming a potentially volatile situation. Once again, links can clearly be made with PSHE and citizenship (see Chapter 6).
- Maintaining a cumulative list of key words and new terminology arising through the season.
- Using a second language in making announcements during the end of season festival, in the festival programme or in one of the match or event reports produced during the season (linking with work in modern foreign languages).

Mathematics and numeracy

- Collecting a range of statistical data throughout a season. This may include the results of competitive games or challenges involving other teams, goals scored by individuals and the team, points awarded for fair play and penalties incurred for incidents of foul play, data from repeated performances in specific skill or fitness challenges through the season, points awarded from peer evaluation of the performance of officials, and data from assessments of match reports, team logo designs, journals, portfolios or the team board.
- Undertaking specific analysis tasks with selected data.
- Presenting selected data and the results of analysis in a variety of formats, linking with learning activities within mathematics and with the development of ICT skills and knowledge.
- Participating in warm-up activities, drill practices and challenges that demand understanding of set distances, time and/or speed.
- Becoming familiar with, being able to explain and practically demonstrating an understanding of rules that feature a numerical dimension.
- Studying transfer and sponsorship arrangements in the sport that the Sport Education unit is focusing on, from both a monetary and linguistic perspective (thus also linking with literacy). This and the next learning activity present clear opportunities to promote students' 'financial capability' and 'enterprise and entrepreneurial skills' (DfEE/QCA, 1999b). In time, students may be challenged to generate their own sponsorship for the end of season festival and establish a sponsorship committee to undertake this task (linking with citizenship, see Chapter 6).
- Producing a budget for the end of season festival and keeping accounts for spending relating to the festival.

Information and Communications Technology (ICT)

- Using digital cameras to take team photographs and transferring these into a printed form.
- Using video cameras to record playing sequences to use in individual or group evaluation tasks.
- Editing video-recordings for use in a team evaluation activity led by the coach.
- Audio-recording commentaries.
- Producing a compact disc of a music compilation to be used in a team performance or during the end of season festival (for example, in medal ceremonies).
- Scanning images to use in producing materials for team portfolios, boards, festival programmes or posters, linking with learning activities in art and/or media studies.

- Designing and producing certificates to be awarded at the end of the season, linking with learning activities in design and technology.
- Designing and producing a printed form of a team logo and/or team uniform, linking with learning activities in art and potentially design and technology.
- Using heart-rate monitors and/or other specialist technology in learning activities focusing upon aspects of fitness and the development of training programmes (linking with learning activities in science).
- Accessing web based resources to gather information for an individual or group task. For example, officials may be given the responsibility of accessing the relevant governing body of sport website to find out the rules relating to the activity being undertaken or a particular aspect of play/performance (such as the taking of a penalty in soccer). The next stage of this task could be to discuss the rules with the team coach in preparation for a practice session.
- Maintaining a computer based individual learning profile or journal through the Sport Education season.

Participation in some of these learning activities may contribute to an ICT learning portfolio that is developed and maintained across subjects and can thereby help to strengthen linkages in teaching and learning relating to ICT. In some schools in England a similar approach may be taken in addressing the new National Curriculum requirements for citizenship (see Chapter 6).

Conclusion: Sport Education – a connective pedagogy?

In discussing potential cross-curricular developments we have focused on various skills, knowledge and understanding that Sport Education, developed with particular groups of students in particular schools, can seek to advance through collaborative curriculum planning and teaching. In many respects, attention has been on matters of content in relation to learning rather than the processes of teaching and learning. It is therefore important to recall that key characteristics of the Sport Education framework provide an enabling structure for cross-curricular developments. Phases of a season can be used as focal points for introducing links with various subjects and/or key points of progression in the link work. Several of the individual and team tasks that invariably feature in a Sport Education season directly prompt engagement with cross-curricular skills, knowledge and understanding. Various roles and their associated responsibilities reinforce and can serve to bring to the fore particular linkages. Firstly, it is appropriate to consider the potential for the defining characteristics and principles of Sport Education (see Chapter 1) to permeate across schools and provide the framework for some of the learning within other subject areas. In primary schools, many class teachers may already be pursuing some of this potential, with group project work (relating to various subject areas) spanning several weeks. They and colleagues across secondary schools may also be actively developing journal and portfolio based activities. Others will be experienced in supporting students to produce displays of their work and/or use new ICT in their learning. Discussions with staff across schools and phases will therefore be crucial in furthering the development of Sport Education in relation to 'whole school pedagogy' and maximising its potential to enhance teaching and learning within and beyond physical education.

Note

1   With respect to requirements to address the use of ICT across the curriculum it was stated that 'At key stage 1 there are no statutory requirements to teach the use of ICT in the programmes of study for the non-core foundation subjects. Teachers should use their judgements to decide where it is appropriate to teach the use of ICT across these subjects. At other key stages, there are statutory requirements to use ICT in all subjects, except physical education (DfEE/QCA, 1999a: 38).

References

Awdurdod Cymwysterau Cwricwlwm Ac Asesu Cymru (ACCAC) (2000). *Physical Education in the National Curriculum in Wales*, Cardiff: ACCAC.

Cutforth, C. (2003). Are We Up to the Challenge?, *PE and Sport Today*, 11, pp. 6–9.

Department for Education and Employment (DfEE)/Qualifications and Curriculum Authority (QCA) (1999a). *Physical Education: The National Curriculum for England*, London: DfEE.

Department for Education and Employment (DfEE)/Qualifications and Curriculum Authority (QCA) (1999b). *Citizenship: The National Curriculum for England*, London: DfEE.

Griffith, R. (2000). *National Curriculum: National Disaster? Education and Citizenship*, London: Routledge.

Harland, J., Moor, H., Kinder, K. and Ashworth, M. (2002). *Is the Curriculum Working? The Key Stage 3 Northern Ireland Curriculum Cohort Study*, Slough, UK: National Foundation for Educational Research.

Hickey, R. and Dinan-Thompson, M. (2003). Collaborative Curriculum Making: The Interplay of Ownership and Dialogue, *Curriculum Perspectives*, 23, 3, pp. 24–33.

Physical Education Association of the United Kingdom (PEAUK) (2001). *PEAUK Policy Statements*, http://www.pea.uk.com/menu.html, accessed 21 January 2001.

Siedentop, D. (1994). *Sport Education: Quality PE through Positive Sport Experiences*, Champaign, Illinois: Human Kinetics.

World Summit on Physical Education (1999) *The Berlin Agenda for Action I* http://www.education.man.ac.uk/pecrisis/agenda_eng.htm, accessed 30 July 2002.

Appendix A: Vocabulary and match reports

(From Sport Education Soccer, Mountbatten School and Language College)

Words/phrases to be used for match reports:

opponents	hat-trick
crossbar	post
goal	midfield
attack	defence
forward	defender
goalkeeper	space
right-wing cross	left-wing cross
half-time	full-time
crunching tackle	composure
possession	rebound
technique	striker
glorious chance	foul
performance	a wave of attacks
conceding a goal	stunning volley
clinched the points	clean sheet
basement boys	crucial goal
steely determination	floated corner
close range	snatched the points

6 Sport Education, citizenship and leadership

Dawn Penney, Gill Clarke and Mandy Quill

Introduction

Sport Education has been recognised internationally as offering rich potential for the development of citizenship and leadership. Specifically, a number of 'citizenship issues' (of behaviour, attitudes, values, rules and traditions) have been addressed in active and 'authentic' ways via Sport Education and adaptations of it (see Chapter 1). In focusing attention upon matters of fair play, respect for all participants, respect for all abilities, the development of leadership and social skills, and in the challenges that it presents to students to work collaboratively, Sport Education seems an important vehicle for citizenship education.

In considering the prospective development of Sport Education in England, it is notable that the government has emphasised the qualities and values that physical activity and sport can instil in young people. Indeed, the Prime Minister has openly stated that 'Sport is a powerful and often under-used tool that can help Government to achieve a number of ambitious goals' (Blair in DCMS/Strategy Unit, 2002: 5). In an accompanying statement, Tessa Jowell, the Secretary of State for Culture, Media and Sport, provided further insights into the political and social goals that sport is associated with:

> I agree with the teachers, police and community workers who all find that sport can also make a valuable contribution to the way people live their lives. It helps to improve their all round educational performance, to build confidence, leadership and teamwork in our young people, to combat social exclusion, reduce crime and build stronger communities.
> (Jowell in DCMS/Strategy Unit, 2002: 7)

The government's proposals for changes to the curriculum for 14–16 year olds in England were also notable in identifying a specific role and focus for physical education, together with citizenship, religious education, sex education and careers education, in shaping young people's lives. Collectively, these curriculum areas are intended to ensure that children will 'continue to learn to be responsible and healthy adults' (DfES, 2003: 6).

Policy statements relating to both sport and education have thus 'cemented' the education–sport–citizenship linkage. In parallel, the link has been reflected in and further promoted by specific initiatives. 'Dreams and Teams' is one such initiative designed to pursue the 'citizenship education' role that sport can play. It is an international project developed by the British Council[1] and Youth Sport Trust[2] promoting leadership skills, confidence and international links in and through opportunities in which young people learn to lead sport.[3] 'Step into Sport' is another project developed by sporting agencies (specifically, the British Sports Trust,[4] the Youth Sport Trust, and Sport England[5]) with clear links to citizenship issues. 'Step into Sport' has focused on volunteering in sport, and the development of Sport Education in physical education has been an integral part of the project.

Against this political and policy backdrop this chapter explores ways in which personal, social and health education (PSHE), citizenship and leadership education can be taken forward in practice in Sport Education. Discussion further illustrates the diverse potential of Sport Education as a pedagogical framework. It links directly with the National Curriculum for PSHE and citizenship at key stages 1 and 2 (DfEE/QCA, 1999a) and citizenship at key stages 3 and 4 (DfEE/QCA, 1999b) in England. But before considering specifics, it is worth first reflecting upon different views of what is, and indeed should be, involved in citizenship education.

Education and citizenship: a commitment to different futures

In England and internationally, there is considerable variation in the practices developed under the banner of 'citizenship education' (and similarly PSHE). In England the National Curriculum requirements for citizenship established a three strand focus for teaching and learning, comprising knowledge and understanding about becoming informed citizens; skills of enquiry and communication; and skills of participation and responsible action (DfEE/QCA, 1999b). However, there has been no consensus about how to approach implementation of these requirements. Further, while many physical educationalists may see obvious connections between their subject and citizenship, it is notable that frequently publications offering guidance for the development of citizenship totally overlook these connections. Instead, it is invariably subjects such as English and history that are the focus of attention. We have a long way to go before there is widespread recognition of the rich potential of physical education and school sport to contribute to the development of citizenship education. A proactive approach to promoting that potential is undoubtedly needed. Yet, as Theodoulides and Armour (2001) have emphasised, it is equally important to avoid making sweeping claims about the personal and social dimensions of learning in physical education that cannot be substantiated (see also Theodoulides, 2003). If we believe that physical education can or does instil in children particular attitudes, values and behaviours, and that it presents them with learning experiences that directly address these matters, we need to be able to provide evidence of both appropriately focused provision, and progress towards specific learning outcomes.

Sport Education may provide an important means of adopting a well structured approach to citizenship education in and through physical education, which also incorporates formal assessment of skills, knowledge and understanding that are central to citizenship. But again, there is a need firstly for clarification of the visions being pursued.

Bottery and Wright (2000) discussed the significance of teachers taking varying stances in relation to their role as professionals. They presented a spectrum of possibilities. At one end are professionals 'of limited technical rationality', who 'believe that their job can be encapsulated by teaching a subject, handling the problems of children, and conforming to predetermined external dictates' (p. 3). At the other are what they term 'ecological professionals', who 'believe that they must understand that to do their job effectively it is insufficient to deal just with classroom and institutional matters' (p. 3). This chapter reflects our support for Bottery and Wright's (2000) view that 'a crucial function of teachers as professionals needs to be their engagement with matters beyond the classroom' (p. 10) and, more specifically, with a form of citizenship education that is directed towards the development of inclusive futures and societies. We hope to prompt reflection about what citizenship education 'is really about' and therefore the types of learning experiences that we should be looking to create under the banner of 'citizenship'. As Gill and Reid (1999) observed in commenting upon civics education in Australia, one approach may be to seek the development of 'safe citizens': 'individuals who will accept current social and political arrangements and who will limit their political involvement to voting at periodic intervals' (p. 64). They also highlighted that tendencies to 'historicise' citizenship may well contribute to a 'retrospective orientation . . . which may not be the best way to involve young people in active engagement with contemporary issues' (p. 67). Citizenship may become 'seen as a product of history and the legal system' and citizens 'those who have gone before' (p. 68) or, alternatively, 'others' rather than oneself.

A 'detached' and historical perspective is not one that we wish to dwell on or promote here. We recognise that Sport Education could provide a focus for exploring historical practices and long-established sporting and social traditions in an essentially unquestioning manner. But it is also our contention that Sport Education presents exciting potential for physical education to contribute to a citizenship education that is characterised by a so called 'futures perspective', involving critical and creative thinking about 'possible, probable and preferable' futures (Hicks, 2001). We believe that Sport Education can provide opportunities for children and young people to envisage, explore, evaluate and re-envisage their *preferred* futures in physical activity, sport, their school and local communities (see Hicks, 2001). This reflects the view that neither citizenship nor community should be seen as static and monolithic concepts, but instead things that young people have a key role to play in shaping for themselves (see Hall and Williamson, 1999). Arguably we need to encourage this same sort of active and influential thinking in relation to physical activity and sport. Indeed, Hicks stresses that an absence of visions of '*alternative* futures' represents an important barrier to citizenship education contributing to 'the betterment of society' (p. 232). We might well say the same about physical education or sport. Unless we encourage creative and critical thinking about the forms that sport and competition can take, and the rules that might be adopted, we will effectively limit the potential futures that young people will see for themselves in sport. Many will struggle to see a personal future that involves positive experiences of physical activity and sport. In encouraging students to take greater responsibility in shaping their learning experiences, and by using modified forms of play and competition, Sport Education can encourage students to think seriously about preferred forms, rules and roles. Importantly, Sport Education also offers them the chance to develop and experience those preferred forms, rules and roles. Sport Education can therefore be empowering, both in an immediate sense (with students playing a greater role in shaping their own learning experiences) but also in relation to young people's visions of possible futures and their ability to make their visions a reality. This chapter explores ways in which such empowerment can practically be developed. Chapter 7 then extends discussion of the 'futures' dimension of citizenship in looking at how Sport Education can relate to the development of lifelong learning and lifelong learners.

Active citizenship: involvement, influence and authenticity in learning

> Personal, social and health education (PSHE) and citizenship help to give pupils the knowledge, skills and understanding they need to lead confident, healthy, independent lives and to become informed, active, responsible citizens.
>
> (DfEE/QCA, 1999a)

Adopting the view that young people have an active role to play in shaping their own futures demands that we take a particular stance in relation to the prospective development of citizenship education. It necessitates a particular approach to the implementation of the National Curriculum requirements in England for PSHE at key stages 1 and 2 and for citizenship at key stages 3 and 4. Implementation of the new requirements needs to be concerned with 'changing behaviour and relationships throughout education' (Alexander, 2001), transforming schools and their relationship with local and national communities. Priorities are students having a sense of ownership of their learning, an appreciation of its purposes, and 'a sense of competence that qualifies one for whatever opportunities may arise in future, and also the capacity to *create* opportunities' (Alexander, 2001: 31, our emphasis). As Alexander states, 'this is about learning *as* citizenship' (p. 31, our emphasis). 'Citizenship is learnt above all through experience, by taking part in activities, discussion and decisions which have a real influence on what happens' (p. 32). It is about 'sharing responsibility for learning, so that teachers involve young people in planning their own learning as far as possible' (p. 66).

Sport Education can encourage these kinds of development in various ways. There are a number of opportunities for students to be offered the chance to consider and debate arrangements within their Sport Education season and the likely consequences of particular decisions. Selection of teams or roles, decisions about points and/or reward systems that will be applied throughout a season, and the format of the end of season festival are all times when this type of critical reflection and responsibility can be encouraged. Undoubtedly, developing this requires planning and structures to suit learners of differing ages and capabilities and with different prior learning experiences. While some students may be encouraged to come up with their own ideas, others will need to be presented with a range of scenarios and prompts about their varied implications (particularly in relation to concerns for inclusion, see Chapter 3). As we emphasise below and illustrate in the chapters that follow in Part 3, there are many opportunities to 'empower learners' in Sport Education.

Negotiating roles and relations: empowering learners in Sport Education

'Empowerment', rather like 'citizenship', is a problematic term. It is all too easy to make assumptions about what is (or is not) involved in teaching and learning. There are, however, several dimensions to empowerment in learning, and of learners, that Sport Education can address. It can encourage and enable students to take progressively greater responsibility for their own learning, for supporting others' learning, for contributing to collective achievement, but also for deciding upon the direction that learning should go and the forms it should take. From this perspective, empowerment therefore includes encouraging reflection on the consequences of decisions and, in particular, how particular decisions will impact upon everyone's learning opportunities, likely progress and enjoyment. But there is no guarantee that Sport Education will achieve any of this. Rather, progressive empowerment and the development of a shared, collective responsibility for learning will be achieved through appropriate structures and strategies. The defining principles and characteristics of Sport Education identified in Chapter 1 provide signposts to a number of key structures and strategies for empowering learners.

New roles, new learning opportunities and new responsibilities

In addressing roles other than that of 'player', Sport Education may positively involve some students in physical education, perhaps for the first time. To have the opportunity to act as an official or a match reporter may be empowering for the students involved. But this will depend upon the process via which decisions are made about which students will take on the various roles and in what circumstances, and also the reactions to an individual's performance in a role. Taking on a new role can dis-empower as well as empower students and it is something that therefore needs to be treated with great sensitivity. Thus, teachers have an important role to play in allocations and in supporting students in taking on the responsibilities that come with a role.

Developing 'job descriptions' for roles can help to clarify expectations and, as we see in Part 3, students can be creative in progressively extending job descriptions/roles and taking clear ownership of their roles. Another approach is for students to sign up to a charter or contract, either as a member of a team or in relation to a specific role. Charters or contracts can be presented by a teacher in a set form, or be a matter of negotiation and shared development (see Hastie and Buchanen, 2000). An example of a team captain's contract developed in a Sport Education soccer unit at Mountbatten School and Language College (see Chapters 10–12) is provided in Appendix A.

The specific roles within Sport Education also provide opportunities for empowering students to take greater responsibility for their own learning and actively support the learning of others. The roles of captain, coach, fitness adviser, warm-up coordinator, official, statistician and publicity officer all require students to undertake 'independent' preparation prior to making an input to a group learning activity. Guidance and support in this process will be crucial, with students therefore being directed towards appropriate resources and provided with a structured framework for their task. Providing pointers for students to follow in undertaking some of the responsibilities associated with a role will be vital if experience of the role is to be positive and enjoyable for the individual student and their fellow learners. In Chapter 13 a trainee teacher explains the way in which a Sport Education handbook produced for the students provided this sort of structured guidance. The handbook supported them throughout the season in taking on both individual and shared responsibilities for learning. Meanwhile at Mountbatten School and Language College, students within the Sport Education groups have been provided with special passes to the ICT rooms to encourage and facilitate individual and group progress with a variety of tasks (see Chapters 10–12). At Mountbatten role sharing has also been used as a way of supporting students taking on new roles and responsibilities, and prompting cooperative learning within teams. Several possibilities have emerged for sharing arrangements. Two students can share responsibility for a role throughout the season with neither student having had prior experience in the role. Alternatively, a rotation system can be developed, whereby, having played a role, the next step is to mentor a team-mate in the role. In the latter, responsibility is extended to a more supportive and instructive role in mentoring. The former arrangement poses challenges for two students to negotiate their respective contributions to the 'job-sharing' situation and establish effective ways of working together.

Once again, it is important to stress the flexibility of the Sport Education framework and the need for adaptation to suit individual school, activity and group contexts. In the Sport Education netball unit at Mountbatten (see Chapter 10), the role of 'warm-up coordinator' was one that students were happy to share. The following different arrangements for sharing this role were tried at Mountbatten:

- A different person in the team has responsibility for leading the warm-up each week.
- The person in the team with the title of 'warm-up coordinator' has responsibility for coordinating the warm-up, and therefore delegating different parts of the warm-up to various team members.
- The role is a shared role between two members of the team who work collaboratively to plan and lead the warm-up each week.
- The role is a shared role between two members of the team, with the pairings rotating. One member of the team leads with another assisting. The next week the assistant takes the lead role and a third team member takes up the role of assistant. This pattern of rotation through the team continues throughout the season.

These or other variations may be appropriate to use in other schools with particular groups. More generally there is a need to acknowledge that, with or without arrangements for role sharing, some of the responsibilities associated with roles may be very challenging and/or daunting for some students. Arrangements need to be sensitive to this and be able to accommodate students choosing *not* to take a role/responsibility (see Clarke and Quill, 2003). Sport Education offers important opportunities for group discussion of the nature and demands of various responsibilities and the reasons for students feeling that they are able to take on a responsibility or, in contrast, do not feel comfortable in doing so. As we discuss further below, developing a collective responsibility for learning that engages with students' feelings and self-perceptions in a sensitive and supportive way is a key challenge in Sport Education.

Collective responsibility within teams

The team basis of Sport Education and, in particular, the fact that teams are maintained throughout the season, clearly establishes learning as a collective responsibility. Mutual support is fundamental to the enjoyment and progress of all individuals and to the team's success. Students involved in Sport Education have highlighted that they enjoy and see value in the continuity of their team membership through the season (Clarke and Quill, 2003). Nevertheless, we need to recognise that positive team dynamics are not assured, but rather will only result from careful planning and ongoing guidance and support from teachers (see Azzarito and Ennis, 2003).

Teachers' guidance in team selections and selection of captains/leaders is likely to be crucial in the first Sport Education season that students experience. At Mountbatten the staff have been successful in progressing student responsibilities in the selection process. Following teachers determining the teams and appointing team leaders, students have taken on the task of selecting teams and electing captains using criteria provided by the teachers. The next logical progression is to prompt students to develop their own criteria for these selections. In Chapter 13 Emily, a trainee teacher developing Sport Education at Brookfield Sports College, explains how she utilised two students' knowledge of different strengths in learning amongst their classmates and her own knowledge of the demands of the various roles, within a collaborative team and role selection process.

Guidance from teachers will similarly be a key factor in teams establishing and maintaining ways of working together that are effective (in relation to individual and group learning priorities) and inclusive. We cannot expect students to instantly understand differences in individual learning needs or recognise ways in which they may best support each other in making progress, or ways in which they are currently failing to do so. Ongoing prompts, set structures (or rules) for the allocation of responsibilities in specific learning activities, and structured collaborative assessment tasks (see below and Chapter 4) will all help to ensure that responsibilities are shared in ways that take account of individual learning needs, preferences and progress. Without adequate guidance there are dangers that teams become dysfunctional and fail to facilitate sustained progress in learning for at least some students. It is interesting to note that at Mountbatten some of the students expressed a preference for 'ability based teams' to be developed in certain activities, and teachers have similarly seen benefits in these arrangements. In both gymnastics and athletics, ability based teams have proved effective and supportive. These arrangements and the mutual support that was then generated between the various teams helped lower skilled students in particular to feel that their performances were valued (see Chapters 11 and 12). Yet, we can also reflect that in some instances ability based teams will be in danger of sustaining negative and stereotypical attitudes relating to physical ability and participation in various sporting activities. Membership of an ability based team gives an explicit label to learners in different teams and, furthermore, one that may dis-empower them within or beyond the Sport Education curriculum setting. That said, there is a need to be aware that mixed ability settings can similarly produce tensions in relation to concerns to be promoting inclusion and a 'transformative perspective' in developing Sport Education (see Chapters 1 and 5). Familiar, hierarchical and stereotypical positioning of learners (and more specifically of girls as compared to boys, or of students of a particular body shape or from a particular ethnic group) can easily be reaffirmed and actively reinforced as responsibilities are established and shared amongst team members. Furthermore we can reflect that, while it may be easy to talk of students developing acceptance of one another as members of a team, an issue to pursue is whether that acceptance goes beyond acceptance of being a strong or relatively weak player. Is there acceptance of others as *equal* in the team (Azzarito and Ennis, 2003)? An important and undoubtedly challenging collective responsibility to prompt within Sport Education is the responsibility to critically reflect upon both the attitudes and values that underlie decisions and the attitudes and values being promoted or suppressed as a consequence of decisions.

For many students the real challenges will lie beyond Sport Education lessons. Francis's (1998) study of students' behaviours and interactions within primary school settings has vividly illustrated that we should not assume that the collective responsibility and mutual support fostered within lessons will be maintained beyond them. In Francis's research girls were positioned 'on the periphery of the boys' football space', facing resistance to their involvement in the game '*because* they are girls' (Francis, 1998: 92, original emphasis). The girls explained that occasionally a few of them would be 'allowed' 'the privilege' of participation but boys would then often belittle them. Similarly, Claire's (2001) research involving children in key stage 2 led her to stress that:

> Identity, acceptance and belonging may be central to a healthy citizenry but pride in one's personal identity is not always confirmed by others; they may use the very aspects of your personal identity [such as ethnicity or sexuality] which are most important to you to 'diss' you and your family.
>
> (Claire, 2001: 47)

Claire (2001) reminds us that 'Positive identities do not develop in a social vacuum but are sustained or undermined through positive or negative experiences in the wider political, economic and social arena' (p. 49). Furthermore, other research has directly illustrated ways in which inequity may be institutionalised in schools and in school sport (see Lynch and Lodge, 2002). Collectively these research findings reaffirm the relevance of Sport Education to teaching and learning in both primary and secondary school contexts, the appropriateness of focusing upon PSHE and citizenship issues in developing Sport Education and, thirdly, the need for the development of Sport Education to extend beyond lesson contexts.

Finally, in relation to matters of team composition and responsibility for learning, we report a more pragmatic issue that we have faced. In the Sport Education netball unit at Mountbatten (see Chapter 10) student absences left very obvious 'gaps' in teams.[6] If players were moved from other teams then the sense of affiliation was lost. To overcome this, a simple transfer system was introduced. Teams were also increased in size to form squads. Bonus points were awarded for full attendance and if a full squad was present then the captain had to rotate the players so that everyone had an opportunity to play in the games. Teams short of players could negotiate the loan of a player from another squad. An extra bonus point was awarded to the team loaning a player. In situations where Sport Education teams are graded or in more than one league, promotion and relegation rules could also be introduced linked to attendance. Arrangements such as these illustrate one way in which specific attitudes and behaviours can be very directly encouraged and explicitly celebrated within Sport Education lessons and seasons.

Extending involvement and responsibility to assessment

As discussed in Chapter 4, one of the most significant ways in which Sport Education can empower students in their own learning is via new developments in assessment. There are many ways in which self- and peer assessment can be incorporated in Sport Education and for successful completion of an assessment task to be established as a collective responsibility. But in considering links to PSHE, citizenship and more specifically 'active citizenship', there is a need to be posing some critical questions of assessment tasks and processes, and furthermore actively engaging students in such questioning. We should be looking for team and group talks, and discussions between teachers across the school, that involve debates about:

- the hoped-for learning outcomes of the season;
- what and whose values and interests these are recognising or overlooking;
- the tasks that would be appropriate as a means of tracking progress towards particular outcomes;
- within those tasks, what might constitute appropriate criteria for assessment of progress towards the outcomes;
- how and when assessment should occur, and what roles teachers and students should have in the assessment process.

We see Sport Education as offering important opportunities for students to take far more active roles in 'assessment for learning' (see Chapter 4) and for their responsibilities in the learning process to thereby be significantly extended.

Rules, rewards, behaviours and values

Sport Education is concerned with children developing a respect for and understanding of rules, their purposes and implications (Siedentop, 1994). Again, we emphasise the need for critical questioning to be embedded in

Sport Education. Students need to be encouraged and enabled to explore not only the 'status quo' formal and informal rules and regulations within sports, sport organisations and events, but also possible alternatives to the status quo. Sport Education has an important role to play in extending students' knowledge and understanding of dominant attitudes, beliefs and values within physical education, sport, schools and society and the ways in which these shape (and constrain) individual lives. As we discussed in Chapter 4, Sport Education point and reward systems can promote very clear contrasts to arrangements that students are familiar with in other physical education and sport settings. The intention is that, in time, ideas relating to alternative rules and rewards will come from students themselves and that they will engage in negotiation to decide upon the arrangements to be applied at various points in a season. Some Sport Education units may also involve students reaching collective decisions about penalties to be applied for incidents of arguing with officials, intimidating members of the opposing team or players on one's own team, or deliberate fouls. In some schools behavioural and disciplinary matters may be passed on to a student sport council (or sub-committee of it) for a 'hearing'. Discussions in these forums can be significant in developing students' communication skills.

Relevant and active citizenship

We have already highlighted that maintaining student interest and commitment in citizenship education demands that they feel that their learning experiences, roles and responsibilities are relevant to their lives and learning needs as they perceive them. During a Sport Education season students will reach a view of whether they feel that they are being given 'real', rather than tokenistic, decision-making opportunities. The extent to which they are able to take ownership of the design of some of the learning activities, and in particular the end of season festival, will be crucial in this regard. As Alexander (2001) pointed out in his discussion of student councils, tokenistic developments are likely to be counter-productive. He explains that, 'If pupils can only discuss minor issues decided by teachers and cannot have any influence on school life, the council soon loses credibility and increases cynicism' (p. 84; see also Taylor and Johnson, 2002). All of the responsibilities promoted within Sport Education need to be viewed in a similarly critical way and claims about the extent of responsibility that is being encouraged made with an appropriate element of caution.

Festivals may offer tremendous potential to extend a wide range of responsibilities that have been introduced during a Sport Education season. For example, students may take on the production of publicity materials, booking equipment, preparing and decorating facilities, officiating and administrating during the event, commentating and reporting on the event. All of these aspects of organisation can be firstly discussed amongst the group, with arrangements and responsibilities negotiated. Planning for the event may be coordinated by either a sports council or a specially formed festival working group. Some students can be given the task of documenting the decision-making processes during the planning of the festival and on the day itself, with their reports then providing the focus for a group reflection and debate. Activities such as this can serve to engage children directly with issues of empowerment in teaching and learning. As Colley (2001) has discussed in relation to mentoring, important inequities in the power-dynamics inherent in new learning relations need to be revealed, debated and also researched further.[7]

Ultimately, if the learning experiences and responsibilities developed within Sport Education are to have real and sustained meaning for students, opportunities will need to be provided for responsibilities to be pursued outside of Sport Education lessons. This may include opportunities for students to become mentors to younger children, take on leadership or officiating responsibilities in activities provided for younger students, act as reporters travelling with a school team throughout their season, or take up positions within a school sport council. Alexander (2001) rightly points out that, if we are concerned to develop things such as confidence and responsibility, positive relationships and skills of participation and action, then

> Simulated action in the classroom is not enough. A child may develop self-esteem and confidence in class, but get emotionally crushed at home or by other children away from school. A young person may create a stunning project at school, but lack the ability to transfer their skills into life beyond school. To be effective, citizenship education has to engage pupils as people living in particular social circumstances which they can influence as citizens. This presents teachers with considerable challenges. For one thing, teachers cannot do it alone.
>
> (Alexander, 2001: 62)

As we discuss further in the next chapter, establishing learning connections with lives and communities beyond schools is vital if either Sport Education or citizenship education is to be valued by children and young people.

Conclusion

Significantly, a recent study of views towards citizenship education suggested 'a strong preference for citizenship as an active enterprise', that is directly relevant to young people, with inclusivity and diversity as defining perspectives, with the outcomes valued by a diverse range of participants, with a local focus and with realistic procedures and expectations (Davies and Evans, 2002). In this chapter we have discussed some of the potential for Sport Education to be developed as this kind of 'active enterprise'. The chapters in Part 3 provide important insights into the ways in which schools, and teachers and students within them, can take forward this potential. The professional and pedagogical challenges for the teachers and students involved are notable, but not insurmountable.

Notes

1   The British Council, founded in 1934, is the UK's international organisation for educational opportunities and cultural relations. It is represented in 109 countries and 'connects people worldwide with learning opportunities and creative ideas from the UK and builds lasting relationships between the UK and other countries' (http://www.britishcouncil.org/who/index.htm, accessed 02 June 2003).

2   The Youth Sport Trust is a registered charity established in 1994 by Sir John Beckwith. Its stated vision is to 'create opportunities for all young people to receive a quality introduction to physical education (PE) and sport and structured pathways for them to continue participating and progressing' (http://www.youthsporttrust.org/yst_yst_about.html, accessed 02 June 2003).

3   See the British Council website for details of the Dreams and Teams initiative (http://www.britishcouncil.org/who/index.htm) or contact The British Council at: 10 Spring Gardens, London, SW1A 2BN.

4   The British Sports Trust is a registered charity that focuses upon 'using sport to give people a better chance' specifically through leader award programmes. These 'use the medium of sport to help people learn essential skills such as working with and organising others, as well as motivational, communication and teamwork skills' (http://www.bst.org.uk/about.html, accessed 02 June 2003).

5   Sport England (the English Sports Council) is accountable to Parliament through the Secretary of State for Culture, Media and Sport. Sport England's primary role is to develop and maintain the infrastructure of sport in England. It is also responsible for distributing National Lottery funds to sport in England (http://www.sportengland.org/about/about_1.htm, accessed 02 June 2003).

6   Absenteeism was also a problem reported by teachers trialling Sport Education in Australia (Medland *et al.*, 1994) and noted in the development of Sport Education at Brookfield High School (see Chapter 13).

7   Colley specifically discusses the need to investigate mentoring in relation to the operation of power at institutional and structural levels and thereby develop an understanding of mentoring 'as a process of producing specific forms of cultural capital ("employability") in both mentors and mentees' (Colley, 2001: 1).

References

Alexander, T. (2001). *Citizenship Schools: A Practical Guide to Education for Citizenship and Personal Development*, London: Campaign for Learning.

Azzarito, L. and Ennis, C. (2003). A Sense of Connection: Toward Social Constructivist Physical Education, *Sport, Education and Society*, 8, 2, pp. 179–98.

Bottery, M. and Wright, N. (2000). *Teachers and the State: Towards a Directed Profession*, London: Routledge.

Claire, H. (2001). *Not Aliens: Primary School Children and the Citizenship/PSHE Curriculum*, Stoke on Trent, Trentham Books.

Clarke, G. and Quill, A. (2003). Researching Sport Education in Action: A Case Study, *European Physical Education Review*, 9, 3, pp. 253–66.

Colley, H. (2001). Understanding Experiences of Engagement Mentoring for 'Disaffected' Young People and their Student Mentors: Problems of Data Analysis in Qualitative Research, Paper presented at the British Educational Research Association, 13–15 September, University of Leeds.

Davies, I. and Evans, M. (2002). Encouraging Active Citizenship, *Educational Review*, 54, 1, pp. 69–78.

Department of Culture, Media and Sport (DCMS)/Strategy Unit (2002). *Game Plan: A Strategy for Delivering Government's Sport and Physical Activity Objectives*, London: Strategy Unit.

Department for Education and Employment (DfEE)/Qualifications and Curriculum Authority (QCA) (1999a). *The National Curriculum for England: Non-statutory Frameworks for Personal, Social and Health Education and Citizenship at Key Stages 1 and 2; Personal, Social and Health Education at Key Stages 3 and 4*, London: DfEE.

Department for Education and Employment (DfEE)/Qualifications and Curriculum Authority (QCA) (1999b). *Citizenship: The National Curriculum for England*, London: DfEE.

Department for Education and Skills (DfES) (2003). *14–19: Opportunity and Excellence*, London: DfES.

Francis, B. (1998). *Power Plays: Primary School Children's Constructions of Gender, Power and Adult Work*, Stoke on Trent: Trentham Books.

Gill, J. and Reid, A. (1999). Curriculum as Political Text: The Case of 'Discovering Democracy', in B. Johnson and A. Reid (eds), *Contesting the Curriculum*, Australia: Social Science Press.

Hall, T. and Williamson, H. (1999). *Citizenship and Community*, Leicester, UK: Youth Work Press.

Hastie, P. and Buchanen, A. M. (2000). Teaching Responsibility through Sport Education: Prospects of a Coalition, *Research Quarterly for Exercise and Sport*, 71, 1, pp. 25–35.

Hicks, D. (2001). Re-examining the Future: The Challenge for Citizenship Education, *Educational Review*, 53, 3, pp. 229–40.

Lynch, K. and Lodge, A. (2002). *Equality and Power in Schools: Redistribution, Recognition and Representation*, London: Routledge.

Medland, A., Alexander, K., Taggart, A. and Thorpe, S. (1994). *Sport Education in Physical Education (SEPEP): Introducing the Findings from the 1994 National SEPEP Trials, Executive Summary*, Perth, Western Australia: Sport and Physical Activity Research Centre, Edith Cowan University.

Siedentop, D. (1994). *Sport Education: Quality PE through Positive Sport Experiences*, Champaign, Illinois: Human Kinetics.

Taylor, M. and Johnson, R. (2002). *School Councils: Their Role in Citizenship and Personal and Social Education*, Slough: National Foundation for Educational Research.

Theodoulides, A. (2003). 'I Would Never Personally Tell Anyone to Break the Rules, but You Can Bend Them': Teaching Moral Values Through Team Games, *European Journal of Physical Education*, 8, 2, pp. 141–59.

Theodoulides, A. and Armour, K. (2001). Personal, Social and Moral Development through Team Games: Some Critical Questions, *European Physical Education Review*, 7, 1, pp. 5–23.

Appendix A: Sport Education Captain's contract

(from Mountbatten School and Language College Sport Education Soccer)

Team Captain's
CONTRACT

The Captain's Responsibilities are to:

Demonstrate Fair Play
Report Improper Dress
Assign Playing Positions
Organise the Team on the Field
Have a Good Knowledge of Rules
Demonstrate Good Safety Practices
Demonstrate Good Conduct

_____   _____

Captain's Signature   **Co-Captain's Signature**

Team Signatures:

Failure to comply with the responsibilities of this contract as
Captain, Co-Captain, player, etc. could result in loss of position and
possibility of removal from the league.

7 Sport Education and lifelong learning

Dawn Penney and Gill Clarke

Introduction

In preceding chapters we have presented Sport Education as a pedagogical framework well suited to the development of citizenship and the promotion of inclusion in education, sport and society. We have indicated our own and also government interests in Sport Education having an impact both beyond the school gates and beyond the compulsory years of schooling. This chapter further develops that vision of Sport Education and of citizenship as 'futures orientated'. It explores the belief that, 'by encouraging and enabling active citizenship, young people can be drawn into society – at neighbourhood, community and national level – as *participants*, not just spectators looking from the outside in' (Hall and Williamson, 1999: 13, our emphasis).

Sport Education: *how* does it relate to lives beyond school?

The interesting paradox with Sport Education is that it is modelled on sporting practices and culture, but at the same time actively seeks to present some contrasts to established practices and dominant sporting culture. It also encourages critical reflection on behaviours and practices in sport. There is an underlying interest in the creation of 'something better' in sport, such that some of the physically and socially damaging behaviours and attitudes that run through much professional sport, such as stereotyping, elitism or abusive behaviours, may become things of the past, or at least less prevalent. As we explained in Chapter 1, some of the adaptations of Sport Education have specifically brought these social interests to the fore. Yet, Sport Education literature also talks of interests in children becoming 'initiated into' and thus serving to 'sustain' sporting practices and culture (Siedentop, 1994, 1995). Arguably there is a strong element of conservatism in commentary such as this:

> to become a member of a sport practice, one must learn to accept the standards of excellence in that sport, accept the authority of those standards, and subject oneself to the rules and traditions that define the

practice as one attempts to achieve the goods that are defined by participation in that sport and respect the admiration of those with whom you
are engaged in that sport practice.

(Siedentop, 1995: 15)

Such commentary raises key questions about the sort of 'lifelong learners'
that we are hoping to develop in and through Sport Education. Personally,
we see a need to move beyond uncritical and unconditional acceptance of
existing sporting and social structures, rules and traditions. Our interests are
in encouraging children and young people to be proactive in taking forward
concerns for more socially just and inclusive practices within both sport and
society. One of the identified 'long-term' purposes of Sport Education is:

> to make sport more widely accessible so that gender, race, disability,
> socio-economic status and age are not barriers to participation. Sport in
> all its forms for all the people is a good slogan, but for it to become
> fully operational as a cultural ethic will require a new generation of
> sportspeople committed to making the slogan a reality.
>
> (Siedentop, 1994: 2)

Teachers developing Sport Education thus face the challenges of developing
inclusive visions and values amongst students but also enabling and
empowering them to take those visions and values forward in their lives and
local communities. This chapter explores what is involved in these challenges
and their implications for pedagogical practices and relationships. As Quicke
(1999) stressed:

> It is imperative that these [educational] systems do not close things down
> for students but open them up . . . No-one should leave school feeling a
> failure or feeling that what they have learned in school has been a waste
> of time, and everyone should be willing and able to continue their
> education.
>
> (Quicke, 1999: 162)

A lifelong responsibility for learning

We have also previously identified greater student responsibility for their
own learning and for supporting others' learning as key characteristics of
Sport Education. It is anticipated that during a Sport Education season
much of the teacher's managerial responsibility will be progressively transferred to students. Teams and individuals within them will take on responsibility for recording attendance, collecting equipment for lessons, organising
warming-ups or drill practices, and ensuring things are put away at the end
of lessons. Teachers should become free to work in a more facilitating
way, guiding and supporting students in their new learning roles. Their time

should become focused on working with and alongside students acting in the various roles and supporting the development of teams as positive, supportive learning communities.

As emphasised in preceding chapters, substantial planning will be needed if students are to successfully extend their roles and responsibilities in planning, organising and evaluating their own learning activities as a Sport Education season progresses. Furthermore, strategic intervention by teachers will be critical to achieving this intended growth in students' responsibility for their own and others' learning. For example, stepping in to support an official facing a confrontational situation, or assisting a coach in preparing feedback points for their team, will reaffirm that learning is intended to be a *collaborative* activity, with responsibility for progress *shared*, between teachers and learners and amongst students within the class. The teachers that we have worked with have all confirmed that a shift from often quite strongly teacher-directed to more negotiated modes of teaching and learning cannot happen instantly. Rather, the process has to be one in which the teachers and students involved take structured steps forward, and in which teachers have support from colleagues who are understanding of the professional challenges involved (Brooker *et al.*, 2000; Medland *et al.*, 1994). As we discussed in Chapter 4, creative thinking about assessment in physical education is important, with self- and peer assessment coming to the fore.

Encouragingly, while the shift in pedagogical approach and relationships with students may present some initial anxieties and feelings of insecurity for some teachers, many overseas practitioners have come to advocate the model, and have grown to enjoy and prefer their new instructional and managerial roles (Alexander, Taggart and Thorpe, 1996; Medland *et al.*, 1994). Yet, with lifelong agendas in mind, the challenges of encouraging self- and collective responsibility for learning go beyond the bounds of the curriculum. As emphasised in Chapter 6, arguably the 'real test' for Sport Education is whether students' new found responsibility for their own learning and support for their peers are sustained beyond school. In our view the development of Sport Education must therefore become a *partnership based activity*, undertaken by teachers working with parents and leaders or instructors working in club and community activity settings.

But before taking a closer look at prospective partnerships, it is appropriate to consider when developing responsibility for one's own and others' learning can start. In Chapter 1 we acknowledged a tendency for Sport Education to be associated first and foremost with the secondary years of schooling. Leadership is now explicit within the National Curriculum for Physical Education (NCPE) requirements at key stage 4 in England (see Chapter 1). Fulfilment of the leadership requirements may be the foundation for accredited leadership courses for 14–16 year olds (see below). Stidder and Wallis (2003) recently commented that 'Externally accredited courses in PE such as examinations, national governing body awards (NGBA's) and sports leader awards (SLA's) are continuing to gain support amongst teachers reflecting the evolving nature of the subject and the government's attention to raising academic standards' (p. 41). Key stage 4 may therefore be seen by some teachers as the most appropriate context in which to first try Sport Education, particularly if there are concerns that physical education at key stage 4 is not succeeding in maintaining the interest and commitment of many students. Sport Education can hopefully present a means of enhancing motivation within physical education amongst more students and ensuring that their experiences of physical education 'set them up for success in the rest of their lives' (DfES, 2003a: 43). There are, however, strong arguments for Sport Education to be developed in the preceding key stages. The observation that 'Success is much more likely if pupils enjoy learning and if the curriculum and the way lessons are taught stimulates students and fires their imagination' (DfES, 2003a: 43) is one that is relevant to every year of schooling. Furthermore, the teachers that we have worked with have increasingly seen both the opportunity and need to be building foundations for Sport Education further down the curriculum. They are agreed that there is no need to restrict our thinking to what we might see as Sport Education in its 'full form'. Selected aspects, including some of the responsibilities associated with working effectively in teams, can usefully be introduced before others. The responsibilities and associated learning relationships can be modified to suit the particular learning capabilities, prior learning experiences and learning needs of students in any key stage. The chapters in Part 3 aim to illustrate that at all key stages Sport Education can be used to engage learners in and through physical education.

Sport Education: pathways and partnerships

> It is not enough to say to someone, learn and you will increase your life chances. The learner needs to know that they have the power to apply their learning and to benefit from it.
>
> (Alexander, 2001: 30)

In Chapter 3 we highlighted the importance of students feeling that they have a real and valued place as participants in the activity and as members of a team. Sport Education does much to try to instil that sense of belonging. Its team structure, the opportunities to focus on new roles and the demand for teams to work together through the season are all things that have been associated with the creation of a positive learning environment for more students. But there is still a need to pose some critical questions of the affiliation and authenticity associated with Sport Education:

- Will the sense of affiliation and value last? For everyone?
- Having facilitated enjoyment of a unit of Sport Education in the curriculum and possibly instilled in many students a desire to continue

involvement in the activity, are we able to offer them *all* the opportunity to do so?

- How does the programme of extra-curricular or 'out of hours learning' activities at school, and provision at local junior sports clubs, compare to Sport Education?
- Do these forums provide the chance for students of all playing abilities to become involved, to make further progress in terms of their own playing ability, but also to pursue interests and talents that they have found in other roles?
- Coming from the Sport Education context in which the emphasis has been that winning is certainly not the only or necessarily the main concern, how will students find the physical activity and sporting contexts that they try to move on to and into?

Elsewhere we have drawn attention to the fact that, in moving either beyond the curriculum or beyond schools, students may well face situations in which the values and principles that have been at the fore of their Sport Education experience no longer shape provision (Penney *et al.*, 2002). Doors to continued participation and continued learning may regrettably be closed for some students, and most likely those less able in terms of their personal playing performance. The question that we therefore pose is whether, having transformed the experiences and outlooks of previously marginalised students through the development of Sport Education in the curriculum, we are in real danger of merely setting them up for failure and rejection elsewhere. Furthermore, having embedded key skills that enable students to take greater responsibility for their own learning and play an active role in supporting the learning of others, can we point them to contexts in which they will be challenged to develop those skills further?

Undoubtedly, these are interesting and timely points to debate. In October 2002 the Prime Minister launched a PE, School Sport and Club Links (PESSCL) strategy that reaffirmed a commitment to inter-agency partnerships being at the heart of enhanced opportunities for ongoing participation and performance in sporting activities (DfES/DCMS, 2003). Several of the programmes within the PESSCL strategy have a key role to play in strengthening pathways to lifelong involvement in sporting activities for young people:

- the Specialist Sports College programme (enabling secondary schools to apply for specialist school status and act as local hubs for the development of physical education and sport in schools and the community);
- the School Sport Coordinator programme (focusing on enhanced provision of quality physical education and school sport across families of secondary and primary schools, usually centred on a Specialist Sports College);
- the Gifted and Talented programme (directed towards encouraging more talented young sportspeople to join junior sports clubs and enhancing

relationships between schools and National Governing Body of Sport performance programmes); and

- the Step into Sport programme (encouraging young people and adults to become involved in leadership and volunteering in sport and involving the development of Sport Education in physical education at key stage 4 particularly).

(see DfES/DCMS, 2003 for further details of these programmes)

Within the strategy there is a commitment to seeking to 'improve the understanding of how quality PE and school sport can be used to support healthy lifestyles and physical activity' (DfES/DCMS, 2003: 11); to increasing the proportion of students being guided into sports clubs from schools; and to ensuring pathways into elite sport for talented students. Partnerships are central to the programmes within the PESSCL strategy and, as we have indicated, there is a strong case for developing Sport Education across partnerships and with learning and participation pathways in mind. This type of 'extended development' has the potential to link directly with the government's vision of an education system that extends and transforms the roles of schools, such that they become the sites of a range of community services (that can clearly include physical activity and sport provision) and community based learning (DfES, 2003b). The envisaged 'extended schools' will:

- pursue joint planning of service provision;
- seek more active involvement of parents, local community, sport and voluntary organisations in activities;
- endeavour to ensure that programmes developed are sustainable over time; and
- feature activities that are presented as 'teacher-free' and a contrast to school activities.

(TeacherNet, 2003)

Learning is thus presented as a 'whole community' as well as a 'lifelong' activity and, further, as something that we need to view in increasingly flexible ways. In addition, there is renewed encouragement for work related learning to be incorporated within the key stage 4 curriculum and for vocational provision and pathways to be strengthened through the 14–19 phase (DfES, 2003a). The stated purpose of the 14–19 strategy was 'to transform the learning experience of young people so that they have a commitment to continued learning, whether in school, college or the workplace, so that all young people can fulfil their potential' (DfES, 2003a: 45).

Many secondary school teachers trying Sport Education have recognised the potential that it offers to secure firm foundations for students to progress to certified courses at key stage 4 and beyond. The Junior Sports Leader Award (JSLA), Community Sports Leader Award (CSLA), Basic Expedition Leader Award (BELA) and Duke of Edinburgh's Awards[1] all present clear opportunities for teachers and learners to build on skills, knowledge and understanding developed through the roles, responsibilities and learning relationships that characterise Sport Education. Pathways relating to leadership are, however, not the only vocational pathways that Sport Education engages with and should arguably seek to strengthen. Rather, the potential here is as extensive as the roles that are encompassed within a Sport Education season. With any introduction of a role comes a new challenge for teachers, schools and other agencies in the community: where can it lead for those young people who develop an interest and ability in taking their learning further?

Flintoff (2003) recently highlighted that, for many young people and perhaps particularly many young women, 'the school may not be the primary context for meaningful learning' (p. 247) and that an important aspect of School Sport Coordinators' work (see above) 'will be to identify contexts beyond the school and its immediate setting that can provide positive learning environments for different youngsters' (p. 247). Given this emphasis it is notable that to date there are few examples of Sport Education being adopted as a framework within sports club or community settings. Undeniably these contexts may prove the most critical in consolidating and sustaining learning and participation.

> It is in their actual engagement with and within their own communities that young people's citizenship is at its most visible. This is where knowledge is put to work, where ideas and aspirations direct and inform a tangible outcome. Needless to say, there are hard realities to this: ambitious plans may go awry or fizzle to nothing when it comes to implementation; expectations may have to be lowered in the face of unforeseen obstacles.
>
> (Hall and Williamson, 1999: 19)

Lister's (2001) account of the development of Sport Education in cricket is notable in incorporating a focus on school–community links. In developing Sport Education cricket in school, an aim was to reflect the structure and pathways for junior cricket in states and territories in Australia. Teachers therefore worked with development officers to facilitate enhanced school–community links. These included increasing the opportunities for girls to play in weekend competitions. Research identified a number of areas in which there was a clear need for collaborative development work, and certainly not only in cricket. For example, students involved said that they would like to perform officiating, coaching, administrative and publicity roles in a community club setting. Many students also expressed preferences for modified forms of cricket rather than the full 'adult' version of the game.

In many respects the apparent lack of developments of Sport Education that extend into club and community settings is not surprising and reflects the extent of the challenges that such development poses. Initiatives that call for critical reflection upon established institutional practices and then seek changes to those practices can be expected to give rise to opposition. As Hall and Williamson (1999) explain, this is an inevitable and inherent part of 'real' 'active citizenship' (see Chapter 5):

> it is important not to have too rosy a picture of active citizenship. Even, and especially, when it is working well, community and democratic participation is an argumentative business. Active citizens are not just good neighbours; they can be quarrelsome and dissatisfied; this is part of active citizenship too. As active citizens, young people ought to be able to ask questions of their communities, not just contribute to them as they stand. Adults may find this uncomfortable but such questioning must be seen as part of any active citizenship worth the name.
>
> (Hall and Williamson, 1999: 14)

One example of an initiative that has sought to (re-)locate learning firmly in a community context is the 'Playing for Success' scheme in England. Launched in 1997 and subsequently extended to other countries, this initiative established professional football and other sports clubs as sites for targeted study support in literacy, numeracy and ICT, particularly for 'underachieving' students (Sharp *et al.*, 2001, 2003). In some schools, it may be possible to create a direct link between Sport Education and 'Playing for Success', and thereby strengthen the learning, vocational, participation and performance pathways that Sport Education in the curriculum can lay foundations for.

Authentic experiences: diverse futures in diverse communities

Above we have highlighted that notions of authenticity in Sport Education may be short lived for some students and that ensuring continuity of experience is an important challenge for schools and other agencies. But in considering authenticity and continuity we need to look beyond provision for students of different playing abilities and with interests in different roles in sport. We need to also review some of the values embedded in the Sport Education experiences that we develop and consider if, in reality, we are promoting connections to culturally diverse local communities. Are we connecting with the current and future lives of all learners, acknowledging particularly their differing cultural contexts and values? This question arguably raises a number of dilemmas in planning Sport Education, including the activities that we choose as a focus for a Sport Education season, the roles and responsibilities that we encourage particular students to take on, the sporting behaviours that we promote or discourage, the types of event that we have as 'culminating festivals', and the uniforms and logos that we encourage teams to adopt. In all of these respects there are dangers that

Sport Education may be culturally narrow and offer authenticity for only some students. Yet when developed sensitively and with recognition of diversity of cultures, community sport practices and values represented amongst a student population, it can be an important means of promoting pathways to diverse futures. Enhancing Sport Education in these terms may demand a rethink and extension of the activities that provide the focus for units and the arrangements (for seasons, sessions and competitions) that are central to Sport Education (see Shehu, 1998).

It is also appropriate to highlight that, from a lifelong perspective, many of the activities that continue to dominate physical education curricula and, further, have also been prominent as a focus in Sport Education are not activities that for many students will retain their authenticity over time. Transferable skills, knowledge and understanding arguably need to be a clear focus for teaching and learning in Sport Education. The model, ways of working within it, the responsibilities and the enjoyment are all things that need to be acknowledged as of greater lifelong value than sport specific physical skills. In this book we have endeavoured to promote the association of Sport Education with many and varied physical activities and with school, community and club contexts of physical activity and sport. We have also sought to encourage linkages between these contexts and thereby enhance the extent to which a lifelong perspective is reflected in the development of Sport Education.

Note

1 The British Sports Trust (www.bst.org.uk) has developed a series of leadership awards for young people: the Junior Sports Leader Award for 14–16 year olds, the Community Sports Leader Award for over 16s and, building on that, the Higher Sports Leader Award, including units in event management, first aid, sports development and coaching. The Basic Expedition Leader Award builds the ability to organise safe expeditions and overnight camps.

References

Alexander, K., Taggart, A. and Thorpe, S. (1996). A Spring in their Steps? Possibilities for Professional Renewal through Sport Education in Australian Schools, *Sport, Education and Society*, 1, 1, pp. 5–22.

Alexander, T. (2001). *Citizenship Schools: A Practical Guide to Educational for Citizenship and Personal Development*, London: Campaign for Learning.

Brooker, R., Kirk, D., Braiuka, S. and Bransgrove, A. (2000). Implementing a Game Sense Approach to Teaching Junior High School Basketball in a Naturalistic Setting, *European Physical Education Review*, 6, 1, pp. 7–26.

Department for Education and Skills (DfES)/Department of Culture, Media and Sport (DCMS) (2003). *Learning through PE and Sport: A Guide to the Physical Education, School Sport and Club Links Strategy*, London: DfES Publications.

Department for Education and Skills (DfES) (2003a). *A New Specialist System: Transforming Secondary Education*, London: DfES.

Department for Education and Skills (DfES) (2003b). Schools to Provide a Full Range of Community Services by 2006 – Ashton, Press notice, 13 March 2003, http://www.dfes.gov/uk/pns/DisplayPN.cgi?pn_id=2003_0038, retrieved 24 March 2003.

Flintoff, A. (2003). The School Sport Co-ordinator Programme: Changing the Role of Physical Education Teachers?, *Sport, Education and Society*, 8, 2, pp. 231–50.

Hall, T. and Williamson, H. (1999). *Citizenship and Community*, Leicester, UK: Youth Work Press.

Lister, A. (2001). SEPEP Cricket and School–Community Links: 'Taking sport education beyond bell times', Paper presented at the AARE Annual Conference, University of Notre Dame, Fremantle, Western Australia, 4 December 2001.

Medland, A., Alexander, K., Taggart, A. and Thorpe, S. (1994). *Sport Education in Physical Education (SEPEP): Introducing the Findings from the 1994 National SEPEP Trials, Executive Summary*, Perth, Western Australia: Sport and Physical Activity Research Centre, Edith Cowan University.

Penney, D., Clarke, G. and Kinchin, G. (2002). Developing Physical Education as a 'Connective Specialism' (Young, 1998): Is Sport Education the Answer?, *Sport, Education and Society*, 7, 1, pp. 55–64.

Quicke, J. (1999). A Curriculum for Life: Schools for a Democratic Learning Society, Buckingham: Open University Press.

Sharp, C., Kendell, L., Bhabra, S., Schagen, I. and Duff, J. (2001). *Playing for Success: An Evaluation of the Second Year* (DfES Research report 291), London: DfES.

Sharp, C., Kendell, L. and Schagen, I. (2003). Different for Girls? An Exploration of the Impact of Playing for Success, *Educational Research*, 45, 3, pp. 309–24.

Shehu, J. (1998). Sport Education: Ideology, Evidence and Implications for Physical Education in Africa, *Sport, Education and Society*, 3, 2, pp. 227–35.

Siedentop, D. (1994). *Sport Education: Quality PE through Positive Sport Experiences*, Champaign, Illinois: Human Kinetics.

Siedentop, D. (1995). Junior Sport and the Evolution of Sport Cultures, Paper presented to the Junior Sport Forum, Auckland, New Zealand, November 1995.

Stidder, G. and Wallis, J. (2003). Future Directions for Physical Education at Key Stage Four and Post-16, *British Journal of Teaching Physical Education*, 34, 4, pp. 41–7.

TeacherNet (2003). Extended Schools Guidance – Overview, http://www.teachernet.gov.uk/educationoverview/briefing/extendedschools/Overview/, retrieved 24 March 2003.

Part 3

Sport Education in action

Editors' note

Throughout Part 2 we have emphasised that without skilful, committed teachers Sport Education is meaningless as a curriculum and pedagogical innovation. The chapters that follow provide invaluable insights into the key role of teachers in planning for and developing learning environments and experiences that prompt students to play an active role in shaping their own learning. Sport Education is shown to involve a shift in the teacher's role, not a reduction. Planning emerges as vital to the success of Sport Education. This includes planning for active involvement of students in various roles, and planning 'for the "what ifs" ' (Siedentop, 1994:19).

The following examples of Sport Education being tried out in practice and at various stages of development draw attention to the many decisions to be made by teachers and some of the 'what ifs' that they need to be aware of. Importantly, the teachers involved explain the reasons for particular decisions, about team size, ways of selecting teams, allocation of roles and the format of festivals or tournaments. They share their reflections on the challenges that they have faced in taking Sport Education from 'rhetoric to reality' in their schools. Certainly, they deserve credit for the openness of their accounts. There is no pretence here of everything being perfect, or of innovation being a totally smooth process for either teachers or students. These are invaluable 'warts and all' accounts of developing Sport Education. We see, for example, that we cannot assume that students will immediately or automatically be able to take on roles such as that of coach or official. Rather, 'we must define those roles, teach them, design good practice with feedback so that students can learn their roles well' (Siedentop, 1994: 15).

Deliberately, the authors were asked to contextualise their accounts by providing a description of the school and specific teaching and learning setting in which the development of Sport Education occurred. The need for Sport Education to be adapted for the individual school and learning contexts is repeatedly reaffirmed, as is the need for the teachers involved to remain highly reflective and be willing to view their own plans as only provisional. We thus see plenty of evidence of Sport Education's inherent flexibility being well exploited, and also maintained. The developments described here are ones that are clearly ongoing and destined to remain subject to critical review and further adaptation.

All of the authors of the chapters in this part of the book were asked to write to a set framework that provided headings for prospective sub-sections within chapters. It was hoped that this would enhance the 'readability' of the chapters as a set of 'case studies' of Sport Education in practice in schools without unduly constraining authors in their writing.

Reference

Siedentop, D. (1994). *Sport Education: Quality PE through Positive Sport Experiences*, Champaign, Illinois: Human Kinetics.

8 Laying the foundation for Sport Education

Gary D. Kinchin and
Valerie K. Kinchin

Later chapters of this book give considerable credibility to the view that Sport Education experiences can be regarded as some of the most educationally worthwhile in physical education. They demonstrate that engagement in physical activity can provide students with feelings of affiliation and see them taking considerable responsibility for learning, cooperating, exercising leadership, and supporting others' participation and achievement. The detailed accounts of Sport Education in key stages 2, 3 and 4 that follow in Chapters 9–14 make explicit many of these outcomes. We are of the view, however, that it is possible to direct students towards these benefits at earlier stages of their formal education. Ultimately, the interests are in providing a foundation that will enable and encourage students to 'extend their participation and involvement beyond the physical education program' (Metzler, 2000: 256). With Sport Education in mind as an important element of the key stage 2, 3 and 4 physical education curriculum, it would appear sensible to develop positive dispositions towards both the concept of and conduct of sport at the earliest possible stage. Developing the necessary attitudes and personal, social, emotional and physical skills which Sport Education demands will prepare students for experience of fuller versions of Sport Education in later years and should also accelerate their readiness to engage with its expectations in terms of participation and learning.

Recent documentation provided by the Department for Education and Skills (DfES) and the Qualifications and Curriculum Authority (QCA) can certainly be seen to justify an examination of the degree to which, and ways in which, a 'foundation' for Sport Education can be established. Before progressing with that examination, it is appropriate to acknowledge concerns expressed in literature regarding the lack of specialist physical educators teaching in primary schools in England and Wales and the limited specialist input to primary training courses (Warburton, 2000). While there have been many calls for greater support for physical education in the primary sector (Warburton, 2000), there are still far too many beginning and more experienced teachers who lack the necessary knowledge and skills to provide quality physical education curriculum experiences for their students. National strategies for literacy and numeracy have compounded the situation, by impacting upon the time, attention and resources given to other areas of the curriculum including physical education (National Association of Head Teachers, 1999).

We realise that some of the issues and suggestions that are raised in this chapter may challenge some teachers with limited backgrounds in physical education. The chapter is written, however, with the intent that some of the learning possible via Sport Education can and might be developed (and sustained) through connections to other areas of the curriculum. Our approach therefore matches with concerns for coherency in teaching and learning across the whole curriculum.

It is also important to acknowledge cautions expressed within some literature in relation to when reasonably 'full forms' of Sport Education would be appropriate for boys and girls in physical education. An assessment of the extent to which younger students are able to support the peer teaching and cooperative learning elements of Sport Education is certainly necessary when contemplating initial planning and implementation. With these demands in mind, it has been claimed that Sport Education may not be possible until students reach the age of 7 or 8 (Metzler, 2000): in effect the commencement of key stage 2. As will be apparent in this chapter, we have seen some evidence to the contrary and retain a view that students are often capable of far more than we typically give them credit for when considering their prospective roles and responsibilities in teaching and learning.

What evidence is there that Sport Education can be developed at an early age and what might young students tell us about their experiences? As indicated in Chapter 1, research and literature on Sport Education have typically targeted secondary (high) school students. The literature does, however, include some examples of Sport Education developed with children of primary age taught by both specialist physical education teachers (Bell, 1994; Darnell, 1994) and non-specialists (Strikwerda-Brown and Taggart, 2001). Also the experiences of the very youngest students in general physical education have been documented. Research has outlined ways in which 4 and 5 year olds describe and critique their lesson time (Sanders and Graham, 1995), and this work concluded that very young students are able to talk about what they do and do not like about physical education.

Notwithstanding questions that have been posed regarding the suitability and timing of the introduction of Sport Education, we explore the possibilities for it contributing to foundation experiences in and of physical education. We also consider connections between some of the characteristics of Sport Education and the language of key contemporary documents focusing upon learning, teaching and assessment of very young children. In outlining the contribution Sport Education that can make to students' learning, we offer some practical examples of how such a foundation might be established in Reception/Year 1. We conclude by providing a summary of one study which was carried out with children aged 5 and 6 years, and served to illustrate how some of the ideas presented may be realised in practice.

Early years education

Any effort to develop the beginnings of lifelong health, enjoyment and participation in sport and physical activity should acknowledge some of the philosophy of early years education. The DfES and QCA (2000) identified a number of principles of early years education. Below we list those principles which are pertinent to the demands of participation in a unit of Sport Education:

1   that children should feel included, secure and valued;
2   that no child should be excluded or disadvantaged;
3   that relevant and appropriate content should match the different levels of children's needs;
4   that there should be opportunities for children to take part in activities that they plan or put in place themselves.

(adapted from DfES/QCA, 2000)

Developing qualities of responsibility, consideration and support amongst students, such that they will be able to demonstrate the ability to care for and invest in their peers, should not only be a major objective for teachers using Sport Education. They are qualities and characteristics of learning and behaviour that are desirable in the very early stages of students' education.

The Foundation Stage and Early Learning Goals

We begin by examining the mandatory guidance within some key policy documents relating to the Foundation Stage and Early Learning Goals, and outlining contemporary developments of interest to those working with students aged 3 to 5. We then consider the content of these documents as a basis for discussing what might be achieved, with connections to Sport Education in mind.

The development of the Foundation Stage has been described as 'a significant landmark in funded education in England. For the first time it gives this very important stage of education a distinct identity' (DfES/QCA, 2000: 3). As a statutory stage of the National Curriculum in England and Wales, the Foundation Stage begins when the child reaches the age of 3 and finishes in the term in which they have their fifth birthday. This is typically when a child is in the Reception (year) of schooling. Guidance for the Foundation Stage was issued in September 2000 (DfES/QCA, 2000) which built upon the Early Learning Goals document issued in October 1999 (QCA/DfEE, 1999). Termed the *Curriculum Guidance for the Foundation Stage*, this document aims to help teachers to make sense of the Early Learning Goals and it also outlines what they need to do to help children make progress towards these goals.

Of considerable relevance to this chapter is the statement that the curriculum for the Foundation Stage 'should underpin all future learning' (DfES/QCA, 2000: 8). Indeed, the following extract from the Foundation Stage guidance makes reference to and links with some of the intended learning which has been repeatedly identified in Sport Education research. The Foundation Stage is identified as making:

> a positive contribution to children's early development and learning. During this time we cannot afford to get things wrong. The early years are critical in children's development. Children develop rapidly during this time – physically, intellectually, emotionally and socially. The foundation stage is about developing key learning skills such as listening, speaking, concentration, persistence and learning to work together and cooperate with other children.
>
> (DfES/QCA, 2000: 2)

Many of these learning skills are referred to in Sport Education research. The socialising and affective benefits are regarded as some of the most positive outcomes from students' participation in Sport Education (Carlson and Hastie, 1997). Some students interviewed following Sport Education units have also described the development of productive working relationships within their teams and identified the importance of cooperating and supporting each other (Kinchin and O'Sullivan, 2003).

In the United States we have seen examples of Sport Education failing to achieve some of its intended aims in terms of student participation. In their study of inner-city secondary-aged students, O'Sullivan *et al.* (1999) detail the inability of some students to either accept responsibilities or take direction from their peers. It is quite possible that sharply contrasting experiences of and expectations within earlier physical education programmes may have impeded the ability of some students to adjust to the demands and expectations inherent within Sport Education. The responsibilities and relationships called for in Sport Education may have been ones that students had not experienced previously and were not prepared for. It seems prudent for educators to give attention to the attitudes and skills that are fundamental to successful development of Sport Education sooner rather than later within the curriculum. Below we expand upon how this may be done in the Foundation Stage. Closer examination of the Early Learning Goals and intended outcomes from teaching and learning within the Foundation Stage provides a starting point from which to identify the possibilities that exist for laying a foundation for Sport Education.

The Foundation Stage, areas of learning and aspects of teaching and learning

The Foundation Stage curriculum is organised into six areas of learning, as follows:

- personal, social and emotional development;
- communication, language and literacy;
- mathematical development;
- knowledge and understanding of the world;
- physical development;
- creative development.

(DfES/QCA, 2000: 26)

For each of these areas of learning the guidance identifies 'stepping stones' that outline 'progress towards the early learning goals' (DfES/QCA, 2000: 26). These goals 'establish expectations for most children to reach by the end of the foundation stage' (DfES/QCA, 2000: 26). The stepping stones detail the knowledge, skills and understanding required to meet these Early Learning Goals.

Within Table 8.1 we set out some competencies, skills and concepts for each area of learning that are relevant to both initial and later engagement with contexts of Sport Education, that could form part of the observation and assessment of students in the Foundation Stage.

Table 8.1 Aspects relevant to the areas of learning

Area of learning	Aspects of learning and teaching
Personal, social and emotional development	➢ Children working in small and large groups ➢ Children developing independence skills ➢ Children learning to respect others ➢ Children being with the same children with time to develop relationships ➢ Children having chances to engage in problem solving ➢ Children developing sensitivity to the needs of others ➢ Children learning about the value of trust and support
Communication, language and literacy	➢ Children learning to communicate with others
Physical development	➢ Children exploring and refining movements ➢ Children using a range of equipment ➢ Children learning the language of negotiation (share, take turns) ➢ Teach skills and have chances to practise them ➢ Children learning to evaluate what worked and what they would do differently next time
Creative development	➢ Support children in reflecting upon and improving their work and the work of others

(adapted from DfES/QCA, 2000)

Assessment: the Foundation Stage Profile

In 2003 the Foundation Stage Profile (DfES/QCA, 2003) replaced the statutory baseline assessments which were carried out when children first enter primary education. Building upon the 2000 guidance (DfES/QCA, 2000), which set out what should be achieved by the end of the Foundation Stage, the Foundation Stage Profile provided a framework for teachers to record children's progress and attainment across all six areas of learning. In incorporating the Early Learning Goals, it encouraged teachers to make multiple observations of students, in order to present a holistic picture of their learning and development.

A foundation for Sport Education

Following this outline of expectations for teaching and learning in the Foundation Stage, we now present a number of features that we regard as crucial to orientating students to the expectations and demands of participation in Sport Education, and which can be achieved very early in primary school education.

Developing and using routines

It is worthwhile considering how some of the teaching formations and organisational routines, which have supported the Sport Education experience with older students, might play a part in early years settings. Routines are an integral part of most primary classrooms (eating snacks, accessing book-bags) outside of physical education. Routines provide structure for students' behaviour and support instruction in the primary classroom. With an emphasis upon repeated routines, it is possible for primary teachers to implement particular managerial and organisational elements of Sport Education (for example, sustained teams, assigned practice areas, equipment managers) without actually attempting the progressive shift from teacher-led to a more student-centred pedagogy. As we shall see later, these predominantly managerial tasks proved beneficial in lessons. They have enabled some lessons to begin more quickly and have reduced the workload experienced by some teachers in organising students, equipment and space.

Sustained groups and affiliation

'The potential positive influence of persisting small groups seems sufficiently powerful that ways to better implement this pedagogical strategy should be explored at all levels in physical education' (Siedentop, 1996: 259). Siedentop (1996) has discussed 'the much neglected and yet powerful pedagogical factor in learning communities' (p. 258) which he refers to as grouping and affiliation. Siedentop (1996) argued that the groupings in most physical education settings are not sustained, which 'greatly reduces the potential positive influence of the strategy' (p. 258). He therefore encouraged teachers to set up groups that persist, where individuals can develop and maintain an affiliation with a group. The curriculum and student organisation within primary schools supports continuous contact with one class teacher, and with a group of peers throughout at least one year. The arrangements present a window of opportunity for teachers to employ sustained small group arrangements both within and outside of the physical education setting, with the intention that students will develop feelings of affiliation, membership and a sense of belonging. Darnell (1994) has shared how one Sport Education programme involved primary students remaining in the same groups for the complete academic year.

The physical organisation (and particularly the desk/table layout) of most primary classrooms also promotes opportunities for paired and group discussions. The table arrangements can provide an ideal setting for groups/teams to meet and work cooperatively on tasks which focus upon developing feelings of attachment and group identity. Providing opportunities for groups to draw and colour team emblems or badges, to then be displayed, will certainly emphasise the cross-curricular potential of Sport Education at this stage and at the same time address aspects of the Early Learning Goals and areas of learning discussed earlier.

Having responsibility

Considerable opportunities also exist for young students to assume responsible roles that support the running of their school (for example, students can act as register monitor, lunch-box monitor, line-leader, teacher's helper). In a physical education context there is much potential and opportunities for boys and girls to assume roles that serve their team/group/class. We have seen examples of very young students being placed in charge of bibs and other small pieces of equipment on a daily basis, and being expected to collect and return this equipment to the appropriate location (Lewis, 2001). Such responsibilities are an ideal introduction to the role of equipment manager and the responsibilities of a 'duty team' in Sport Education.

The foundation 'in action': exploring the potential for Sport Education in primary physical education

Key stage 1: a case study

This section provides an insight into a study which set out to examine the impact of some of the foundational characteristics of the Sport Education model on one class of students in a small Bedfordshire lower school. Lewis (2001) applied some features of Sport Education to a considerably modified eight day unit in key stage 1 with 22 children aged 5 to 6 years of both mixed gender and race. Data was collected via participant observation and focus group interviews with teams.

The following features of the Sport Education model were established in the unit: sustained affiliation with teams, non-playing roles with associated responsibilities, and opportunities for competition. A simplified invasion game which incorporated some features of netball provided the activity focus for the unit. Students were placed into one of four teams. Teams were selected by the teacher on the basis of information provided by the regular class teacher with respect to ability and how well they got on with peers. The individual teams came up with the following names: The Red Rockets, The Green Monsters, The Blue Bell Bombers and the Yellow Suns. All teams were assigned an area of the court with students taking on one of the following roles with their attendant responsibilities:

- spokesperson: team representative and point of contact with the teacher;
- court person: sets up and dismantles the home playing court;
- equipment person: collects and returns team's equipment (hoops and balls);
- team uniform person: collects and returns bibs;
- scorer: records scores during the unit.

Teaching was predominantly teacher-led. All individual and group practices and modified lead-up games occurred within teams (throwing, catching, retaining possession). The final two days were devoted to a round-robin format competition where some records were kept of results and goal scorers.

Over the course of the short unit, increasing examples of students helping each other during practices were observed. This was mainly through students showing each other how to catch and throw. Affiliation was developed within lessons but also beyond them. For example, students requested that they be able to sit in their teams in non-PE class time, wanted to line up in their Sport Education teams, and were also seen sitting in their team during lunchtime and around the playground.

The non-playing roles were generally successful. Lewis (2001) commented upon student adjustment to these roles, stating that:

> as the weeks past the pupils became more accustomed to their roles and performed them with great efficiency. By the end of the six weeks the pupils were skilled enough to complete their jobs without any major interference, prompting, or reminding.

(p. 29)

Lewis (2001) continued by describing the impact that these roles had upon the time taken for lessons to begin: 'the need to plan for and organise the setting up of lessons was greatly lessened leaving more time to concentrate upon the teaching and coaching part' (p. 31).

Having roles was clearly enjoyable for some students as the following extract from an interview with the Green Monsters illustrates:

> Pupil 1: Yeah, I put out the cones, so we know where we are supposed to go.
> Pupil 2: I'm the scorer . . . when we play against other teams I keep score.
> Pupil 3: My job is to get out all the balls. Sometimes we all have a ball. Sometimes we only have one ball.
> Pupil 1: I liked my job because I got to set things out . . .
> Pupil 3: My job was alright, if I didn't get the balls we couldn't play.
>
> (Lewis, 2001: 51)

As the following comments from the Blue Bell Bombers indicates, students of this age could explain *why* jobs had been allocated:

> Pupil 1: So that we could all take part.
> Pupil 2: We all had jobs so that no-one is left out.
> Pupil 3: Yes, so that no ones left sitting down.
>
> (Lewis, 2001: 51)

While competition was enjoyable for some members of the Green Monsters, some students in this team also described other outcomes from working as a team. Notably, they explained how they had seen less desirable teamwork and possible examples of exclusion:

> Researcher: Did you think your team was the best?
> Pupil 1: Yes.
> Pupil 2: We didn't win all our games though.
> Pupil 1: I know, but we did pass the ball a lot to each other.
> Pupil 3: Yeah and the blue team only passed to the boys, they left the girls out a lot.
> Pupil 4: And they argued quite a lot, we didn't do that. We get on.
>
> (Lewis, 2001: 52)

While admittedly implemented over a period considerably shorter than that expected in Sport Education, this study has highlighted ways in which a foundation for Sport Education can be realised in practice at the Foundation stage of education. It also provides some encouraging evidence that very young children are able to talk at an introductory level about the benefits of Sport Education's pedagogical features and outcomes, and that they can demonstrate engagement with the behavioural and attitudinal expectations that it demands and seeks to promote in students.

Conclusion

Sport Education in its fullest form has certain expectations of students and teachers and demands that attention is directed towards fulfilment of specific learning outcomes, including team affiliation, developing a sense of belonging, supporting and cooperating with others, developing independence and taking responsibility. While we are of the view that young students are unlikely to be able to engage pedagogically with 'full' versions of Sport Education, it seems evident from recent documentation relating to the Foundation Stage that the expectations and intended outcomes of Sport Education are nevertheless at the heart of the learning and development at this stage. Building early learning of Sport Education as a 'foundation' around the notion of routines, sustained team affiliation and grouping, and having responsibility has been quite successful. A window of opportunity now exists for other early years teachers to develop this flexible and broad foundation in order to promote a more holistic emphasis to their instruction across the curriculum at this stage of the education process.

References

Bell, C. (1994). Elementary Gymnastics, in D. Siedentop, *Sport Education*, pp. 47–60, Champaign, Illinois: Human Kinetics.

Carlson, T. B. and Hastie, P. (1997). The Student Social System within Sport Education, *Journal of Teaching in Physical Education*, 16, pp. 176–95.

Darnell, J. (1994). Sport Education within the Elementary Curriculum, in D. Siedentop, *Sport Education*, pp. 61–71, Champaign, Illinois: Human Kinetics.

Department for Education and Skills (DfES)/Qualifications) and Curriculum Authority (QCA) (2000). *Curriculum Guidance for the Foundation Stage*, London: HMSO.

Department for Education and Skills (DfES)/Qualifications and Curriculum Authority (QCA) (2003). *The Foundation Stage Profile Handbook*, London: HMSO.

Kinchin, G. D. and O'Sullivan, M. (2003). Incidences of Student Support for and Resistance to a Curricular Innovation in High School Physical Education, *Journal of Teaching in Physical Education*, 22, pp. 245–60.

Lewis, J. (2001). Is It Possible that Siedentop's Sport Education Model Can Be Used with a Key Stage 1 Physical Education Class to Aid Pupil Development?, Unpublished undergraduate dissertation, De Montfort University, Bedford.

Metzler, M. (2000). *Instructional Models for Physical Education*. Boston, Massachusetts: Allyn & Bacon.

National Association of Head Teachers (1999). Survey of PE and Sports in Schools, *British Journal of Physical Education*, 30, 2, pp. 29–31.

O'Sullivan, M., Tannehill, D., Knop, N., Pope, C. and Henninger, M. (1999). A School–University Collaborative Journey towards Relevance and Meaning in an Urban High School Physical Education Program, *Quest*, 51, pp. 225–43.

Qualifications and Curriculum Authority (QCA)/Department for Education and Employment (DfEE) (1999). *Early Learning Goals* (ref. QCA/99/436), London: Qualifications and Curriculum Authority.

Sanders, S. and Graham, G. (1995). Kindergarten Children's Initial Experiences in Physical Education: The Relentless Persistence of Play Clashes with the Zone of Acceptable Responses, *Journal of Teaching in Physical Education*, 14, pp. 372–83.

Siedentop, D. (1996). Physical Education and Education Reform: The Case of Sport Education, in S. Silverman and C. Ennis (eds), *Student Learning in Physical Education: Applying Research to Enhance Instruction*, pp. 247–67, Champaign, Illinois: Human Kinetics.

Strikwerda-Brown, J. and Taggart, A. (2001). No Longer Voiceless and Exhausted: Sport Education and the Primary Generalist Teacher, *ACHPER Healthy Lifestyles Journal*, 48, 3–4, pp. 14–17.

Warburton, P. (2000). Initial Teacher Training: The Preparation of Primary Teachers in Physical Education, *British Journal of Teaching Physical Education*, 31, 4, pp. 6–8.

9 Sport Education in key stage 2 games

Ann MacPhail, David Kirk and Gary D. Kinchin

Introduction

Mountfields Lodge Primary School is a predominantly middle-class state nursery and primary school based in the Midlands region of England. It caters for over 540 students between the ages of 3 and 12. Students in Years 1 through to 6 are aged between 5 and 11/12 years and, in relation to the National Curriculum, are organised into key stage 1 (5–7 years) and key stage 2 (7–11 years) groupings. Approximately 10 per cent of students are formally identified as having special educational needs. Approximately 8 per cent of students come from ethnic minority backgrounds and have English as an additional language. The attainment of 11 year old students in national tests for English, mathematics and science in 2001 was close to or above national averages when compared to all schools. The 2002 OFSTED report for Mountfields Lodge noted that the school makes very good provision for sport (and music). Students' standards in physical education at the end of Years 2 and 6 are in line with national expectations. The school is involved in national and local initiatives that aim to increase the range and quality of the sporting activities available to primary age children.

Mountfields Lodge's physical education provision is directed and supported by two classroom primary generalist teachers who have taken on the shared role (one responsible for key stage 1 and the other for key stage 2) of 'Physical Education Coordinator'. This includes organising sport in and out of school, maintaining resources, health and safety issues, updating the school physical education policy, liaison with the community and monitoring innovative ideas related to the delivery of sport and physical education. All the teachers in the school teach physical education and primarily rely on the physical education content that they were introduced to while training to be a teacher. Some have attended professional development courses to update their knowledge and ideas. Key stage 1 and 2 physical education lesson plans and related support materials are available for all teachers to collect from the staff room.

All physical education lessons at Mountfields Lodge are grouped by class. Year 5 and 6 students receive two timetabled sessions of physical education, one lasting one hour and the other 30 minutes. The hour session tends to be delivered by people external to the school, including sports coaches and Sport Development Officers, who concentrate on particular games. Within games activities as presented in physical education in the National Curriculum for Physical Education (NCPE) in England, children at key stage 2 are expected to be taught to play and make up small-sided and modified games, use skills and tactics and apply basic attacking and defending principles and work with others to organise and maintain game play (DfEE/QCA, 1999). The 30 minute physical education lesson is delivered by the classroom teachers who are encouraged to promote dance, gymnastics and athletics and thus extend the breadth of activities experienced at key stage 2. When the school made the decision to introduce Sport Education to Year 5, the established hour that was serviced by external people became the Sport Education unit time.

The development of Sport Education at Mountfields

Staff at Mountfields Lodge had previously worked with two of the authors in an earlier physical education related study and were approached and asked if they would be interested in introducing Sport Education at the school. The introduction of Sport Education resulted in the key stage 2 Physical Education Coordinator, another female primary generalist teacher and the male Head Teacher restructuring the physical education programme to accommodate the introduction of Sport Education. There was very little disturbance to the physical education timetable and teachers appreciated the prospect of introducing student-centred learning into the primary school physical education programme as it was currently structured. The same three teachers were also responsible for planning and teaching the Sport Education unit. None of the teachers had heard of or had any prior experience of Sport Education. It was very much the key stage 2 Physical Education Coordinator who 'drove' the Sport Education initiative at Mountfields.

Before beginning Sport Education the three teachers met and decided on the time scale for the initiative and what they would ideally like to happen during each week of this key stage. The authors worked with the three teachers to introduce them to the key elements of Sport Education and provide support for development of lessons and clarification of content for the season. On most occasions one or two members of the research team attended each Sport Education class and were there to support the initiative and collect data that would aid the assessment of teachers' and students' experiences of Sport Education.

A total of 76 students from three classes took part in the Sport Education season. Two of the classes contained students from Year 5 and the third class was a composite Year 5/6 class. There were ten Sport Education teams, four each from the first two classes and two from the composite class. Before the official start of the Sport Education season, teachers spent two weeks assessing the students' ability. In the first week this entailed keeping notes on how the students passed and received the ball and how well they shot at a given target. Team skills, including how well students moved into space, stayed 'in tune' with their team-mates and how they interacted and made decisions were assessed in the second week when playing two versus two invasion games. Teacher observations from weeks one and two informed the formation of teams, so that each team was co-educational and mixed ability. The teachers believed that if students had been given responsibility for team selection, those who were proficient games players would have gravitated together. Teachers thus made a conscious effort not only to split up the more able students into different teams but also to allocate the less able students to teams where they were not necessarily with a close friend. This, they believed, would enhance the extent to which students in teams would have to work together, get to know each other and play 'as a unit'.

After the teacher observations and before beginning the Sport Education unit, the three teachers who were to be involved in teaching the unit held a meeting with all Year 5 students. The purpose of this meeting was to inform the students of what was going to be happening over the next two terms in Sport Education. Time was spent sorting students into their working teams (decided previously), encouraging teams to choose a team name and explaining the individual roles within a team that would be undertaken (e.g. coach, warm-up officer). Teams were encouraged to discuss role selections. Arrangements for the upkeep of portfolios and team display boards outside the classrooms were explained. The purpose of keeping a portfolio, the opportunity to design logos for team shirts, the format of the season and the rules of the game and points scoring were also outlined to the students. The notion of awarding points to motivate students to carry out behaviour that the teachers believed to be important was also introduced (Bell, 1998). Criteria for collecting team points were based not only on playing ability, but also on punctuality, fair play, cooperation, having the equipment ready for each Sport Education session and working on the team's display boards. It was also explained to students that the season would end in a Festival Day, when all the teams would play one final match to determine their finishing position.

The three teachers were anticipating that Sport Education would not only encourage the notion of team affiliation and team-building skills amongst the students, but also act as a positive reinforcement of sport and promote the importance of maintaining involvement in sport and an active lifestyle.

Planning the unit

The Sport Education unit initially planned at Mountfields Lodge is outlined in Table 9.1. The basic features that it was intended would feature in the unit were pre-season, formal competition and a final tournament. Although 12 weeks was to be timetabled for the Sport Education unit, the teachers

Table 9.1 Sport Education unit: initial plan

Season week	Content
1	Teachers observe and assess ability of students' individual skills.
2	Further teacher observation and assessment of students' team skills and formation of mixed ability teams.
3	Meet with all Year 5 students to explain and discuss Sport Education. Students informed of teams and encouraged to discuss and agree a team name. Introduction of portfolios and team display boards.
4–7	Pre-season training – teacher led. Students encouraged to practise the role of reporter, warm-up officer, scorekeeper and equipment officer while also being active playing members of the team.
8–11	Round-robin formal competition (5v5). Team T-shirts designed and printed.
12	Festival Day. All teams play one match (5v5) to decide their finishing position. Medals awarded to all students as well as the winning team, most improved team and most improved performer.

allowed two weeks' leeway in the event of a need to spend more time on certain aspects of the unit. The Sport Education unit ran during the spring and summer terms of 2001.

The game for the Sport Education season was a generic invasion game. This entailed scoring a point by bouncing a ball in a hoop placed on the ground, behind a back of court line. Any team member was allowed to score as long as they avoided crossing the line that defined where they could shoot from. It was a non-contact game and a free shot was awarded for deliberate contact. Players who were marking others were to stand at least 1 metre away from the player with the ball. Players in possession of the ball were not allowed to move with the ball, with a sideline throw being awarded to the opposition if they did so. A ball going out of play resulted in a free throw from the sideline for the opposition. A jump ball started play.

The official start of the Sport Education unit was to be termed '*pre-season training*' (weeks 4 to 7). During this phase students were to practise their Sport Education roles, including that of reporter, warm-up officer, score-keeper and equipment officer. They would also practise playing skills with the teacher initially leading sessions, before allowing the 'coach' of the team to lead. An example of a coach worksheet that was prepared by the teachers is provided in Appendix A. The students were to be given a list of possible roles – team representative, warm-up officer, scorer/timer, umpire, reporter, coach, equipment manager – and the corresponding responsibilities for each.

Formal competition was then scheduled to take place during weeks 8 to 11. All teams were to compete in a round-robin format where they would have the experience of playing all teams. To facilitate this, teachers devised a fixture list of game play for two playing areas, with relatively short games (of three minutes each way). This schedule would allow four teams to be on court at any one time and enable teams to quickly experience play against the nine other teams. The games were to be a '5 versus 5' format, allowing teams to substitute players from their squad and have team members producing match reports and encouraging the team.

Once all teams had played each other, the ten teams were to be split into one of two 'zones' in a ladder system. Teams would then play against the other four teams in their zone. The teachers used the term 'zone' instead of 'league' in an attempt to deflect the competitiveness that some children would relate to a league structure. The zones were called 'alpha' and 'omega' rather than '1' and '2' in a further attempt to downplay the implication that one zone was better than the other. The team with the most goals at the end of playing all other nine teams was to be put in alpha zone and the second team in omega zone, the third team in alpha zone and the fourth team in omega zone. This was to continue down to the ninth team in alpha zone and the tenth in omega zone. The odd number placings (1,3,5,7,9) from the initial fixture list consequently made up the alpha zone and the even placings (2,4,6,8,10) made up the omega zone. Thus, each zone would have five teams of mixed levels, i.e. one zone was not of a higher standard than the other.

The final week (week 12) was to be *Festival Day* with a chance for all teams to play in front of spectators made up from family and friends. By this stage teams would have made it into either a grand final or play-off matches. The play-offs would be between the teams placed fifth, fourth, third and second in each zone. The grand final would be between the team that had finished first in each zone. It was expected that only one game would be played at a time so that everyone could focus on the game and that the teams waiting to play would sit in their teams around the outside of the court. At the end of the Festival Day, medals for *all* participants and for the most improved player and team were to be presented as was a trophy for the winning team.

Researching Sport Education at Mountfields

A comprehensive range of data was generated throughout the Sport Education season at Mountfields Lodge in an attempt to assess teachers' and students' experiences of Sport Education. Data was generated from individual students and team interviews, teacher interviews, motivational profile questionnaires administered to all Year 5 students before and after the Sport Education season, team portfolios, video evidence of game play and students' drawings. The reports of experiences of Sport Education at Mountfields Lodge below draw predominantly on data from interviews conducted before, during and after the Sport Education season.

The interviews that were conducted with students and teachers were informal in nature. Exploratory questions were developed by the research team. The first interviews were carried out in May 2001 with one particular Sport Education team, four individuals from four different teams who were pursuing the role of coach, and two individuals whom the teachers thought it would be interesting to talk to in relation to their experience of Sport Education. The two individuals were a girl who had previously disliked school physical education and a boy who had difficulties in interacting with other students. Two group interviews were conducted, one with the members of the same Sport Education team and the other with the four coaches. The two individual students were each interviewed on their own. The focus of the interviews was the Sport Education experience, including students' impressions of Sport Education, their likes and dislikes in relation to the experience and whether Sport Education was viewed differently from their previous involvement in physical education at school.

Additional interviews, asking 24 students what the word 'sport' meant to them, their involvement in sport, and whether Sport Education was similar to their notion of sport, were conducted in the playground on a day of round-robin formal competition in July 2002. Members from each team were purposefully chosen at random, making sure that they were not engaged in play at the time, and were interviewed individually. Interviews were also conducted in the playground during the Festival Day the following week. Two or three members from each of the ten Sport Education teams were asked as a group what the Festival Day meant to them and the importance of being part of a team. The final interviews were conducted with three Sport Education teams, including the winning team, during the week following the Festival Day. These interviews were designed to encourage students to reflect on their Sport Education experience.

In addition to the interviews with students, the two classroom teachers involved in delivering the Sport Education season were interviewed before the 2001 Easter break to assess how Sport Education was progressing, to consider the decisions made in delivering the unit and to identify any difficulties or concerns regarding implementation. One of the two teachers was interviewed again at the completion of the unit, to establish the impact of the Sport Education season and ways in which the delivery could be improved. These interviews took place in the school staff room.

Experiencing the unit

Team selection: The team selection was undertaken by the teachers, to reflect a mix of abilities and gender. Initially this resulted in 'a few niggles' with students. Some of the more able students realised that the promotion of mixed (ability and gender) teams reduced the likelihood of being a member of a winning team. Some students were not happy with the team selection and it took them a couple of weeks to accept that they would have to work together.

Team names: Students chose their own team names with guidance from the teachers in order that the names were not offensive! The teams were given a week to think of names and when it came to finalising a name some teams had three or four suggestions. At this point the teachers introduced a ballot in order to decide names and teams drew up voting papers for each of their team members. The agreed team names were Simpson City, South Park United, The Cheeky Monkeys, The Comets, The Daggers, The Invaders, The Persians, The Rattlesnakes, The Smashers and The Thrashers. Some members of teams gave themselves a nickname within their team.

Roles: There were no major issues in relation to students deciding (within their teams) the roles that they were initially going to pursue. As explained above, students were given a list of possible roles – team representative, warm-up officer, scorer/timer, umpire, reporter, coach, equipment manager – and the corresponding responsibilities. They were encouraged to choose two or three roles that they would be happy to undertake in the event that some-one else desperately wanted one particular role. One team had difficulty in appointing a coach, as they all wanted to pursue the role of coach. They were, however, convinced by the teachers that they should rotate the role on a weekly basis and that they would all work cooperatively with the coach. If they did not, they would not be given the opportunity to be the coach.

The students were encouraged to experience a number of roles through-out the weeks but this was not 'policed' by the teachers. It was consequently left to individual teams and team members to decide upon rotations or switching of roles. The teachers were keen that all students should have an opportunity to practise scoring and umpiring, and the skills and responsi-bilities were introduced to the whole year group during one particular Sport Education session.

The notion of roles within the teams was clearly something that enhanced team affiliation, with team members believing that they had some investment in their team, whether they were the coach, warm-up officer or reporter. In the event that someone from the team was absent, the team members tended to be efficient in either placing someone else into that particular role, or merging the role within the team. Teachers cited numerous instances where the role had been 'the making' of particular individuals. Those students who had been less prominent in classroom activities and had an appointed role within their Sport Education team now conveyed a level of confidence that had not been evident before.

Team portfolios and display boards: Each team kept a portfolio that included details of their team, fact files about the individuals in their team (nicknames, favourite sport, role within Sport Education) and reports from the games that they had played. Display boards were put up in the school corridor and each team was allocated a section where, under their team name, they chose to display team photographs, drawings and team chants. While the teachers requested that the team portfolios include certain information, teams were allowed to change and add whatever they wished to their display boards.

Team points: Team points were introduced for punctuality, fair play, cooperation, having the equipment ready for each Sport Education session and working on the team's display boards. It was evident, however, that there was some lack of consistency in how teachers awarded team points, and the students were quick to notice that teams in one class might have more team points than teams in another class.

During the formal competition phase teams scored a point for each goal that they scored. Teachers were aware that giving points only for the scoring of goals could potentially be very demotivating for teams not scoring goals. Teachers kept a check on teams that were not scoring goals and made a conscious effort to allocate points for things such as their Sport Education display board or team organisation.

Teacher experiences: The intention to meet on a regular basis to discuss the unit's progress was difficult due to one of the teachers being the Head Teacher and consequently having other priorities and engagements at allocated Sport Education times. The teachers assessed their role on a week to week basis, not being sure what their role should or would entail as the weeks progressed. They were aware as the weeks progressed that they moved from leading the majority of a session to a situation in which students were running the session and they were interjecting where and when they felt it was necessary to do so. The teachers were aware of a significant change in their usual role from being expected to teach throughout the whole lesson to now acting as facilitators and having a supporting role. This allowed the teachers more time to assess what was happening and to spend more time with each group of students. As the weeks progressed they were also aware that, in order to make the Sport Education unit more beneficial to the children, they had to be flexible in relation to the number of weeks they allocated to each of the phases that they were attempting to incorporate in the season (see Table 9.2).

Cross-curriculum links: Possibilities for cross-curriculum links between Sport Education and literacy, numeracy and artwork were clearly evident. Literacy opportunities included writing a match report, writing about their Sport Education role, i.e. referee, coach, reporter, and keeping team portfolios. Numeracy opportunities arose when students worked out average points per team and discussed the scoring system for the zone games that would lead up to the Festival Day. Students began to calculate how many points they needed in each game to be at the top of the zone. Artwork was addressed through designing team T-shirts and team display boards. One teacher commented on the noticeable development in cooperation between students, when they were now working in art and design and music, with the task of thinking creatively and working together to design something.

Pre-season training: The teams practised in half team groups on small grids marked out on the playground, with the intention that every team member would get an opportunity to practise playing and umpiring, advise and evaluate team performance and keep score of the game. Understanding the rules of play and the consequences should these be broken was also a focus at this stage.

Teachers reported that, when teams initially split in two to play the other half of their team, some teams chose to play the better three performers against the poorer three performers. When it was explained to them that they were going to be playing other teams as a complete unit and not only with their three better performers, they began to realise the benefits of working to improve and include all team members in game play.

The game itself evolved as the teachers observed what was happening during the pre-season phase. In response to what they were observing during this phase, the teachers tightened the game play to include rules such as no movement of the feet when in possession of the ball, and the requirement to stand a metre away from the person with the ball. These points were introduced and reinforced to the children during the first three weeks of the pre-season phase. This allowed individual teams to practise suitable game play before playing against other teams. The teachers made a conscious effort to keep the rules of the game simple in order to minimise confusion about the rules and enable students to concentrate more on game play.

The teachers encouraged regular 'time-outs' during games and facilitated team chats with the coaches where they would prompt teams to address issues pertinent to their team game play. As the weeks progressed the teachers prompted the teams to take time out from practices and (without gathering the coaches together) encouraged the coaches to stay with their team and discuss what they, as a team, felt that they needed to work on in order to improve their game play. Decisions were then seen to be made more quickly in the time-outs and teams were spending less time reaching consensus on issues.

During the pre-season training phase teachers assessed the performance of the students and were prepared to swap players from team to team if necessary. No changes were made. The pre-season training phase was extended to allow teams to play short, three-sided matches against other teams. The teachers decided to spend a further two weeks on pre-season as they believed the students were substantially benefiting from it socially and were benefiting from practising umpiring and scoring in their own teams before competing against other teams in a more formal competition format.

The teachers then introduced '5 versus 5' friendly six minute matches against other teams to allow students the experience of playing on a full court, shooting and the basic rules of the game. The games were informal and not part of a league structure. Because of the short playing time, all teams had the opportunity to play each other during the sessions. By this time the teams were well versed in conducting their own warm-up, deciding the first five players to represent their team in the matches, and who would swap in at half-time. While they were doing the warm-up and making team decisions, the teachers had time to chalk the court lines on the playground. It was clearly evident that the students were getting an enormous boost from putting into practice a lot of the tactics that they had discussed as a team.

Formal competition: As planned, two playing courts were marked out so four teams were playing at any one time. When a team member was not playing they were encouraged to take notes as a reporter and/or conduct the team talk at half-time, where they were expected to give feedback on the team's performance. The teams decided who was to play in either half. Those who had not played for their team in the first half swapped on in the second half. Individuals from non-playing teams were chosen to keep the time and collect stray balls. Other non-players were encouraged to either practise with their team in a space away from the main playing court, or sit and watch the games and evaluate the teams.

Teams were given the opportunity to play against all other teams, making sure that the one team did not play two consecutive matches. On some days when teams who were timetabled to play only had three members of a team in attendance at school, that team swapped a time slot for the following week with another team. This resulted in teachers spending time before the following session making sure that they had a routine that would accommodate those teams who had not had the opportunity to play match games. A ladder detailing the games to be played was pinned on to a classroom door and as the weeks progressed results of each game were filled in. Teachers included a reminder at the bottom of the ladder that although it might appear that your team was doing well you might in fact have played more games than other teams had, at that point in time.

To maintain consistency in decisions and experience in refereeing, the teachers refereed the matches and focused on four points related to playing the game – no travelling with the ball, 1 metre away when marking the person with the ball, no barging and throw-ins. The two teachers took responsibility for managing and refereeing one of the two zones, alpha and omega, that had been constructed after the round-robin phase of formal competition.

Ultimately two outdoor sessions had to be cancelled due to bad weather. Although the students did not get to go outside in these conditions, they were able to work on their portfolios in the classroom, design team T-shirts and recap on the notions promoted through Sport Education and the rules of the game. This, and an extension of the pre-season training feature of the Sport Education unit, resulted in the unit running for 16 weeks and not, as had initially been expected, 12 weeks. The modified unit is outlined in Table 9.2.

As the Festival Day approached time was spent ordering medals, trophies and T-shirts. Students were encouraged to design and paint a team logo on the T-shirts and this was done on a day when it was too wet to go out and play any games.

Student reactions to relationships and roles: It was clearly evident that the students at Mountfields Lodge could see the benefits of having increased interaction time with the same team-mates. Ahmed admitted: 'I like being in a team since Christmas because . . . you don't have to keep swapping teams

Table 9.2 The actual Sport Education unit

Season week	Content
1	As planned – see Table 9.1.
2	As planned – see Table 9.1.
3	As planned – see Table 9.1.
4–6	As planned – see Table 9.1.
7–9	Extension to pre-season training. Students lead the sessions and not the teacher.
10–13	As for weeks 8–11 of planned unit – see Table 9.1.
14–15	Outdoor sessions cancelled due to bad weather. Time spent on team display board and portfolio work.
16	As planned – see Table 9.1.

so you get to know them and play with them.' John commented that remaining in the same team had been 'quite good because if you swap teams round all the time, then you just wouldn't get to know how all the other players do it and you wouldn't be very good at the sport'. The notion of getting to know people better in Sport Education than in other sporting opportunities outside of school was illustrated by Jacob:

Jacob:	I go to the Q— football club on Wednesday nights 6–7 and we do some warming up, do some skills and then have a game. When you're doing Sport Education you're working not just on sport, you're doing portfolios and stuff . . . you're not on a different team all the time and you can get to know them more.
Interviewer:	How do you feel about getting to know people more?
Jacob:	It feels quite good because you can make more friends.
Interviewer:	Have you made more friends?
Jacob:	Kind of a bit more because I know more about the people in my team.

The opportunity to get to know students other than current friends was also appreciated. Sue commented that working in a team that was not necessarily made up of your friends might let you find out that someone who you thought was 'really horrible' was 'actually quite nice'. Billy and Leigh, members of the same team, commented that the Sport Education teams allow you to get to know other people and make new friends. John admitted: 'it's [Sport Education] made me get a lot more friends because Isaac is in my team, and before this started me and Ahmed didn't like each other very much but now we're best friends, just because we're in the same team.' The impact of friendship within a team is illustrated in the following extract involving two members of the same team:

Interviewer:	How important is your team to you?
Kevin:	It means a lot to me because all my friends are in here, we work great as a team and it's great fun . . . To be able to trust people, to be friends with people, to know what you're doing and work as part of a team.
Interviewer:	What do you think is the best thing about Cheeky Monkeys' team?
Robbie:	Most of my friends are in it. We all work great as a team.

Grant, Tredinnick and Hodge (1992) identified that, while some students appreciate having to interact with others who were not necessarily their friends, others can become frustrated at different levels of enthusiasm for participation. This reaction was not apparent at Mountfields Lodge. Less-enthusiastic players tended to be ignored, but frustration was not overt in the behaviour of more motivated team-mates. The Daggers shared their experience of having a team member who appeared to be disinterested in being involved in Sport Education:

Leigh:	[Joanne] just likes to sit there. A person always has to go out [swap over], or two people, and she's always 'I don't want to go on the pitch.'
Joanne:	On the gala day, I said I'd be off for the first game. Then I came up at half-time and none of them wanted to go off so I had to be off again and I didn't play and I just had to sit there on the rug and I was a bit bored. I'm not a very good player so I didn't bother to play.
Lance:	She is a good player but she just never plays.
Leigh:	She just stands there lazing around daydreaming. She just looks at her nails and you have to go 'Joanne! Wake up!' and she says 'What?'
Stuart:	'I'm painting my nails!'
Leigh:	We do a game where you have to pass the ball around the circle and run and someone passed it to Joanne and she just stood there!
Stuart:	It hit her in the head and she didn't notice!
Interviewer:	But you don't really mind do you?
All:	No.

Without getting upset or appearing bothered, Joanne implies in the above extract that she has a low perception of her sport competence and that she was not encouraged to play in the second half of the game. Joanne did not appear bothered by what her team-mates were saying about her and the team did not get upset at Joanne's apparent lack of interest. The Daggers may have favoured the strength of team affiliation amongst the remaining members over the disinterest of one individual member.

There was a lot of support from the students for the increase in responsibility that was promoted through Sport Education, with students appreciating the autonomy that they were encouraged to have in practising a number of roles. The students appeared comfortable in dealing with this level of autonomy:

Sue: Outside [in Sport Education] we've got more of a say because Sarah's the coach. She watches what people are doing wrong and she can tell them what to do, when usually Mrs — would. Like if someone's talking in class she would tell them not to talk but if Sarah sees someone not marking very well she tells them to mark somebody ... We're meant to have more of a say in Sport Education.

Laura: You can become more independent and work out what's good and what's bad and work things out and do stuff that teachers wouldn't normally let you do.

Teacher reactions to relationships and roles: There was a feeling from one teacher that it was both the social and physical skills promoted through Sport Education that brought teams together, suiting the diversity of abilities and skills in each team. While some students were known for having good communication skills, others were more physically talented at either sport or art. A reported attraction of the Sport Education model is its effectiveness in catering not only for highly skilled students but also for girls, less skilled students and less 'popular' students (Alexander and Luckman, 1998). Improved outcomes for lower skilled students include increased opportunities for involvement and greater peer support (Hastie, 1998). At Mountfields Lodge, teachers commented that students began communicating more with their peers and, rather than dismissing a team member who could not carry out a particular skill successfully, other team members were encouraging and advising them on how to improve:

They're talking to each other a lot more. Rather than getting cross with people who can't do a particular skill and saying 'Well, you're rubbish' they're saying 'Well perhaps if you can't do that then if you move into a particular space', 'Perhaps if you were looking at the ball' ... They've started talking to each other more and they've started to respond well to ... the encouragement and the advice ... I think really they feel happier because they've got more to focus on and they have got this role and it's their team now and they feel quite protective about it.

(Alison, Teacher)

This statement suggests the students' appreciation of the responsibilities (Hastie, 1998) that they have for their team members. The teachers observed an increase in some of the children's confidence when they took on their particular role as coach, reporter, etc. and encouraged them to talk with each other and to make decisions:

> Their ball skills have amazingly improved . . . they've really thought about what they are doing and they'll sit down and say 'We're not filling spaces enough' or 'We need to vary the passes.'
>
> (Claire, Teacher)

> They've started to talk to each other . . . team coaches were talking and advising . . . when I came back to them and said . . . 'Do you feel that what you said wasn't happening before has improved?' and they said 'Oh yes, because we had to do this to mend that.' And they're starting to look for a space, they're starting to watch the ball more and [saying] 'We're concentrating on marking and staying with a particular person rather than all chasing the ball.'
>
> (Alison, Teacher)

The roles such as player, coach and official promoted through Sport Education offered students an opportunity to experience a legitimate role throughout the season. The above extracts attribute, to an extent, the improvement of students' ability levels and understanding of when to use particular tactics within a game situation to the roles undertaken by students and the subsequent reflection and discussion that arose in teams. To some extent, teachers were attributing the improvement in students' ability to the level of autonomy that students were encouraged to have in reflecting and discussing issues pertinent to their specific teams. As a team, students were appraising their own performance and discussing how they could improve. However, one of the teachers at Mountfields Lodge commented that, owing to the usual promotion of teamwork in her classroom, some of the students experienced difficulty in taking on leadership roles, such as that of coach. While the students had experienced the teacher acting as facilitator for group projects, they had never been given the opportunity to make decisions and carry them out without verification from the teacher.

One teacher attributed an increase in students' confidence to team-mates encouraging each other rather than to the individual skill levels of individuals. She noted that students welcomed improvement in their performance and observed an increase in confidence when teachers commented on how well the team was working. The confidence that students had acquired through involvement in Sport Education was also evident in dance lessons. One teacher also reported that a couple of girls who had previously been very shy and reticent before the introduction of Sport Education had since joined the school netball team. One of the teachers reported that, when she first took over as a Year 5 teacher, the class was made up from 'small groups of cliques of children'. The students were prone to complaining if they were asked to sit next to anyone who was not a member of their established group of friends. The same teacher introduced the notion of working with different people in the classroom and this was extended to Sport Education. Once the Sport Education teams had been established students were less bothered about working in the classroom with other people that they would not normally choose to work with. Teachers hinted at the Sport Education groupings beginning to be used to group students when doing other group activities, for example in science or art. Identifying groups by Sport Education teams was a quick way of arriving at mixed ability groupings in the (non-physical education) classroom.

Reflecting on the unit

The teachers agreed that the promotion of team affiliation and having an appointed role throughout the Sport Education unit had enhanced the enjoyment and involvement of students in a sporting environment. They believed that because the students had to work in teams they had become much more prepared to talk to others and work through issues and problems that the team were experiencing.

Teachers also noted that the Sport Education unit allowed individual teams to spend time addressing things that they felt would improve their own team's performance and that the class were not confined to following what the teacher believed the majority of the class would benefit from practising. Sport Education was thus perceived to be more responsive to varied learning needs.

One teacher admitted that the introduction of roles within the Sport Education model may have benefited from more time being allocated to the explanation of what specific roles entailed. Some of the students had never experienced having such responsibilities and it was difficult for them to understand what they were being encouraged to do. It was felt that perhaps the expectations that students would 'pick up' the meaning of Sport Education, the new game being introduced to them and the roles being promoted were too much for students to comprehend within a matter of weeks.

One of the enduring problems was that the Head Teacher had various engagements and appointments that resulted in him not being able to attend every Sport Education session. This was more of a problem in the early weeks of the unit when the students and teams were not as independent as they were after three or four weeks. The unit might have benefited from the presence of a third teacher, at least in the initial weeks.

Looking to the future

The school has continued to offer Sport Education to all Year 5 students and, in the third year of offering the unit, was forced to review and re-evaluate the original game in an attempt to accommodate special educational needs considerations. The Sport Education unit plan, however, remained very similar to that used when introducing the Sport Education unit for the first time in the school, and the elements of portfolios, team names and team T-shirts were maintained.

The playing area for the game remained divided into three areas but game play was different. A 'live play area' was created in the centre of the court and at either end of the court a dead ball line (previously the line which teams had to shoot from) was established. On leaving the live play area the ball has to be thrown to and caught by the team's 'roving catcher' who then passes to one of two shooters sitting at either sideline of the dead ball area. The shooter then attempts to score a goal by shooting at a hoop placed on the ground. If either the roving catcher or the shooters drop the ball it is a throw-in for the other team. The two seated shooters on each team allow a visually impaired girl and a cerebral palsy boy, who relies on the use of a trolley or wheelchair, to take part in every game without having positions or rules different to the rest of the students. A team-mate of the visually impaired girl who is not playing at the time stands beside her and catches the ball on her behalf and then gives it to the girl who is then encouraged to shoot. In a similar arrangement to the original unit offered in the school, six players from each team play at any one time and are encouraged to swap on and change playing positions at half-time. Three members of the team play in the live play area, one acts as the roving catcher and two sit by either sideline to shoot into the hoop.

Teachers have commented that reducing the number of students vying for the ball in the live play area to '3 versus 3' has encouraged much more accurate passing and catching than previously. Teachers are still refereeing the matches but hope to begin to introduce students to the task and responsibility of refereeing matches.

The teachers are keen to continue with Sport Education with Year 5 groups as they believe that it not only encourages a focus on tactical game play but also, through a block of time, encourages and allows teachers to evaluate the learning taking place. The teachers feel that the opportunity to evaluate their own work and student learning is enhanced by the duration of Sport Education units. They also believe that there is a greater impact on student learning if students are encouraged to evaluate their own work rather than the teacher being solely responsible for evaluating.

The teachers at Mountfields Lodge believe that their understanding and management of Sport Education can only improve now that they have experienced Sport Education. The workload related to Sport Education is expected to decrease now that they have templates for games and tournaments.

The teachers have decided to keep Sport Education as an upper school activity for Years 5 and 6, with the Year 5s taking what they have learned and experienced in Sport Education into Year 6. At the time of completing this chapter there is support for Sport Education to be promoted within the next three years in the local area surrounding Mountfields Lodge Primary School. That is, Sport Education is planned to be a partnership group activity in the local primary and middle schools. Thus, an expanding collaborative learning community is emerging with a common interest in Sport Education.

References

Alexander, K. and Luckman, J. (1998). Teachers' Perceptions and Uses of the Sport Education Curriculum Model in Australian Schools, Paper presented at the British Sports Council's Seminar on Sport Education, Loughborough University, UK.

Bell, C. (1998). Sport Education in the Elementary School, *Journal of Physical Education, Recreation and Dance*, 69, 5, pp. 36–9, 48.

Department for Education and Employment (DfEE)/Qualifications and Curriculum Authority (QCA) (1999). *Physical Education: The National Curriculum for England*, London: HMSO/QCA.

Grant, B.C., Tredinnick, P. and Hodge, K. P. (1992). Sport Education in Physical Education, *New Zealand Journal of Health, Physical Education and Recreation*, 25, 3, pp. 3–6.

Hastie, P. (1998). Applied Benefits of the Sport Education Model, *Journal of Physical Education, Recreation and Dance*, 69, 4, pp. 24–6.

Appendix A: Guidance for Sport Education coaches

<u>PRE-SEASON TRAINING 2</u>

POINTS TO REMEMBER WHEN COACHING YOUR TEAM

PLAYER WITH BALL	LOOK UP
	PASS TO TEAM-MATE IN SPACE
	TYPE OF PASS TO USE
PLAYER WITHOUT BALL	MOVE INTO SPACE
	SIGNAL FOR A PASS
	DODGE FROM MARKER
ENCOURAGE TEAM TO	INTERCEPT BALL
	MARK PLAYERS

10 Sport Education in Year 8 games

Mandy Quill and Gill Clarke

Introduction

This and the two chapters that follow all report on the introduction of Sport Education in physical education at key stage 3 (see Chapter 1) at Mountbatten School and Language College, in Romsey, Hampshire. To set the context in which Sport Education has been developed at Mountbatten in games (discussed below), gymnastics (discussed in Chapter 11) and athletics (discussed in Chapter 12), we begin with a general introduction to the school and physical education within it.

Mountbatten School and Language College

Mountbatten School and Language College is a large, co-educational comprehensive school for students aged 11 to 16 years. It is situated in a semi-rural area on the outskirts of a small market town in Hampshire. It caters for close to 1,500 students with approximately 280 in each year group. The intake is predominately white and middle class, with the majority of students coming from five local primary schools.

The facilities for physical education in the school include a sports hall, gymnasium, hall, dance studio, weight training suite, tennis and hard court area and extensive fields. As is the case in all too many educational institutions, at various times throughout the year the large indoor spaces are taken to accommodate formal examinations and other statutory tests. The dance studio is a shared space with drama and community use. The fields also present problems. An area floods in wet weather and is unusable for games. There is also a large dip in the centre of the field which means that there is only space for a 300 metre (rather than full size 400 metre) track to be marked for athletics. These various limitations mean that the timetable for physical education has to be carefully planned to minimise disruption to teaching and learning. Local facilities off-site are also used in curriculum time for some activities within key stage 3 and for the key stage 4 options programme. The off-site facilities include a swimming pool, badminton and squash courts, golf, ten pin bowling and outdoor education centres.

A further point to note in relation to the provision of physical education generally, but the development of Sport Education in particular, is that the school operates a two week timetable.

Physical education at Mountbatten

For many years physical education has had a high profile within the school. The physical education faculty aims to encourage and increase participation in sport and physical activity by helping all students to appreciate and enjoy physical activity. It endeavours to support the development of independent learners by extending students' ability to select and apply physical skills that will make them effective performers, and raise standards in learning by increasingly giving students greater responsibility in lessons. Involvement in planning, leading and establishing relevant and appropriate targets for learning is designed to help students make sensible decisions about the types of physical activity that they become involved in, and at what levels. A further intention of the faculty is to promote healthy lifestyles, by increasing students' knowledge and understanding of the benefits of regular exercise. The firm belief is that 'challenge and enjoyment equals success' and that if students experience success through physical activities then this can only be worthwhile, and will contribute to their development into positive and responsible adults.

At key stage 3 all students receive one 2-hour session and two 1-hour sessions within a two week period. At key stage 4 they receive one 2-hour session and one 1-hour session. In key stage 3 all students follow a common curriculum focused on five areas of experience: athletics, dance, games, gymnastics and outdoor education. All students experience a minimum of two terms study of a game, and this may be increased to three if they opt to stay with the same game in Year 9. Some students will, however, opt to change games in Year 9. The choice that they have is between basketball, netball and soccer.

In Year 7 students are taught the principles of the game in what may be termed a 'traditional way'. Students are taught set skills relating to the game and then incorporate these into game situations. In Year 8 they have their first experience of Sport Education, described below and in Chapters 11 and 12. The experience of Sport Education has now been extended to Year 9, in order to provide a firm foundation for physical education studies at key stage 4. At key stage 4 the skills learnt in Sport Education are used to enhance learning experiences and attainment in the context of accredited courses (particularly GSCE Physical Education and the Junior Sports Leader Award (JSLA) course) (see Chapter 7) and in core National Curriculum Physical Education.

In Years 7 and 8, students are taught in both mixed ability and mixed gender groupings in all areas of experience. This enables the faculty to foster personal and social development. In Year 9 students are set in ability groups.

The most able may be mixed gender or single gender grouping depending on group numbers. The remaining students are then divided into single gender groups. These grouping arrangements were established several years ago specifically to increase levels of participation amongst lower skilled girls in particular.

During key stage 4, the physical education faculty respects the need for students to have the opportunity to select a more personalised physical education programme, directed towards their lives beyond school and into adulthood. This key stage therefore features a blocked programme within which students can select specific programmes of study for each term of Years 10 and 11. This arrangement aims to encourage identification of a personal preference for specific activities and sports. The physical education faculty is also aware of the need to promote certificated courses that enable students to record their standards of performance, their leadership and organisational skills. Students are therefore offered the opportunity to follow the JSLA course and can select physical education as a GCSE subject in addition to core physical education. Finally, students throughout key stages 3 and 4 are encouraged to participate in the wide variety of out of hours learning clubs and activities that are on offer at the school.

Staffing and resources for physical education at Mountbatten

The physical education faculty has seven full time members of staff, four male and three female, who collectively have a wealth of experience. All have been teaching at the school for between 15 and 27 years. They are therefore a firmly established team of staff. Faculty staff also hold other positions of responsibility in the school. Two members of the physical education faculty are heads of year. Others respectively hold positions of key stage assistant, primary liaison teacher, examinations officer and PSHE coordinator. The faculty work well together in diverse teaching situations. They work very much 'as a team', with the team atmosphere maintained by constant support for each other. The faculty is arguably very fortunate in that all of the teachers within it are comfortable teaching mixed ability or ability set groups and mixed or single sex groups. When timetabling arrangements demand, male teachers teach girls only groups and the female teachers teach boys only groups.

The head of faculty is very good at managing the team of staff in the light of individual strengths. He uses their specific subject knowledge to create programmes of study for each activity, which are taught by each member of the faculty. Collectively the faculty are passionate about their subject and enthusiastic about innovation, not wanting to 'fall behind' and always wanting to remain at the forefront of new initiatives. The diversity of expertise within the faculty contributes to its success and gives students the opportunity to develop and perform to a high standard in basketball, cricket, athletics, dance, gymnastics, trampolining, skiing, netball, tchoukball and soccer. In addition the faculty organise various residential experiences for a large number of students including camping, multi-activity outdoor courses, skiing, water-sports and team-building youth hostelling weekends.

The head of faculty coordinates the timetable and delegates teaching responsibilities to individual teachers. Everyone in the faculty is, however, confident and willing to teach everything that is offered within the curriculum. The faculty are committed to staff development and are constantly updating, reviewing, extending and expanding their qualifications and experience in various activities, through continuing professional development activities and 'cascading' to the rest of the faculty.

The interest in Sport Education

The idea of introducing Sport Education into the physical education curriculum at Mountbatten School and Language College was first mooted in the summer of 1999 following discussions with Southampton University staff. Shortly after these discussions, between Mandy Quill (then a physical education faculty member at Mountbatten) and Gill Clarke, the prospect of introducing Sport Education was considered at a faculty meeting. The teachers in the faculty were largely positive, seeing it as a 'Good idea – always willing to try something new'. They welcomed the opportunity and were 'optimistic about the benefits to the physical education faculty'. The concept of Sport Education and the notion of creating skilful, intelligent and enthusiastic sportspeople were things that the staff could all identify with. They recognised that through this teaching model they could continue to encourage all students to maintain an active interest in sport and to pursue excellence, while at the same time developing their knowledge of the importance of fitness gained through participating in physical activity.

Some concerns were, however, raised at this stage. Specifically it was felt that potentially:

- it would take students too long to organise themselves and therefore waste lesson time;
- the students would not have the subject knowledge or experience to structure successful practices themselves; and
- students would not warm to the concept or approach.

As we will see in this chapter and those that follow these concerns were to prove unfounded.

Sport Education in Year 8 games

It was decided that initially Sport Education would be introduced into the Year 8 winter games programme for several compelling reasons. Firstly, it was felt that the Sport Education model lent itself to the games programme. Teachers were competent and confident with games teaching and this also meant that every member of the faculty would be involved in the initiative. With a third of the Year 8 students being timetabled together, the competition dimension also seemed likely to be more authentic and the organisation of leagues and the end of season festivals easier. The teachers also agreed that some students in Year 8 were ready to take on more responsibility for their own learning in a controlled situation and it was felt that the requirements of the NCPE relating to key stage 3 and specifically games (see below and DfEE/QCA, 1999) could be comfortably met through Sport Education. In addition it was recognised that existing programmes of study could be adapted to be used as a starting framework for Sport Education, so that the additional workload demands would not be too great for staff. Further, staff believed that, if they were expecting students to recognise and appreciate the different roles involved in sport and to successfully adopt these roles at key stage 4, then they needed to be providing opportunities for students to experience the roles and their associated responsibilities during key stage 3. It was felt that early experience of Sport Education would particularly enhance certain aspects of the GCSE course, where students are assessed for their ability to take on different roles, and the JSLA course, where there is a need for students to make informed decisions about their suitability to train as a sports leader. At key stage 4 at Mountbatten students also have the opportunity to apply to be a *sports prefect*. The designated prefects are responsible for organising lunchtime sports leagues, reading results and notices in assembly, keeping display boards up to date, coordinating inter-house sports fixtures and running the school's Sports Council. Through participating in Sport Education the students would be gaining experience of using these skills and gathering evidence to support a prefect application.

It was felt that by beginning with one year group, and one activity, the chances of success in trying Sport Education for the first time would be greater for teachers and students alike. The physical education staff believed that, once students had become familiar with Sport Education in one activity, the model could be used in other areas of the physical education curriculum.

To begin with it was agreed that the major focus in introducing Sport Education would be upon learning roles and responsibilities, learning to compete, learning to prepare for a sporting event and learning to celebrate sport through an organised festival. These four components provided a framework within which there was a clear emphasis upon the learning of sporting skills in context and sport being an important aspect of physical education. A more fundamental concern underpinning the identification of these components was the desire to be transferring responsibility for learning to young people and involving them more closely in shaping their own learning.

It was hoped that a Sport Education games unit would give students an authentic experience of the game through a season and make the learning process more relevant for them. Although at this stage the experience of organising and running a festival of sport would be new to the students, it was hoped that within the framework of the unit and with structured support from teachers they would learn how to do this.

A progressive and structured development

Having decided on the starting point, taking into account factors such as the timetable, groupings, choice of activity, resources, etc., the next step was to produce a comprehensive plan for taking Sport Education forward in practice. A planning framework was put together that could be used with different activities within the physical education curriculum. The following set of planning principles gave a starting point that each teacher could identify with and relate to the particular activity that they were teaching:

1   *Units as seasons:* The unit of work would be described as a 'season' with an early, mid- and late phase. The start of the season would incorporate the introduction to the concept of Sport Education as an approach for teaching and learning, the team selection and affiliation to the team, and selection of a team name. The main part of the lesson would still be teacher led at this stage. The setting up of the leagues and recording of scores would initially be done by the lead teacher. Mid-way through the season additional roles would be introduced and students would begin to take more responsibility within the lesson. Towards the end of the season roles would be re-allocated and a tournament or festival would be organised. Again students would take on more responsibility and have more input to planning.

2   *Selection of leaders:* Specific students would be selected as appropriate leaders within each activity. The lead teacher would meet with these students before the beginning of the season, so that the leaders had some prior knowledge of the expectations associated with their role. Clearly, knowledge of the students was essential in order for effective leaders to be put in place from the start. Qualities to be considered in selections included: those who demonstrated good organisational skills, were highly motivated themselves and good at motivating others, and those who were confident, and popular with their peers. Potential leaders would need to display some of these qualities and therefore be more than merely the most skilful players in the group.

3   *Selection of teams:* This was designed to achieve balance between teams, taking into account ability of individual children, gender, peer groups, etc. To begin with, selection was made by teachers. It was envisaged that in the future different selection strategies would be used, with captains working with teachers and, in time, captains having sole responsibility for selections.

4   *The selection and allocation of additional roles:* A framework was outlined for the introduction of other key roles. Depending on the group these would sometimes be allocated to individuals by the teacher, and sometimes decided on by the students themselves.
5   *Competitions and festivals:* Every unit would involve the organisation of a league competition to run the length of the season, with a festival or tournament at the end to celebrate the season's work.

Once the Sport Education programme had commenced, ways of making connections with and thus supporting learning in other curriculum areas became apparent. The cross-curricular dimension of Sport Education (see Chapter 5) was therefore developed over a period of time. Staff particularly focused on the use of key skills such as numeracy and literacy, citizenship and use of ICT. Links to other subject areas such as art and design and science were also developed and are explored in some detail below and in Chapters 11 and 12.

It is also pertinent to note that, since the initial development of Sport Education at Mountbatten, adaptations have been made to students' introduction to physical education at the school in Year 7. Specifically, in Year 7, time is now devoted to teaching the principles of warming up. Students are given a large repertoire of warm-up exercise and gradually throughout the year take on responsibilities for warming up. In skill practices students are also encouraged to identify problems and work out solutions. A foundation is therefore being established for Sport Education, in terms of prospective roles and responsibilities but also expectations and standards in physical education.

Putting plans into practice: Sport Education in games in Year 8

The winter games selected for the initial trial of Sport Education were netball and soccer. Year 8 students would be moving into their second term of these activities and would therefore have the basic skills and understanding to play the game with some success. It was anticipated that in the Sport Education units the four aspects of skills, knowledge and understanding identified within the NCPE (DfEE/QCA, 1999) would be addressed:

- 'Acquiring and developing': students would be taught to refine and adapt their existing skills of passing, shooting and receiving and to develop specific techniques such as attacking and defending to become more effective in the game.
- 'Selecting and applying': students would be taught how to plan, modify and develop simple strategies of play to improve their own performance. This would be done by involving the students, encouraging them to take

the initiative and to lead and organise practice situations. The students would also be taught the rules and to apply their knowledge by being actively involved in refereeing and umpiring games.

- 'Evaluating and improving performance': students would be taught how to make value judgements about their own and others' performance and so begin to make informed decisions about how to improve the quality of their game.
- 'Knowledge and understanding of fitness and health': students would be taught how to prepare for the game using general and specific warm-up techniques. They would also develop an activity specific training programme designed to raise their level of fitness in preparation for the festival/tournament at the end of the season.

Throughout the season students would also be encouraged to experience different roles such as leader, coach, official, etc. Opportunities for links across the curriculum might also arise throughout the season, such as use of ICT and links with literacy, numeracy, art and design and science.

Success of this first trial was important in order to give the teaching staff the confidence to continue their development of the new approach. Input from the students at this stage was therefore deliberately limited. As staff and students became more familiar with the model and approach, student input was increased and gradually the teacher was able to become more of a facilitator (see below).

It was hoped that for all of the students involved the experience of Sport Education would be a positive one and specifically one that would give them the necessary skills to make informed choices at key stage 4 and beyond about participation in sport as young people. Sport Education was also intended to help students to become informed spectators and enable them to acknowledge success and to accept defeat. This emphasis upon the development of positive attitudes and behaviour in sport was synonymous with the established aims of the physical education faculty:

- to understand and appreciate the importance of valuing the contributions of others, whether male or female, whatever their level of ability or social and cultural background; and
- to appreciate the importance of fair play and of abiding by the rules and codes of conduct in different activities.

Developing the Sport Education games units

Unit length: The length of the season would be the same as the length of one unit, i.e. a term. It was intended that students would have one 2-hour session every two weeks, amounting to seven sessions over the term. Six of these would be Sport Education lessons and the last would be given over to the festival or tournament.

Team selection and groupings: This was a very important issue and a good knowledge of individual student abilities was essential. Captains were identified by teaching staff and were approached prior to the start of the unit. Students were then allocated to teams to ensure that the teams were even as far as numbers and ability were concerned. This is something that is done routinely in physical education lessons, but the difference here was that once in a team students would be affiliated for the whole season. The importance of getting the balance right at the outset therefore cannot be stressed enough.

Role selection: The lead teachers for the games unit identified core roles that would be introduced: that of player/performer, coach (warm-up, skills or game coach), official (scorer, recorder, umpire, etc.) and duty manager. Again initially individuals were selected by the teachers to undertake the different roles. As they were new to this way of working, teachers did not want to place students in situations where they might fail. It is recognised that this selection process may have been more teacher defined than was perhaps desirable, and that these actions may appear to undermine the integrity of Sport Education. Staff hoped, however, to progressively extend student responsibilities over the key stage, so that they were supported in becoming independent learners and informed sportspeople.

The season structure: Within the season students would hopefully gain an authentic experience of sport, sometimes being successful and sometimes not. As the season progressed they would be given the opportunity to take more of an active role in planning sessions until they became capable of devising and leading practices themselves. At the outset the lead teacher would use the existing programme of study for the unit to plan the content and sequence of the lesson. Gradually students would become more involved in making decisions for themselves and their teams, developing the ability to set relevant targets, plan specific skill practices and undertake constructive game reviews.

Assessment: Initially the assessment of individual students would be done by the teaching staff as they did before the introduction of Sport Education. Neither the assessment criteria nor focus would change from that already in place for Year 8 games. The aspect of learning formally assessed through Year 8 games was 'selecting and applying' and this was identified in unit planning. Teachers would assess the students' ability to plan and implement a warm-up specific to the activity, their ability to modify and develop skills practices and their knowledge of the rules and conventions of the game.

Competition: As the season progressed students would learn how to keep records and how to organise league fixtures fairly. They would learn the rules of the game and how to apply them, and also, through umpiring and refereeing, how to recognise when rules were not adhered to. This would be good preparation for the festival or culminating competition at the end of the unit. Points would be awarded for the league games throughout the season and these would be posted on the notice board in the physical education corridor alongside school team fixture results.

Festival or culminating competition: This would be organised by the students towards the end of the season. They would plan the number of games, the length of each game, organise the rotations, record, score and time keep. All this would give the students enhanced ownership of their learning and hopefully foster a more positive attitude towards physical education.

In the planning it was noted that learning in other areas of the curriculum would potentially be advanced with the adoption of Sport Education. Specifically, connections were identified with literacy (through the writing of reports and players making verbal evaluations of their own and others' performance); numeracy (through the collection of results and scores); ICT (students would be given the opportunity to photograph their team and possibly some playing situations); art and design (through the production of a team logo); and citizenship (see Chapters 5 and 6).

Materials to support the first trial of Sport Education were developed by lead teachers and, as the season progressed and ideas emerged, other members of the faculty became involved in producing material for lessons. Faculty meetings would be held regularly and Sport Education would always be an item on the agenda, so that discussion could lead to the sharing of observed benefits and shortcomings of the approach. Tracking and monitoring developments was recognised as important for collective learning and improvement.

The realities of teaching and learning in Sport Education

The unit structure and sequence: Dividing the unit up into early, mid- and late season gave the students a clear structure to follow, with logical progressions linking the phases. The skills and game development progressions were similar to those in the established programme of study. There was therefore a familiarity about the content and unit layout. National Curriculum requirements and terminology provided a further common reference point for staff and students alike.

Team identities: In netball the students enjoyed identifying with the team for the season. This made the game more meaningful for them and helped to create a supportive learning environment. They felt secure in the knowledge that they knew who they were playing with, where (physically) on the court they would prepare for the session, how many games they were going to be playing and so on.

In the case of soccer, Sport Education tapped into an existing and very powerful sporting and social culture. The sport and prospective role models are prominent in the media for students to relate to. Students frequently see their local town team and often the England team wearing team strip, warming up on the pitch with the trainer immediately prior to the game and having a team talk from the coach. They hear match commentary and see match reports in newspapers.

This context, together with the structure of the season with league matches running each lesson, meant that Sport Education in soccer was extremely successful. Students quickly identified with their team name and enjoyed the idea of affiliation for the season. Team captains in soccer were also issued with an A5 booklet which had a blank circle on the front page for teams to create their own logo based on their team name. The task was appealing and successful because of the existing role models that many of the students had. Several teams therefore likened their team names and logos to their favourite professional team. In tasks such as this, the netballers were, however, at a distinct disadvantage as they did not have comparable reference points or access to examples.

Roles and responsibilities: One of the responsibilities associated with being a member of a sporting team is a responsibility to attend team practices or training sessions. In the Sport Education netball unit particularly, absenteeism was problematic, because of the speciality of positions within the game and consequent impact of particular players missing from a team. A reduced number of players in the game and imbalance in team sizes had a knock-on effect on the students' motivation to play effectively, when they could see they were at a distinct disadvantage. The effects of absenteeism upon games, however, also encouraged students to apply peer pressure to ensure full attendance. To reduce the negative impact of absenteeism and at the same time add pressure to attend, it was decided that teams would become squads of up to ten pupils and that a point system would be introduced. If a team was short of players and a transfer had to be made, i.e. a player was put on loan for the lesson, then the team that the transfer player came from would be awarded a bonus point. Points were not withdrawn for having an incomplete squad or for receiving a transfer as it was felt that this might be de-motivating for the team concerned. A similar arrangement was introduced in soccer and here students were already familiar with the notion of a 'transfer system'.

With all of the roles, staff endeavoured to ensure that students were never put in the situation of leading or being responsible for a part of the lesson without appropriate preparation, or without having knowledge of the skills required to do the job. The learning and teaching demands in Sport Education were recognised as considerable. Structure, guidance, support and progression were acknowledged as critical in the move to greater student responsibility for learning and, specifically, students having specific roles. Thus, students would learn the rules of the game through playing so that they would then be able to recognise when the rules were broken when umpiring. They would learn how to lead an activity specific warm-up and how to develop a progressive training programme over the season in order to be able to take on a coaching role. They would learn how to evaluate the performance of individuals and teams and as a result would be able to set relevant targets for future lessons. Throughout the season all students also learnt how to keep records and how to organise league fixtures fairly. A recorder noted results each week and a league table was produced. This was all part of the authentic experience of being affiliated to a team and playing in a league throughout a season.

Team captains were informed of their responsibilities and the contribution they were expected to make to each lesson in respect of organising their team, equipment, warm-up, motivating their players and leading by example. When additional roles were introduced during the unit, a basic job description was explained to establish the expectations of the person in the role and to enable students to decide who would be most suitable for the role within their team. Sometimes the roles were shared and sometimes it was appropriate to rotate the roles between different players over several weeks. For example, in netball two people from each team were elected as equipment monitors responsible for setting up and checking the playing area each lesson. As the season progressed it was decided that this role would be better shared amongst the whole team. Therefore, each week a different team was established as the duty team and could earn bonus points in this role.

Students responded positively to taking on different roles in netball and being involved with the scoring and umpiring and organising the culminating festival. The start of the lesson became more effective as a result of assigning roles and responsibilities. Equipment was set up quickly and warm-ups were taken purposefully by the warm-up or fitness coach.

In soccer the lead teacher gave each team the responsibility of one particular practice, which they practised as a team. Each lesson a different team therefore led the practice session. In netball the lead teacher set the theme or focus of the lesson and gradually each team would be challenged to devise and develop their own practices based on the theme to improve their play. Task cards were made available for the team coaches to use when devising their practices.

A media representative was responsible for taking photographs of the team in action using disposable cameras. These would be displayed on the notice board in the corridor. In soccer, match reports were also written by identified students and these too were displayed on the notice board. Headings were provided as a beginning structure for match reports. In netball the students wrote player profiles about the players in their team. All of these activities helped to strengthen team affiliation.

'Non-participants', for whatever reason, were fully utilised within Sport Education lessons. Variously, they had the roles and responsibilities of being recorders, umpires, timekeepers and photographers. Thus, they were re-positioned as participants in lessons. Again this is good practice and something that good teachers do already. However, in Sport Education, these other roles have an authenticity and, even if not playing, students can still feel that they are centrally involved. The appointment to a role is not tokenistic. If not playing, students were encouraged to still change into appropriate kit. They therefore looked more like an official and were also able to do the job more effectively. Changing into appropriate kit also gained them the respect of the other players. In soccer it meant that non-playing students did not have to wait off the field to avoid getting their school uniform muddy and in netball it addressed the problem of girls trying to umpire in short skirts and heeled shoes.

With each individual being given the opportunity to have a valued role within the lesson this gave students greater ownership of learning. It was noticeable that students were more motivated to participate in the lesson, they were working with a positive attitude, their interest was maintained, they wanted to learn, they were cooperative and lower skilled players were encouraged. Students were not waiting all the time to be told what to do. With increased confidence they were able to begin to make informed decisions within the lesson about their own learning.

Developing independent learners and changing teacher–learner relationships: Skill development remained teacher led for some time, until students were confident to set up and develop relevant practices themselves. Students' lack of subject knowledge could be a cause for concern if responsibility was passed to them to lead part of the lesson too soon. It must be emphasised here that the role of the teacher in Sport Education lessons involved more than handing out whistles and balls and saying, 'off you go'. The process of passing on responsibility was sometimes more successful than other times. Students made some mistakes but were able to learn from these. It was important at this stage not to try and correct everything. Rather, mistakes needed to be acknowledged as part of the learning process and to therefore be expected, be seen as 'OK', but also recognised and addressed.

In soccer students were able to take on organisational and instructional responsibilities quite early on. Many of the students play soccer outside school for local junior sides. They had a wealth of ideas and experiences from this community link to bring to the Sport Education unit. In netball, shifting the balance of teacher–student responsibility took longer. Students could only effectively take greater responsibility for their own and others' learning once they could make accurate judgements about performance and game play. Practical assessment is not easy and the background knowledge of netball was not as evident as it was in soccer.

Practically, developing and sharing responsibilities demands that students are enabled access to resources appropriate for their new roles, including equipment for additional team practices outside of lesson time. Some changes were also needed to the materials used by teachers. Team lists, record and score sheets had all been written on paper and kept in the teacher's register. Paper was lost, got wet or blew away outside. A portfolio was therefore introduced and students were also encouraged to take responsibility for their own record keeping. Each team was given a plastic wallet which contained team sheets, player profiles, role descriptions, a target sheet, evaluation sheets, a record card of games played, goals scored, penalties incurred and so on, team or action photos and their individual team floppy (computer) disc. The portfolios were kept in a year box (a square plastic box stored in the physical education department). A box of clipboards was also available to use, plus a tin of whistles, pencils and stopwatches. Students were given responsibility for getting this equipment ready for the Sport Education lesson.

Digital cameras replaced the disposable cameras for several reasons and each team was issued with a floppy disc. The disposable cameras did not allow immediate viewing of the pictures. It was the teachers' responsibility to get the films processed and this was extra work that they did not need. It was also not cost effective because while students were learning to take pictures of movement many photos were wasted. With the digital camera, photographs could be viewed instantly and deleted when necessary at no cost. The media representative for each team took on the responsibility for printing any photographs taken during the lesson.

Sport Education students were given a pass to use the IT suite at break and lunchtimes and this was regarded as a privilege. With all the roles students were encouraged to extend their learning opportunities in the extra-curricular setting, continuing and developing the roles that they had experienced within the unit. It was noticeable that, after Sport Education had been introduced, participation in extra-curricular clubs increased. This was not just the performer but staff began to find students who were interested in recording, scoring, reporting, taking photos and umpiring.

Point systems: A point system was used throughout the season. Each team was awarded points for games won but also for a variety of other things. Points were awarded for full attendance, for effective input into the lesson either in the warm-up, or skill development, or game. Points were also awarded for accurate record keeping and relevant evaluations of play. These value added points helped to motivate students. It created positive peer pressure which again helped to maintain standards and often improve them.

Inclusion, assessment and advancements in learning: It was evident that standards of performance had been maintained, that students were well motivated and enthusiastically taking part in the lessons. The lower skilled and the average students were well challenged. The more able students were challenged to take on more responsibility within lessons and their teams. Yet staff rightly questioned whether with mixed ability teams the able performers were being provided with opportunities to advance their personal performance. In netball it was felt that the able students were well integrated and had the opportunity to develop and improve their own play. But this was not always the case in soccer. In recognition of this situation, it was decided to hold a mid-season international mini-tournament for which the Sport Education teams would be disbanded. Teams were rearranged with different names and with the most able players playing against each other (for example, Brazil v Italy) thereby giving these students a clear opportunity of improving game play.

Another task that was introduced enabled students to be more involved in formally evaluating their own and others' performance. A team target sheet was designed, divided into weekly sections with two headings: 'things we did well' and 'areas to improve'. Each week the teams would briefly fill this out.

Verbal assessment was also used. For example, students were asked to discuss appointment of 'player of the match', the best goal scored and why. The title of 'champagne moment' was used to prompt students to identify, discuss and agree upon a special incident in a game. This need not always be related to exceptional playing performance. Rather, it may identify an incident of positive sporting behaviour to be celebrated.

Notably, teachers found that in Sport Education assessment tasks became easier to manage. Teachers had more time available during the lesson, once the skills practice or game was set up, to step back and observe individual students in different situations. It also became possible to use self- and peer evaluations in assessment.

The festival or culminating competition: Towards the end of the season some time within the lesson was allocated to the preparation of the festival or end of season tournament. In netball a 'versatility tournament' was organised where the players rotate positions in a set order every game. In soccer a tournament where individual players are conditioned according to their ability was organised. Students were given a list of things that they needed to organise such as a rota of play, timekeepers, umpires or referees, scorers and recorders. It was easier organisationally to allocate each team a particular responsibility. Some of the preparation could be done outside the lesson time. The whole of the last lesson was then set aside for the tournament to take place organised and run by the students.

Reflections and future directions

As explained above, Sport Education was a regular item on the physical education faculty meeting agenda, in order that the implementation could be reviewed and discussed on an ongoing basis. This was undoubtedly crucial to success. With seven teachers involved in Sport Education there was a great deal of sharing of good practice, ideas and feelings about what was not so successful and needed to be changed. The meetings were also a time for supporting each other in the task of taking on board a new and unfamiliar initiative within which teachers may well feel uneasy or insecure. The strong team commitment and mutual support meant that those feelings did not arise.

The key criteria by which success of the initiative was measured were as follows:

- that standards of performance were maintained;
- that there was evidence of increased participation;
- that the students demonstrated increased knowledge of exercise and its benefits to health; and
- that this model of teaching contributed to the creation of independent learners.

In reviewing teaching and learning we looked at the benefits and shortcomings from the students' perspective and the benefits and shortcomings with reference to the National Curriculum requirements.

The unit: The structure of the unit was successful and the design was appealing. The idea of modelling the unit on a season worked. The students could identify with this and the lessons as a result had more purpose from the students' point of view.

Team format and selection: The students were more motivated within the lessons as a result of being affiliated to a team. Although most mentioned that they were happy with the selection process, some suggested that they would like to have known *how* and *why* they were selected in a particular way. In reviewing the unit several other methods of team selection were suggested and it was decided that these could be used successfully once students were familiar with Sport Education. For example:

- There could be a trial period at the beginning of the season – practice games could be used to assess students and changes then made if necessary to address equality of the teams.
- Team captains could be elected and given responsibility for selecting teams of equal ability either independently or together with the teacher. They would not captain the team that they selected. Instead the teams would be linked to a captain either at random or by the teacher. Thus, they would not be picking 'their team' but rather, collectively selecting teams of equal ability, in the knowledge that they might ultimately have the responsibility of captaining any one of the teams formed.

Role selection: Captains could be elected rather than selected by the teachers once it was felt that students were familiar with the expectations of the Sport Education model. With some roles the possibility of rotation within the season seemed appropriate and would give more students the opportunity of experiencing a role. The development of written role (job) descriptions would help students to understand the expectations of the role and would give them guidelines to work from. Specific tasks could be developed to link with specific roles to facilitate development of particular knowledge and understanding. For example, with equity in mind, the statistician could count the number of touches of the ball each player has and then use the data to suggest rule modifications that might enhance involvement of all players in the game. Extended cross-curricular work could be developed relating to the roles and thereby enhance involvement of other departments in Sport Education. The role of interviewer could be developed to engage students as researchers and thereby also give them an explicit involvement and responsibility in the ongoing development of Sport Education (see Chapters 2 and 16).

The progress achieved in Sport Education, particularly in terms of student responsibility, made it possible to consider the idea of introducing a Sports

Council, made up of a mixed group of students who had had some experience of the Sport Education programme. They would be responsible for different tasks including organising a festival of sport for the local feeder schools and overseeing the Sport Education unit, dealing with fair play issues and awards that may be given to teams or individuals. To organise the festival for the feeder schools, the Council would be required to meet in a lunchtime so commitment, enthusiasm and availability were qualities that students needed to show if they wanted to be considered for this additional role. The individuals would initially be selected by the teachers and then in the future students could apply and elections could be held.

Curriculum and pedagogy: Adopting a new approach to the teaching of games was a great motivator for the staff. With a support structure in place and a wealth of existing teaching experience within the faculty, individual teachers felt comfortable trying Sport Education. Staff had already identified with the core concepts and key components of Sport Education and had at various times tried out some of the components. The new units therefore presented the opportunity to formalise and extend practice. Everyone was pleased with the initial outcomes.

It was also notable that at this time (and in line with new National Curriculum requirements, see Chapters 1, 5 and 6) staff were being asked to incorporate issues from the wider curriculum into their teaching. By introducing Sport Education they were doing so, specifically literacy, numeracy, ICT and citizenship.

The portfolios that were introduced could also be used as an assessment tool (see Chapter 4). Potentially this could extend beyond physical education, to become an assessment task and tool formally linked to other subject requirements.

Professional profile: The provision of a Sport Education notice board gave students space to display their records and photos alongside the school team boards. This gave the Sport Education programme a high profile within the school. For some students this was an important opportunity to obtain recognition for their efforts in lesson time. Sport Education was also recognised as having started to fill a gap in school sport, that of the student as an official.

Conclusion

Having had a successful experience to start with, all the teachers involved were positive and enthusiastic about Sport Education as a model for teaching and learning. Yet they felt that it could be even better. They saw it as essential that the reviewing process be ongoing in order to ensure continued progress.

The physical education faculty at Mountbatten unanimously decided to continue development of Sport Education in key stage 3 by extending the netball and soccer units and by looking to introduce Sport Education in the context of other areas of the National Curriculum. Staff decided to take up the challenge of developing Sport Education gymnastics and athletics units. Gymnastics would be delivered in the spring term and athletics in the summer term. This would give students an experience of Sport Education across the whole year. Chapters 11 and 12 continue the story of this development. The appendices to this chapter include examples of Sport Education materials for games produced by teachers and students at Mountbatten.

Reference

Department for Education and Employment (DfEE)/Qualifications and Curriculum Authority (QCA) (1999). *Physical Education: The National Curriculum for England*, London: DfEE.

Appendix A: Extracts from student player profiles, The 'Nutty Netballers'

(Student names deleted)

- Not keen on netball although
) she is an excellent player -
Plays C - She is the fitness
coach.

- Shares the roll of fittness
coach - Brilliant shooter -
Plays GS - Enjoys playing

- team Captain - enjoys playing.
She feels she has improved -
Plays any position - Excellent playe

- Enjoys playing - plays Goal Atta
Has improved - Good shooter.

- team player - enjoys playing -
plays WD - she has improved
since playing in P.E..

- team player - substitute - likes
playing GD - Has improved. likes
playing some time.

- team player - plays GK - not keen
on playing - Has improved. Very
good player.

Vice captain - really likes playing -
Has improved - plays WA

8c

Year 8 Sports Education Netball

Team | GROOVY GREENS

Evaluation Sheet

Focus: **Team work**
                    Match play ✓
                    Practices

- Good passes up the court between all of the players.

- Defeanding is good and they all seem to be getting into good space.

- Very good teamwork going on, all seem to be focused.

- Need to think more when passing, don't rush passes.

- Footwork is good

Target:-

-Think & about when passing!
- Make sure they are marking at all times.

Recorder:-   Emily.

SPORT EDUCATION SOCCER - PLAYER ANALYSIS

Warriors Of Williams

Areas of Strength	PLAYER'S NAME	Areas to improve
Nice first touch and good through balls.		Shouldn't be afraid to have a go at goal.
Good at holding the ball up and passing.		Should come back and defend a little more.
Very good goalie doesn't mind diving and getting dirty		Come out a little more and tell the defence what to do
Good at getting stuck.		Should be more confident on the ball and take people on.
Very good tackler and really gets stuck in well.		Shouldn't be frightened to have a shot at goal.
Likes to take people on and always likes to have a go at goal		Not go up so much and get back and help the defence more
Good on the ball and running at defenders.		Use the wings more and get some crosses in.

INDIVIDUAL AND GROUP TARGET SETTING...

TARGET SHEET

Individual Players	Team
Week 1	Team work (defence - shooting)
Week 2	Dodging finding space work more as a team.
Week 3	getting into space and marking.
Week 4	Dodging and mark ing Working more as a team (cooperating)
Week 5	
Week 6	

PE forms

Appendix C: team logos (Sport Education soccer and basketball)

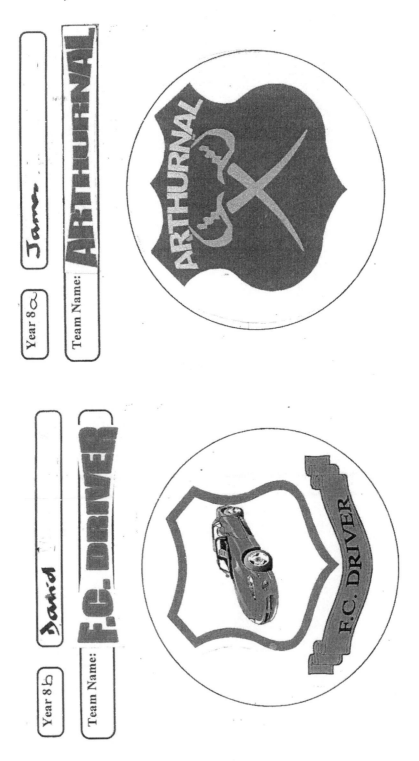

Dukes Flukes

Basketball

Transfer System

One week only, 'FREE' transfer system.

During a transfer 'window' (at the end of two cycles of league games), the league leaders must exchange their 'strongest' player with a designated player from the bottom team.

The 2nd and 3rd teams do the same.

This is a temporary transfer for one week only.

The transfer system is repeated over a 2 games league cycle – or, if directed by the class teacher.

11 Sport Education in gymnastics

Mandy Quill and Gill Clarke

Introduction

At Mountbatten School and Language College all students experience gymnastics at key stage 3. As explained in Chapter 10, a two week timetable operates at the school. In Years 7 and 8, the students have one lesson over a two week period in term one and two lessons over two weeks in term two. In Year 9, students have one lesson of gymnastics over two weeks during both terms.

In discussing the development of Sport Education in gymnastics it is important to acknowledge that there is a strong tradition of gymnastics at the school, particularly in sports acrobatics. Standards and expectations are high. Students are generally well motivated towards gymnastics.

For gymnastics in Years 7 and 8 students are taught in tutor groups of mixed ability and gender. Units of work cover a variety of gymnastic themes including travelling with changes of speed, over and under with twisting and turning, balance, sports acrobatics and flight. In Year 7 students initially work towards producing individual sequences of movement on floor and apparatus that fulfil the task set relating to the particular theme being studied. Towards the end of the second term they begin to work with a partner. At the start of Year 8 they work individually, in pairs and in trios or small groups. In Year 9 students are set into ability groups and in some cases single gender groups for physical education. All students still follow a gymnastics course but the content varies according to the ability of the group. Themes covered include group work, an introduction to rhythmic gymnastics, extended balance and flight work.

Students are assessed in their ability to acquire and develop a wide range of gymnastic skills and agilities that will enable them to create and perform a sequence of movements relating to the theme, sometimes individually and sometimes with others. As a guideline students are expected to be performing at between National Curriculum levels 4 and 5 at this stage (see DfEE/QCA, 1999).

As the games unit developed in the autumn term had been well received by students and the teaching staff (see Chapter 10), it was decided that part of the Year 8 gymnastics course could be adapted to incorporate Sport Education. In term one (the autumn term) Year 8 students had followed a basic introduction to balance work and had focused on developing the theme through pairs and trio balances based on simple sport acrobatics balances. This unit had been teacher led and students were taught the safety issues for supporting their own and others' weight, how to build the balance shapes and then how to creatively get into and out of the balances.

Developing the unit

For this Sport Education unit it was decided that each team would be required to perform a series of set agilities and create and perform a group sequence. The group sequence would incorporate set balances in addition to other balances selected by the group. The sequence would be performed at a festival of gymnastics to be held in the last week of term. The gymnasts themselves would be the audience and the teaching staff would judge the sequences. Every student would receive a certificate acknowledging their performance in the festival. Each group would also have to have a team name and produce a logo for their team to go on the front of their booklet.

Unit length and structure of the season: The unit of gymnastics would consist of ten lessons. This would give students time to practise the set agilities and balances as well as their own chosen balances. They were expected to link them together with agilities and other linking moves and thereby create and choreograph a sequence. The teacher would offer guidance, reinforce safety requirements and help students put their ideas together as a group. It was envisaged that students would have built up their movement vocabulary from the previous term's work on balance and would therefore be able to draw on this knowledge when creating a sequence. Each group would have an allocated matted area of equal size in the gym to work.

Team and role selections: Each tutor group (about 30 students) would be divided into four teams, with team composition negotiated by the teacher and students in order that teams were equal in numbers, boy/girl distribution and gymnastic ability. The teacher would select a leader in each team who would usually be one of the more able gymnasts. It was anticipated that the leader would often also take on the role of the team coach. Each team would elect a number of additional roles including a choreographer, a recorder to write down ideas in their gym booklet, warm-up coordinator(s) and equipment managers. Equipment managers would be responsible for setting out and packing away the mat area each lesson. The teacher would highlight the key responsibilities for each role so that expectations would be clear.

Assessment: Students would constantly be assessing their own and others' work by giving verbal feedback about the shape and the quality of the balances and agilities. They would have access to a camera to take photographs of their balances, which could be used for giving feedback. Before choosing their group shapes and balances, students would have to make an assessment of the group's collective gymnastic ability and then select appropriate balances to use. Teacher assessment would include looking at the quality of the students' performance in terms of the shape of the balance and ways of getting into and out of it. In addition assessment would address how individual students performed within the group and the extent of their movement vocabulary relating to the theme.

The Festival: It was envisaged that planning required for the festival would not be onerous. On the day of the festival the equipment managers would set out the equipment and the team leaders would draw up the order of performance. Certificates would be written beforehand so that they could be presented immediately after completion of performances. Each class would nominate four photographers for the event (one from each team) who would take photographs of the other groups from their class during their performances.

The event was formally placed on the school calendar so that all classes in the year group would be able to attend to observe and perform. The festival ran over a double lesson, lasting two hours. In order to further raise the profile of the event, each team leader would be asked to invite a VIP to the event. This could be a governor, any member from school senior management team, the head of year, their form tutor, etc.

From planning to practice

The idea of the gymnastics course being adapted for Sport Education worked reasonably well. The constraints of the two week timetable sometimes presented a problem as the length of time between the lessons made continuity in teaching and learning difficult but not impossible. At the start of the unit and following the allocation of roles, clear guidelines were provided highlighting what students had to do and by when. They were also notified of the date and time of the festival.

Teaching, learning and assessment: Generally students enjoyed the experience of working in a team and, once the basic structure of the lesson and expectations became familiar, good progress in learning was made. The teacher's role changed from command style to more of a facilitator. The teacher would move around between the groups helping with the balances and the task of putting together a sequence. Resource materials, including photographs and diagrams of balances, were made available for groups to access. Students were already familiar with some of the resources and these were used well by groups.

The beginning of lessons was noticeably more effective. Students were quickly focused and accepted the responsibility of setting up the equipment and warming up together as a group. Early on in the season it became evident that many classes needed structured direction from the teacher and a focus for each lesson in order to make progress. What tended to happen was that teams would keep practising the same parts of their sequences or the same balances and could easily waste time in the lesson going over the same material. The teacher needed to set clear guidelines within the lesson for the students to work to. For example, at the start of the lesson ten minutes might be given to practice balances already learnt; then the class would be stopped and set the next task of, for example, 20 minutes to practise two new balances, then the next ten minutes to find ways of linking the two new balances, and the remaining five minutes to work through from the beginning. This process helped students to remain on task. As the season progressed, in some classes the teacher still needed to give reasonably detailed guidelines or direction for the lesson, but in others students were able to make their own decisions about what the focus for their work was going to be. The teacher encouraged each team to say at the start of the lesson what they hoped to achieve by the end of the lesson, so that they could help them to remain on task. These were all noted on the whiteboard for reference if needed.

Teams had the opportunity to use music as it was felt that this would add to the performances. For ease of organisation the music chosen had to be the same for the whole class. The music coordinators from each team in the class therefore met and decided on the music to be used. Some groups chose to compose or compile an instrumental track just for gymnastics.

As in the games unit (see Chapter 10) one of the problems that arose immediately was absenteeism or students being present but unable to participate in practical work. Group work was disrupted as a result.

Students' assessment of their own and others' performance was generally good. The team coaches and choreographers were able to make accurate and relevant comments about performance and use these to improve the sequence. Other team members were also able to contribute to this and offered suggestions on how to improve the sequence. This involvement encouraged the use of communication skills and specifically the use of gymnastic terminology, helping to develop a greater depth of understanding amongst all. The teacher wrote gymnastic vocabulary on the whiteboard as guidance. This included words such as 'quality', 'timing', 'extension', 'poise', 'moment of stillness', 'spring', 'turn', 'spin', 'jump'.

Teachers again kept notes relating to the unit development and issues arising and these were discussed at faculty meetings as the unit progressed. Success and the shortcomings could thus be monitored, reviewed and addressed.

Team/group selection and identity: The initial team selection worked well, with students responding positively to the process of negotiated selection with the teacher. With even teams in the class, the able and the lower skilled were evenly distributed and this seemed fair to all parties. However, as the season progressed the arrangements started to prove problematic. Basically the teams were too big. Eight students trying to work out a sequence under the guidance of a choreographer was too difficult, the task took too long and sometimes teams achieved very little. The organisation of this number of performers presented particular problems, including some students being inactive for long periods of time within the lesson and also not staying on task. The adjustments to team composition that were made in the light of these experiences are discussed below.

Each team was issued with an A5 team booklet. On the front page this had a list of the different roles required and a space for the team name. Inside there was a list of the required elements (i.e. the set agilities and set balances) and space for writing selected balances down. On the back page there was a space for each team to design their team logo, which was credited with 20 points towards their overall score (see Appendix A).

Roles and responsibilities: The additional roles were democratically decided in each team and sometimes the roles were shared between two or three students. As most members of the team had some kind of responsibility this helped the cohesion of the group and the sense of affiliation increased. Difficulties arose when there was conflict or disagreement between group members. Moving students to another group was no longer an option, as affiliation was for the season. The importance of the initial team selection and the process of negotiation with students was therefore highlighted.

The most difficult role was the choreographer. Choreographers had to motivate the group, make suggestions for the sequence, put the ideas into practice and focus on their own performance. With groups of up to eight students this was a hard task. If students were uncooperative and did not stay on task, then progress was limited.

Points system: As an additional motivator a points system was introduced which worked particularly well. Awarding team points for full attendance encouraged individuals not to miss the lessons. Points for the logo and the team approach to different duties were also awarded and this helped to reinforce the principle goals of Sport Education (creating independent and informed learners, increasing participation especially amongst the lower skilled and raising standards of performance).

The festival: At the end of the unit, the festival was held as an official and formal event. Most students rose to the occasion and the standard of their performance definitely improved under these conditions. For some students, however, and particularly the lower skilled, performing in front of their own peer group was difficult and not always appropriate. Upon reflection staff recognised that they had put students on a public platform in what was a potentially uncomfortable or threatening situation for them. They acknowledged that the arrangements needed careful consideration for the future and, as discussed below, modifications were made.

Nevertheless it is important to emphasise that the festival at the end of term gave students a clear goal to aim for. There was added purpose to the task of creating a sequence. Also, with the knowledge that each class would have to perform their sequences in front of their year group, students were inspired to help each team in their class to ensure that they were as successful as possible. There was also an explicit incentive for collaboration and support.

The overall winners would be the class with the most points collectively. Therefore motivation was good and participation levels within lessons also increased.

Reflecting on the unit

As the gymnastics unit followed on from the games unit, the teaching staff and students were already familiar with the framework and process of Sport Education. Teaching gymnastics using Sport Education was therefore more straightforward than would otherwise have been the case.

The structure of the unit had been discussed prior to the start with colleagues, and team booklets designed and printed. Nevertheless it was decided to discuss the unit at regular faculty meetings, so as to continue to support each other, share ideas and address any problems arising. This process worked well.

As with the games unit, the key criteria by which success of the initiatives was measured were as follows:

- that standards of performance were maintained;
- that there was evidence of increased participation;
- that the students demonstrated increased knowledge of exercise and its benefits to health;
- that this model for teaching contributed to the creation of independent learners.

In reviewing teaching and learning, staff again looked at the unit in relation to the students and the National Curriculum requirements.

Team composition: In the light of the difficulties discussed above regarding team size and also concerns about the performance context of the festival, it was felt that three teams should be selected within each class:

- a mixed gender team of the most able gymnasts, who would be the performance team to represent the class at the festival;
- a boys' development team and a girls' development team. These two teams would still have the task of creating a sequence but they would not perform it at the festival. Their sequence would be judged in lesson time prior to the festival and the points that they were awarded would carry forward to the festival and be added to the performance team score, so as to give an overall class total. The performances of the development teams would therefore still be valued and would contribute to the final points score for the class, but these students would not be required to perform in a public arena.

The reason for deciding upon single gender development teams was that it was felt that the lower skilled students worked better in this way, at this age.

There can be a significant physical difference between boys and girls at this age which will affect performance. In addition, in previous units the team leaders, who were the able gymnasts, had tended to be girls and sometimes the boys did not respect or respond to the leadership of the girls.

The selection process for these modified teams could take the form of 'a trial' in the first lesson using set gymnastic tasks. This would provide a clear reference point for both teachers and students in deciding who should be in each team.

Team tasks and roles: The tasks set were also reviewed and it was decided that the agilities set should be differentiated for the development teams. The able gymnasts were to be given the opportunity to add two more agilities to the standard agilities in order that they could demonstrate their full potential and be further challenged.

Adjustments were also seen as desirable in relation to the way that teams would be required to fulfil the tasks. Instead of eight students trying to create one sequence, each team would be divided into trios or pairs. The mixed performance team would always have nine members, to ensure consistency for the festival (with three trios performing). This grouping arrangement was more manageable and effective for choreographing a sequence.

As mentioned above, the team leader had also often been the choreographer and/or the coach because they were the able gymnast in the team. With the reorganisation of teams this issue could be addressed. There was now the scope for an overall team leader and a choreographer within each trio or pair.

Extending roles: The introduction of digital cameras would give students instant feedback, and teams would be encouraged to record evidence of their progression in learning. A video camera could also be set up for teams or the teacher to video performances, with the recording used in team review and feedback sessions. The media representative would be responsible for printing photographs and these would be displayed on the Sport Education notice board throughout the season. There would also be a festival display at the end of term.

Assessment: Teacher assessment of individual progress had been quite difficult with students working in large, even ability teams. With the division into trios and pairs and the move to three teams based on gymnastic ability, assessment would be easier. This way of organising the Sport Education gymnastics at Mountbatten has now been running successfully for three years.

The festival: As explained above, the idea of everyone performing at the festival was not appropriate for all students. The festival was still calendared so that all the classes in the year group could attend, but the development teams would make up the audience. By watching the performance teams, their appreciation of good performance would be extended.

The organisation of the festival was reviewed annually and it was decided that the teachers would sit with their development teams, and the festival would be judged by Year 11 gymnasts who were also sports prefects at the school (see Chapter 10). This has become better and better each year as students at key stage 4 have now experienced Sport Education through key stage 3. The quality of judging has improved, highlighting that Sport Education can be effective in raising standards not only of performance, but also in relation to the ability to make informed judgements about performance.

The idea of the festival is undoubtedly a good way to share and celebrate work in Sport Education. As well as providing the opportunity for students to perform in a competition, it was a good way for teachers to see work across the year group and address issues of moderation across classes.

Conclusion

The faculty could see rich potential for the use of Sport Education in gymnastics. They recognised that careful organisation was needed in order not to set students up for failure or embarrassment in front of peers. As in the case of games, the staff have remained committed to advancing the initiative. Sport Education has been successfully adopted as a model for delivering part of the gymnastics curriculum at key stage 3 and is seen to be making a valuable contribution to the creation of independent learners, whilst maintaining high standards of performance and increasing participation. The appendices to this chapter provide examples of teaching resources developed and student work produced in Sport Education.

Reference

Department for Education and Employment (DfEE)/Qualifications and Curriculum Authority (QCA) (1999). *Physical Education: The National Curriculum for England*, London: DfEE.

Appendix A: Team logo for Sport Education gymnastics

TEAM LOGO

20 MARKS

Appendix B: Sport Education gymnastics team booklet

YEAR 8 GYMNASTICS

TEAM NAME: ....

Choreographer 1: ....

Choreographer 2: ....

Warm Up Co-ordinators: ....
....

Media Relations Director: ....

Recorder: ....

BOYS/GIRLS GROUP COMPULSORY ROUTINE

To be performed individually by every member of the group.

	Marks
Dish Roll	5
Straight jump	5
½ Turn jump	5
Shoulder Balance	5
	20 marks

FLOOR ROUTINES TO BE PERFORMED IN TRIOS TO INCLUDE:

- Log balance.
- Stand on thighs low
- 2 of your own balances
- Each person in the trio must perform 2 of the compulsory agilities together, or in cannon.

NAMES		
TRIO 1	TRIO 2	TRIO 3
10 MARKS	10 MARKS	10 MARKS

DIAGRAMS

1.

2 BASES
1 TOP

2.

2 BASES
1 TOP

TEAM LOGO

20 MARKS

Appendix C: Certificate for Sport Education gymnastics competition

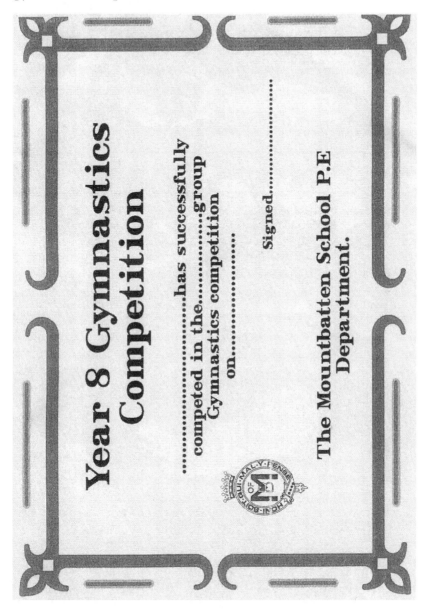

Year 8 Gymnastics Competition

.............has successfully competed in the............group Gymnastics competition on............

Signed............

The Mountbatten School P.E Department.

12 Sport Education in athletics

Mandy Quill and Gill Clarke

Introduction

At Mountbatten School and Language College all students experience athletic activities throughout key stage 3. At key stage 3 Year 7 and 8 students have two lessons of athletic activities during a two week period (a total of two hours). Year 9 have one lesson of athletic activities during a two week period. In Year 7 students receive an introduction to the principles of running, jumping and throwing and are taught the basic skills required in order to perform successfully in athletic activities. Initially the command teaching style is used. Reciprocal teaching is used as students develop their basic knowledge. Year 8 is their first opportunity to experience specific athletic events, learn specific techniques and use these techniques in the context of competition. As explained in Chapter 10, in Year 9 students are taught in ability groups of various sizes, with some of these being mixed gender and some single gender groups. A common programme of athletic activities is followed across the ability groups but the types of challenges are differentiated according to ability.

The National Curriculum for Physical Education (NCPE) states that for athletic activities at key stage 3 students should be taught to:

a) Set and meet personal and group targets in a range of athletic events, challenges and competitions.
b) Use a range of running, jumping and throwing techniques, singly and in combination, with precision, speed, power or stamina.

(DfEE/QCA, 1999: 22)

Sport Education athletics would particularly focus on point a.

As in the units of work introduced in games and gymnastics, Sport Education was seen as connecting with the four aspects of skills, knowledge and understanding within the NCPE:

- *Acquiring and developing*: the students would be taught specific techniques for different events and would be able to draw on their knowledge of the principles of athletics from the Year 7 course.

- *Selecting and applying:* the students would be set different challenges and competitions where they would have to select and combine relevant athletic techniques in order to produce an effective performance both individually and as part of a team. They would also have to demonstrate their knowledge of the rules of the event.
- *Evaluating and improving performance:* this area would be particularly useful in athletics for developing students' ability to analyse performance and to make critical judgements about themselves and others in order to improve the quality of performance. They would be taught how to identify key points to improve performance and what qualities together made a good run, jump or throw.
- *Knowledge and understanding of fitness and health:* the students would develop their knowledge of how to prepare for and recover from specific events. They would also develop a training programme as in the games unit designed to increase their level of fitness in preparation for the sports day at the end of the unit.

The Sport Education model lends itself to giving students the opportunity to assess and evaluate their own and others' performance in a variety of athletic activities. Developments made in this regard are discussed below. Opportunities are also presented for the teacher to make considered judgements about individuals in their performance, as evidenced in students' ability to select and apply effective techniques in specific athletic events and also their knowledge of the rules for different events. Judgements made in the Sport Education context contribute to overall assessment and the selection of the level for physical education that a student receives at the end of the key stage.

Developing the unit

Continuing with the theme of Sport Education in the summer term completed the year and meant that the students had experienced Sport Education in each term in a different activity. This enabled continuity with this model for teaching and added to the authenticity of the experiences of physical education at Mountbatten School. The students were now more familiar with the process and related roles and routines that worked well and could successfully transfer these. Thus setting up equipment and warming up for the lesson were routines that were now well established and accepted by the students as standard expectations for physical education lessons.

The unit structure and organisation: Athletics was developed and structured in a similar way to the Sport Education gymnastics (see Chapter 11). Again teaching was in tutor groups which were classes of mixed ability and mixed gender. Each class was divided into three teams, an Olympic team which consisted of ten pupils, five boys and five girls who were the most athletically able, and two Commonwealth teams one of which was a boys' Commonwealth team and the other a girls' Commonwealth team.

With the format of two lessons in the two week period, it was decided that one would be taught in a largely traditional way, with teacher-led instruction in the specific techniques of athletics. The students would be taught together as a class for this lesson. The second lesson would then be the Sport Education lesson, where different athletic challenges would be set and the three teams in the class would compete against the equivalent teams in other classes who were timetabled for physical education at the same time. (A third of the year group had physical education timetabled together.) The Olympic teams would compete against each other and the two Commonwealth teams would compete against each other. Points from all competitions would be added together to give a class total.

The athletic challenges set within Sport Education would all be based on running, jumping and throwing events and in each lesson the teams would take part in a different challenge. It was decided that there would be a series of different challenges (see Appendix A) and then the sports day festival at the end of the term. Points would be awarded to individuals for good times, for good performances and for winning the events. These scores would be recorded in an athletics booklet given to each team. As with the other Sport Education units (see Chapters 10 and 11) value added points were awarded to teams for things such as full attendance and accurate record keeping.

Team and role selection: The three teams in each class were selected by the teacher using previous knowledge of students' ability. Several different officiating roles were identified for students to take on in the unit: recorder, timekeeper, responsibility for measuring, judging or starting. Teams would also have a designated warm-up coordinator, a team coach, an officials delegate, team photographer, media representative and a team manager. Although the challenges were set by teachers, team selections would be required for specific events and this would be the responsibility of the team manager.

These various roles would be democratically decided within each team at the start of the season. Sometimes teachers would make suggestions to teams about individuals that they felt would be particularly 'suitable' for specific roles. At some point during the term every member of the team would be an official. This involved students being responsible for either timing, measuring, judging or recording performances (times, distances, heights) in the various events. The organisation of the officials was the responsibility of the officials delegate in the team. This student would also keep a record of the officiating roles that team members had undertaken.

Teams would also take turns for being responsible for the equipment each lesson and thus be designated the 'duty team' for that lesson. They would report to the teacher at the start of the lesson to find out what equipment was needed and would be responsible for putting it away at the end of the lesson. Equipment would include specific athletic equipment plus stopwatches, score sheets, clipboards and so on.

To avoid problems of absentees affecting the competitions (as had occurred in other activities, see Chapters 10 and 11), everyone present would compete but only the top five scores would count towards the team total. In challenges such as the continuous relay around the copse, or sprint relay, this arrangement would not apply and teams would need all their members present in order to get the best result.

A master score sheet would be displayed on the Sport Education notice board together with weekly photos of teams in action. Every two weeks, when a round of lessons was complete, a leading class (with the most points) would be identified. This position would be recognised by their team photo appearing in the leader frame on the notice board.

The festival: At the end of the season the athletics festival would be held and organised in a similar way to a sports day. As with the gymnastics festival (see Chapter 11) this would be entered in the school calendar to enable all students in the year group to take part as performers or officials. Students would take on the responsibility of organising the festival, providing officials, recorders and scorers for the events. These roles could be filled by the same students who had done the job throughout the term for their team, or other students could take on the roles with support and guidance from peers.

Across the year group there would be three competitions: the Olympic, the Commonwealth boys and the Commonwealth girls. The festival would be an inter-tutor group event, with each tutor group having a team in each of the three competitions. Planning the festival could take considerable time. Tutor group representatives would therefore meet at a break or lunchtime with a senior sports prefect and/or a member of staff to plan the festival over several weeks.

Assessment: The unit would provide many opportunities for students to evaluate their own and others' performance. Simple set tasks would be assigned, to identify another student's strengths and weaknesses in an athletic event and suggest ways in which they might improve their performance.

Experiencing the unit

The unit and season structure: As with both the games and the gymnastics units the Sport Education athletics worked well. Students responded well to the format of one lesson being set aside for technique and one for competition. They were also more motivated to compete than had been the case in previous athletics units. The lower skilled students in particular liked the idea of being in teams. In the ability group context they did not feel as vulnerable or exposed when performing as had been the case in mixed ability and non-team contexts. Problems only arose during the season when poor weather prevented the planned competition from taking place. In order not to lose continuity, equivalent indoor competitions were devised and points were transferable so that the impetus of the season was maintained. For example, a track relay event using reverser boards in the sports hall replaced the relay challenge, and throws and jumps could be adapted to indoors.

Teams, roles and responsibilities: The division of each class into ability teams was a positive move as far as increasing participation in athletics was concerned, particularly for the lower skilled girls (i.e. those in the Commonwealth teams). This became apparent as the season progressed. They enjoyed competing against students of the same ability and worked well together, encouraging each other. They were also better at 'having a go' at the different events without the fear of failing in front of the more able athletes or boys. The grouping arrangements established clearly helped to increase the girls' self-confidence and also gave some students the opportunity to try roles that in a mixed ability situation would invariably have been taken by a more able peer.

Once the teams had been established and the teacher had explained what the different roles entailed, roles were distributed amongst the team members by a process of election. The additional roles that the team was expected to take on encouraged the team to work together. By involving students in the officiating and coaching, their depth of knowledge of performance and the events was also enhanced.

Giving students the opportunity to officiate within the lesson in a formal capacity increased their knowledge of athletics and again contributed to the development of independent learners. The requirement for all team members to take an officiating role at some stage ensured that the same children did not volunteer for everything, and gave everyone a chance to be actively involved in this capacity. The already confident and capable team members readily took on additional roles of coach and warm-up coordinator.

At the start of the lesson, usually in the changing rooms, the teacher would tell the teams which of the five challenges they were going to do. Students could then go out and warm up appropriately in the designated area of the field. They responded well to this, knowing what they were doing and being able to prepare accordingly.

With the scoring system of the top five scores counting for team points, there was still 'pressure' on individuals to attend the lessons, particularly if they had a particular strength in an event.

Each team was issued with a record booklet which contained an explanation of each of the challenges and score sheets, plus a page for evaluations where each team member could identify areas for improvement. Having participated in Sport Education games and gymnastics the students were now familiar with the booklets used to record results. Continuing with this idea in athletics was considered favourable and booklets were colour coded to distinguish the Olympic and Commonwealth teams.

On a number of occasions homework was set and teams were asked to produce, for example, a logo for their team, or to find out the colours of the Olympic flag, or to find out where the Olympic or Commonwealth Games had been held in a particular year. This extension work reinforced their background knowledge of the subject.

The 'leader board' was successful and generated an ongoing interest in the competition across each two week period. Students were able to compare their results to other classes in different blocks and this again was a motivator, encouraging them to do their very best in each event. There was a real competitive link across the year group. This in turn made the festival both more authentic and more exciting. By then each class had some background knowledge of how the other classes had performed throughout the season and the number of points each class had been awarded for each challenge. This information could be used in team selection decisions for the festival. It reinforced the process of giving students responsibility for making informed decisions about their own learning.

The competitions and festival: As mentioned above, the structure of the competition was successful in involving as many students as possible in competing in an athletics event within a team. Students gained valuable experience in officiating and learnt how to time keep, score record and measure, all with increasing accuracy as the season progressed. This was good preparation for the festival.

For the festival organisation, the class teacher helped each team to select a representative to meet with the senior sports prefects. As an incentive to take on this role students would be allowed to use the IT suite, and a record would be kept which could support their future sport prefect application (see Chapter 10).

Students were familiar with a sports day. The difference in the Sport Education festival was that they now had an input beyond being competitors. They were involved together with the senior sports prefects in officiating each of the events. The collaboration amongst students on the day of the festival was very encouraging to see. Year 8 students worked well with the sports prefects from Year 11.

The events for the festival were based on a combination of the challenges set during the term time competition and more traditional sports day athletic events. The idea was to make it as authentic as possible and thus as like an athletic meet as it could be, taking into account the safety issues with students involved in officiating and judging.

In the Festival Day events, students raised the level of their performance for the occasion and as with the gymnastics festival (see Chapter 11) other members of teaching staff and VIPs were invited to attend. This raised the profile of the event. Certificates were awarded to the winners of each event and the overall winning team. School records achieved or broken in any events in the festival were acknowledged and certificated accordingly. Other certificates and awards were distributed by the head of year in a celebration assembly. This was organised by the senior sports prefects together with the team managers.

Assessment: Worksheets were developed for students to use in reciprocal teaching situations to help them to identify coaching points. 'Tick sheets' were a good format for these. For example:

1   Did the athlete keep their head still when sprinting?
2   Did the athlete use their arms effectively?
3   Did the athlete lift knees high?

Students were also able to use a digital camera to record performance and sometimes a video camera. The video camera was much better for this because students found it difficult to successfully capture athletic performance on digital camera. In contrast the video was excellent for providing instant feedback on performance. Records of times and distances achieved were also used for feedback and review purposes. Using records and coaching points, students were able to establish a plan to improve their own performance.

Reflecting on the unit

For the athletics programme the Sport Education model was ideal and the framework was a sound one for addressing the National Curriculum requirements. Overall participation increased, and standards of performance increased particularly amongst the lower skilled, while the more able students were also clearly challenged. Their standard of performance also rose significantly during the season. The experience of the Sport Education athletics thus reinforced the feeling of confidence in the new model and approach as something that would appropriately continue to feature in physical education at Mountbatten. The appendices to this chapter provide examples of teaching resources developed and student work produced in Sport Education.

Conclusion

With all of the Sport Education units staff were able to give students the opportunity to set themselves, and meet personal and group targets in a range of events, challenges and competitions. Why Sport Education?

- It helped to raise standards of performance by motivating students.
- It increased participation levels in lessons and extra-curricular activities.
- It gave students an authentic sporting experience within the boundaries of the National Curriculum.
- It gave students the opportunity to be involved in leadership.
- It continued to educate students about the responsibility that they have to themselves to lead an active and healthy lifestyle.

With the introduction to Sport Education and the development of it through key stage 3 students were better prepared for the challenges of key stage 4. Sport Education became the training ground for accredited courses such as the Junior Sports Leader Award and GCSE PE (see Chapter 7). Students were able to make far better informed decisions within these courses, creating a situation in which staff recognised the emergence of more confident leaders and more knowledge candidates for GCSE. In GCSE students were more qualified to address 'skill D' (to provide evidence of their ability to analyse and improve their own and others' performance)' having had practical experience of this prior to the GCSE course.

As explained in Chapter 10, at key stage 4 at Mountbatten there is a sports prefect system in place. The sports prefects are held in the highest esteem and these are sought after positions of responsibility at the school. The sports prefects organise and run the inter-house sports programme for each year group which takes place during the lunch hour throughout the year. They are also involved in supporting the teaching staff at clubs by coaching, umpiring, managing and officiating. From early in key stage 3 students see the advantage of taking responsibility within a lesson and are keen to contribute to their team in a positive way in order that they can build up evidence to support their prefect application at key stage 4. The progressive experience of Sport Education through key stage 3 serves to highlight individuals who can take on responsibility and gives them the opportunity to practise the role before they take up the post at key stage 4.

With the introduction of Sport Education and its links with the sport prefect system it has also been possible to select a group of students to form a Sports Council at the school. One of the main responsibilities of the Council has been to set up, organise and run an athletics event for the feeder primary schools. Without the background of Sport Education the qualities that these young people now display may not have been as easy to identify.

Sport Education has many positive aspects that can contribute to lifelong learning. The benefits to the teaching of physical education out-weigh any disadvantages or difficulties that may be experienced. With an enthusiastic approach and careful planning it is a model for teaching that all of the physical education faculty at The Mountbatten School and Language College would recommend without hesitation.

Reference

Department for Education and Employment (DfEE)/Qualifications and Curriculum Authority (QCA) (1999). *Physical Education: The National Curriculum for England*, London: DfEE.

Appendix A: Sport Education athletics challenges

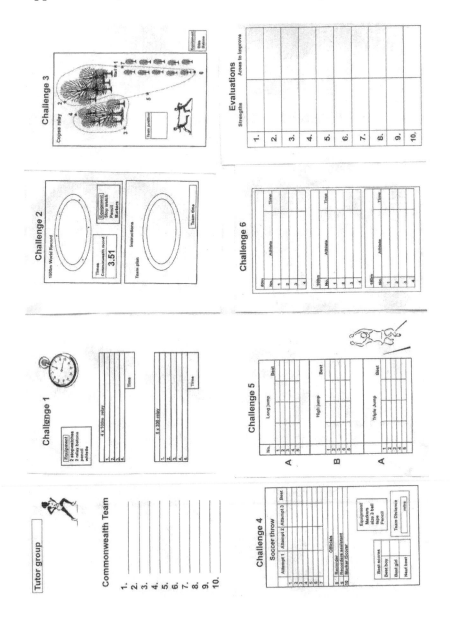

SPORT EDUCATION - ATHLETICS

DESIGN A LOGO TO REPRESENT SPORT EDUCATION : ATHLETICS

SPORT EDUCATION
ATHLETICS

(1) Name the **cities** that staged the Olympic Games in the following years:

2000: Sydney

1996: Atlanta

1992: Barcelona

1988: Seoul, Korea

1984: Los Angeles

1980: Moscow

(2) Draw and colour the Olympic Rings

13 Sport Education in key stage 4 swimming

Emily Scrivener and Dawn Penney

Introduction

This chapter discusses the development of Sport Education within an activity context that to our knowledge has rarely been a focus for Sport Education and that only sometimes features within the key stage 3 and 4 physical education curriculum in schools in England and Wales. Yet, swimming remains one of the most popular adult recreational activities for both men and women in England and one of few activities that can legitimately claim lifelong appeal. It is an activity that variously fulfils people's interest in participating in physical activity for health benefits, as a social activity and/or to compete in sport at club, national or international levels. Further, swimming is now a core programme within the delivery plan for the government's Physical Education School Sport and Club Links (PESSCL) strategy launched in October 2002 (DfES/DCMS, 2003). It has been emphasised that 'All children should be able to have the chance to swim safely and enjoy the sport. Learning to swim can be great fun, has health benefits and can save lives' (DfES/DCMS, 2003: 13).

To talk of 'swimming' in general terms is somewhat misleading. It encompasses a tremendous variety of activities, including synchronised swimming, life-saving, water-polo and diving, in addition to competition on an individual or team basis in events using freestyle, backstroke, breaststroke and/or butterfly stroke. In our view this variety signals rich potential for the development of Sport Education. The possibilities in relation to the form that festivals might take, the roles and responsibilities that students may take on, and the diverse skills, knowledge and understanding that they will thereby develop are all immense. A Sport Education swimming season could concentrate upon one of the forms identified above and therefore lead towards, for example, a water-polo tournament. Alternatively it could include a variety of swimming activities within a 'split season'. Roles and responsibilities might be linked to:

- coaching of particular strokes, of other technical aspects such as turns, starts or specialist movements within water-polo, synchronised swimming, diving or life-saving;

- researching tactical strategies for defence or attack in water-polo;
- developing strength, flexibility or endurance training programmes;
- mastery of one of the many officiating roles in swimming (including starter, touch judge, finish judge, timekeeper);
- choreography for synchronised swimming;
- match analysis in water-polo;
- pool safety checks.

As in other activity contexts, there is also the scope for publicity officers and equipment monitors.

A pool or open water environment also reinforces notions of both individual and collective responsibility. As in the outdoor and adventurous activity setting (see Chapter 14), understanding of and adherence to safety considerations is of paramount importance. Cooperation and responsibility thus take on particular significance.

Swimming is also a sport that is well suited to the phased pattern of a Sport Education season and prompts exploration of important social and cultural issues relating to participation and performance in sport. It is interesting to note for example that, while students in schools in England may struggle to find many examples of newspaper coverage of events or performances, a visit to an Australian newspaper website will readily provide these, and serve to highlight the very different status of swimming in the two countries.

Brookfield High School and Sports College

The Sport Education development that we now turn to took place at Brookfield High School in north Liverpool. Brookfield is an 11–16 comprehensive school for girls and boys. There are some 800 students at the school, which is located in an area of profound and extensive social and economic deprivation. Approximately 50 per cent of students (well above the national average) are eligible for free school meals, and the attainment of students on entry to the school is also recognised as 'well below the national average' (OFSTED, 2002: 5). In 1998 Brookfield established itself as a Specialist Sports College within the government's Specialist Schools initiative,[1] thereby signalling a particular commitment to physical education and sport as a focus in raising standards in teaching and learning throughout the school and across the curriculum. As a result of government initiatives targeted towards social deprivation (including the Excellence in Cities programme[2]), the school acquired funding to improve facilities and develop a 'state of the art' basketball hall. Encouragingly, in 2002 OFSTED reported that students were achieving well in relation to their prior attainment and that both teaching and attitudes to learning were good (OFSTED, 2002).

Physical education at Brookfield

The physical education department at Brookfield is highly respected locally, and has an influential role within the community. It has experienced great success in attempts to improve the sporting achievement of all young people in the area. As a team the department are committed to working together to enable all students, whatever their ability, to achieve their full potential in a caring, purposeful and supportive learning environment and to equip them with the knowledge, skills, understanding and values for successful adult life. They aim to help students to develop positive self-esteem through improving physical confidence, individual success, however modest, and leadership.

At the time of the research study reported here and conducted by one of the authors (Emily), the physical education department comprised a Head of Department/Director of Sport, six physical education teachers with various department responsibilities and a range of sporting specialisms, one technician, one Youth Sports Dance Coordinator on a part-time timetable and a number of outside coaches responsible for the provision of extra-curricular activities. The oldest teacher in the team had been working at the school for 20 years. Two of the staff were newly qualified teachers (NQTs) and others had between six and one year's experience at the school. Two physical education trainees from Liverpool John Moores University were also present in the department for half of the academic year.

At key stage 4 (incorporating National Curriculum Years 10 and 11, for students aged 14–16 years) at Brookfield all students follow a General Certificate of Secondary Education (GCSE) Physical Education examination course. GCSE Expressive Arts is offered as an additional option, and the Junior Sports Leader and Community Sports Leader Award courses (JSLA and CSLA, see Chapter 7) are offered to all students as part of recommended out of hours study. Part of the department ethos is an expectation that all teachers will use a range of teaching styles and in so doing encourage the development of leadership throughout all key stages. Thus, in addition to leadership being formally addressed through JSLA and CSLA courses, it is embedded in, for example, reciprocal teaching in gymnastics (spotting each other) and the development of students' evaluation and feedback skills in dance and swimming.

In Year 10 all students have five practical options which are then repeated in Year 11 (i.e. in Year 11 students revisit their five Year 10 options). The range of practical activities offered during the year is extensive and may be expanded in response to specific student interests and depending upon the costs associated with provision and availability of teacher/coach expertise. Five activities are offered per term, with each activity lasting for six weeks and specific terms being devoted to a particular type of activity. The spring term of 2002 was based around performing/aesthetic emphasis activities and included swimming, various gymnastics activities (Olympic/rhythmic/educational) and dance.

The teaching groups for key stage 4 at Brookfield are decided upon by student choice for a particular activity and teachers are assigned to activities on the basis of their personal sporting specialism. Groups are therefore typically mixed gender and mixed ability. However, in the case of swimming, girls expressed their wish to have a girls only group. Their wishes were accommodated and separate girls' and boys' swimming groups were formed. The department retained a concern to actively encourage girls' participation in physical education and sport, having previously been involved in national initiatives focusing upon increasing the interest and involvement of girls in sport. The Sport Education research project that is reported here, however, specifically involved the Year 10 *boys'* swimming group.

Sport Education: a new development for Brookfield

This was the first time that Sport Education had been developed in physical education at Brookfield. The interest in the model came from outside of the department and the development was a formal research project undertaken by Emily Scrivener. At the time Emily was a training teacher in her final year of a BA (Hons) Secondary Physical Education, Sport and Dance (with Qualified Teacher Status (QTS)) degree course at Liverpool John Moores University. Emily was interested in trying Sport Education as a new approach to teaching as part of her final dissertation study. She was placed at Brookfield for her final teaching practice and approached the Head of Physical Education about the possibility of undertaking a study focusing on Sport Education during her practice.

Discussions between Emily and the Head of Physical Education established the context in which Sport Education would be developed, and shaped the investigative focus of the dissertation study. The development was negotiated and sought to fulfil the department's priorities for student learning in addition to Emily's dissertation requirements. It was decided that the project should focus upon key stage 4 GCSE Physical Education, with the anticipation that by this stage students would be more likely to have acquired the background skills, knowledge and understanding necessary to successfully engage in a Sport Education season. The season would contribute one activity of the five that the students would follow for their GCSE Physical Education course and it would therefore have to fulfil the requirements of the examination course. Within the GCSE course 60 per cent of marks were allocated to practical work and 40 per cent to theoretical work, with the latter assessed via formal examination.

The Head of Physical Education and Emily decided on *swimming* as the Sport Education activity in order to fit in with the physical education timetable and because this was an activity in which Emily had an extensive knowledge base. It was agreed that Emily would teach one of the Year 10 boys' swimming groups. Another teacher would teach the other boys' group, using the established curriculum and teaching framework, rather than adopting Sport Education. Through developing Sport Education in the context of swimming and with the presence of what could loosely be considered a 'control' group, Emily hoped to investigate the following teaching and learning issues:

● Could students' knowledge and understanding be further enhanced by the use of the Sport Education approach to teaching?
● Reflecting the department's established aims, could this change of teaching climate and style benefit the students in becoming more able to cope in leader/coach positions?

The hope and expectation was that knowledge and understanding would be improved by teaching using the Sport Education structure, ethos and approach and that the students involved would enjoy the new atmosphere of teaching and learning. The performance of the Sport Education group and the non-Sport Education group in a cognitive test addressing officials and their responsibilities, rules of swimming, starting techniques, tactics of swimming, teaching points to correct errors in technique, and how to help others, would be compared. Test results would provide an indication of the advancement in knowledge and understanding achieved by the respective groups at the end of their swimming unit.

Planning the unit

Unit length, structure and content

Initially it was envisaged that the season would run for 12 weeks. However, owing to timetable restrictions within the school it was only possible to have a season lasting for six weeks, with one 2-hour lesson per week. This lesson length would enable a large amount of material to be covered in one lesson. It was also decided that extra sessions could be added at lunchtimes or after school if necessary, to accommodate, for example, the culminating festival. In total, three extra 30 minute sessions were included beyond timetabled curriculum time, to allow for video analysis and a swimming gala at the end of the season.

The timetabling arrangements at Brookfield and in particular the restriction to six weeks meant that the typically phased structure of the Sport Education season (see Chapter 1) was not considered appropriate. Instead, it was decided to devise sessions that would each include all of the various types of experience that would usually feature throughout a season. Thus, each lesson would include warm-up activities, skill practices, specific activities linked to coverage of the GCSE requirements, and experience of formal competition. In relation to the decision to design the unit and lessons within it in this way, it is important to note that swimming was not a new activity for the Year 10 boys. They had completed three six-week units of swimming during key stage 3 and had therefore covered the basic elements of all four swimming strokes. In order to now fulfil the GCSE PE swimming criteria within the Sport Education season, there was a need to:

- refine previously acquired skills;
- develop advanced skills;
- introduce competitive diving;
- undertake video analysis of stroke technique; and
- undertake detailed evaluation of others' performances.

The GCSE syllabus that was followed demanded that a number of general water and swimming skills be exhibited, including: water confidence; entry into water/exit from water in varying depth settings; floating; propelling; turns; proficiency in different strokes; differentiation in pace; conservation of energy, breath and heat. For assessment purposes students were required to complete a pre-planned routine demonstrating these skills and were marked against set criteria for swimming competence. Analysis of performance would also be assessed, using question and answer technique, and would account for 10 per cent of the students' overall grade.

In considering the format of the season and sessions within it, it was felt that motivation to attend and to actively participate would be enhanced with weekly competitions. Students would be encouraged to think of the series of lessons as a season that was building towards a finale (the completion of the league and holding of a culminating event). The competition part of each lesson involved races in which students would race in pairs. The pairings and also the set strokes would vary each week, based on coach or captain choice. Races would be conducted in accordance with competitive swimming rules that the students would be expected to become conversant with. Competing pairs did not have to match strokes, adding to the tactical element of the competition. As the season progressed it was also planned that students would take on roles of officials for the races, having learnt the relevant responsibilities for the roles. This learning would also prepare them for their participation in the culminating gala event.

The culminating event

The Head of Department was very keen on the notion of celebrating achievements within the season and was willing to help organise the culminating gala event at a local sports centre. However, owing to the time of year, it was not possible to book the pool facility at a suitable time. It was therefore decided that the gala would coincide with the school's annual sponsored swim. This scheduling would encourage spectators and mean that the students could also use their officiating knowledge and skills in supporting the running of the sponsored swim.

Team selections and role allocations

It was decided that warm-up activities for lessons would be taken by specific team members on a weekly rotation. The skill practices would be delivered by coaches, assistant coaches or captains. Following Siedentop's (1994) advice, the students played a key role in the team and role selection process. Discussions with the Head of Department established agreement upon the best way to proceed with this aspect of the unit organisation. It was agreed that the teacher-researcher (Emily) would discuss the team and role/ responsibility dimensions of Sport Education with the class and also briefly explain the roles to those students who were non-participants at the initial swimming session. It was anticipated that several students would forget their kit for their first swimming lesson of the year, and that therefore they could help with the selection process. This student input was also considered advantageous as Emily had no background knowledge of the class. When they have been in the same class for a number of years, students generally know their own and others' strengths and weaknesses. They are therefore well placed to consider their own and others' suitability for roles.

It was planned that Emily would explain more about the roles after selection, in order to ensure that appropriate decisions had been made and to enable changes to be made if necessary. Emily advised the non-participants that teams evenly matched in ability would be preferable to uneven teams, but to also consider established friendships. She wanted all students to have at least one known friend in their team. Both the non-participants and Emily used descriptions of the roles as a point of reference in their selections of team coach, captain, publicist and statistician. Emily also asked the non-participating students specific questions about ICT skills when she was discussing prospective publicists and statisticians. It was decided that each student would take on one role for the whole unit. The teams did not discuss rotating roles at any point within the unit and Emily decided not to allow switching of roles unless absolutely necessary in order to avoid undue disruption within the short season. During the season the following additional roles would be integrated into the formal competitions: referee, starter, clerk of course, chief inspector of turns, inspectors of turns, judges of strokes, chief timekeeper, timekeepers, chief finish judge, finish judges and desk control officer.

Developing responsibility for learning

A significant feature of this Sport Education unit and the preparation for it was that all students within the group received a copy of a 'student handbook' for the unit. This was produced by Emily and designed as a reference guide for students throughout the season. The handbook was also produced in acknowledgement of the Head of Department's feeling that some students might be somewhat worried about taking on new and unfamiliar roles or taking part in new practices. The handbook incorporated an enormous amount of information on swimming, relating directly to learning and assessment tasks that would be undertaken within the season. It featured the following sections:

- Introduction: this contained information about the concept of Sport Education, job descriptions, the six week timetable, a homework timetable and a sample league table.
- Teaching manual: this section presented each stroke with teaching cards for stroke development, detailing common errors, drills/practices relating to technique, stroke rules, and assessment sheets in diagrammatic and bullet point style. Teaching cards for stages of diving were included in a similar format.
- Official roles and other rules: this included detailed information about roles and specific responsibilities of each official in the authentic sporting situation. It drew upon materials produced by the international governing body for swimming (FINA).
- A section of sheets that could be pulled out or photocopied for use by any member of the teams to plan, implement and evaluate practices, technique and progress.

Students were advised that if they needed photocopies of sheets within the handbook they could ask for these.

As preceding chapters have emphasised, encouraging students to take responsibility for their own and others' learning has to be gradual and, more specifically, acknowledge the nature of their prior learning experiences. In this instance the boys had experienced lessons featuring a range of teaching styles, including reciprocal teaching. This was regarded as beneficial, as the students would therefore have had a 'glimpse' of being a coach and hopefully be well positioned to progress to leadership and evaluative roles with their peers. A number of specific tools were designed to encourage and structure the development of individual and collective responsibility for learning and, specifically, enhanced awareness and understanding of progress in learning. Sheets were provided for the boys to record their progress on a weekly basis and captains also had the responsibility of completing a team progress sheet.

Assessment

The Head of Department and the teacher responsible for observing Emily's lessons throughout the unit highlighted that the Sport Education unit must ensure the completion of the GCSE course requirements and that time needed to be built in to allow for the course assessment to be carried out. As explained below, this ultimately necessitated some modification to the content of the later lessons within the unit.

Experiencing the season

Table 13.1 provides a summary of the content of each of the nine sessions that were ultimately incorporated in the unit and details the respective roles of the teacher and the students.

Table 13.1 Season outline

Session/ lesson	Content	Teacher's roles	Students' roles
One	Choose options. Baseline assessment. Discuss team, decide roles.	Take assessment and use information to select teams/roles.	Participate, decide on teams/roles.
Two	Coaches take warm-up. Reciprocal teaching. Assessment and teaching of dives. Personal survival skills (PSS). Formal competition.	Class leader with some teaching.	Participate in pairs and teams.
Three	Teacher takes warm-up. Coaches take practices on worst stroke with videoing of individuals' technique. Teacher-led practice on PSS. Roles of officials. Formal competition.	Class leader with some teaching.	Participate in teams and as individuals. Coaches teaching.
Four	Video analysis of individuals' technique/ performances.	Guidance on analysis.	Evaluate own and others' technique.
Five	Captain takes warm-up. Assistant coach takes practices on second worst stroke. Teaching of butterfly. Exploration of tumble turns. Formal competition.	Head coach, class leader with some teaching later in lesson.	Participate in teams and as individuals. Assistant coaches and coaches take practices.
Six	Discussion about communication with coach/captain progress reports. Statisticians take warm-up. Practice/learning of racing dives. Formal competition.	Class leader, then head coach for rest of lesson.	Participate in teams throughout lesson. Various roles have duties to complete.

Table 13.1 continued

Session/ lesson	Content	Teacher's roles	Students' roles
Seven	Video analysis of individuals' technique/ performances.	Guidance on analysis.	Evaluate own and others' technique.
Eight	Publicist takes warm-up. Coaches take practices on second best stroke. PSS circuit with assessment. Individuals' swimming assessment. Tactics discussion and formal competition.	Head coach and supplying information for culminating event.	Participate in teams and as individuals. Complete assessments.
Nine	Culminating-event at the sponsored event and helping keep scores for sponsored event.	Spectator.	Team roles and participate. Responsibility for completing scores for sponsored swimmers.

In the first lesson the focus was on affiliation to teams. As planned, non-participating students were directly involved in the selection process. Emily drew upon their knowledge of peer strengths and weaknesses to formulate two teams and discuss prospective role allocations. The two students who worked with Emily in this process seemed pleased to have the added responsibility and input to the decisions about who would be affiliated to which team and play what roles. Students were then given the opportunity to name their own team, which they clearly relished. A sense of ownership had already started to form. The provisional allocation of roles was also presented to students and they were given the opportunity to negotiate the allocations. No-one had any clear objections and the provisional lists therefore became the team sheets for the season.

At the end of the first lesson the whole class also received a team talk that gave them the 'big picture' of the concept of Sport Education and an outline of what the season would involve and demand of them. At this stage an important point was made in relation to inclusion. It was emphasised that the Sport Education setting should be inclusive of everyone, an 'embarrassment free zone' in which the emphasis was that 'we are here to learn, make mistakes, be able to laugh at them and then get on'. Emily reiterated this point numerous times throughout the season. She was aware that two students in one team were self-conscious because of their size, shape and weight. Later in the unit, a supervised class 'bombing' practice took place and it appeared that hints of barriers to inclusion had been countered somewhat by this activity. Emily felt that a relaxed, uninhibited learning environment was generally created and encouraged throughout the season.

At the beginning of each session learning objectives were written on the whiteboard to communicate to the class the aims of the session. This seemed to work very well to focus the teams and also give the coach support in what they were trying to achieve with the team that day. In some respects it was something to fall back on if discipline problems occurred. Notably, this way of working was not new to the students. It was school policy within Brookfield for objectives to be made explicit to students in this way.

During the second lesson the vital importance of the selection of roles became apparent. Encouragingly the students had roles that suited individual personalities well. Over the season they were seen to mature and grow into their roles. However, relatively early on a concern was raised by an observing teacher that the coaches were not receiving sufficient practice time to enable the development of their skill technique and facilitate improvement in their swimming GCSE grade. This tension between the Sport Education format, scope and focus of learning, and that required for GCSE Physical Education was not fully overcome. Difficulties were eased with a modification to roles and responsibilities. Specifically, the role of assistant coach was added. Arrangements were then adjusted so that the assistant coach or captain could take over for a particular session, thereby freeing the coach for personal practice in the pool. This modification caused some worries amongst the students then taking on a coaching role, as they felt that they were not necessarily competent enough in the role and that they would not do as good a job as the normal team coach. Their concerns were addressed by the development of further support resources in the form of laminated teaching cards for each stroke that they could refer to when unsure of technical points. This enabled the assistant coaches/captains to relax somewhat. They used the cards when they felt that they needed to and a situation of minimal direct teacher intervention was thereby retained.

Some of the student coaches were notably innovative in their approach. One boy developed a 'coaching-in-the-water' technique to indicate to individuals exactly where they could improve. He swam alongside other members of his team, watching what they were doing under water with the help of a pair of goggles. There was only a single pair of goggles between the team and the students were seen to work well in sharing this resource in working on their observation and evaluation skills.

The concept of students taking on roles of officials was developed using more teacher-directed teaching styles, simply because none of the students had any previous experience of formal racing competitions and were unfamiliar with the format and rules for events. The weekly experience of competition meant that as the season progressed the students became more familiar with the roles of referee, starter, clerk of course, chief inspector of turns, inspector of turns, judge of stroke, chief timekeeper, timekeeper, chief finish judge, finish judge and desk control officer. They understood how to fulfil each role successfully. Notably, the results of the end of unit test showed that knowledge and understanding of the rules and implementation of them were far more extensive amongst the Sport Education group than the non-Sport Education group. In particular the Sport Education group knew where the various race officials stood, their job title and their responsibilities, whereas the control group only knew that there was a starter of the race. The boys in the Sport Education group also commented on the questionnaires that were administered to them that one of the most enjoyable aspects of the season was the formal competitions at the end of every lesson. They clearly enjoyed and valued the opportunities to race each other and to put new and/or improved skills into practice within this competitive setting.

As the season progressed, the teacher-researcher role definitely became one of facilitating learning and group coherence amongst team members. This involved providing teams with necessary equipment, such as video cameras and coaching materials. Emily found that an important means of supporting coaches was to guide them as to when to move on to a new task or next stage of development with individuals or the team. Emily therefore established the basic overall structure of the lessons and then supported the development of appropriate pace within each part of a lesson. Increasing responsibility was given to the coaches to establish appropriate content, using the handbook that had been provided for them.

Within the class there were a number of less able and SEN pupils. Their needs had to be catered for within practices and roles fully explained to ensure that they had a clear understanding of their responsibilities. The handbook provided essential support in this respect. The intuition of the coaches to adapt practices and experiences was also crucial to ensuring learning needs would be met. This required an element of pre-planning and alertness on Emily's part in order to ensure that all students were provided with opportunities to progress their skills, knowledge and understanding. As the group of ten boys were mixed ability, the teaching staff had some initial concerns that the learning needs of each individual would not be fully met via the Sport Education approach and, about, the greater learning responsibilities that were being placed upon the boys themselves. Staff were, however, pleasantly surprised to see that one coach in particular coped well with the need for differentiation, designing differentiated practices and giving coaching points well suited to individual team members' technique. The other coach struggled somewhat in these respects, due to a relative lack of knowledge about technique. This highlighted once again the need for teachers to be proactive in their support/facilitating role. Emily used a question and answer technique directed at the whole team in order to help advance knowledge and understanding about causes of the ineffective technique. Further questioning with reference to the handbook or laminated teaching cards was then used to clarify the correct technique and the team members were asked to suggest practices to improve specific aspects of technique. This process helped the development of team cohesion with students working together to achieve improvements in technique.

In contrast to this guided discovery and self-directed approach, the sessions focusing upon analysis were teacher directed. Several considerations informed the decision to adopt this approach. Specifically, the short duration of the unit meant that confidence in the team's ability to take responsibility for their own learning was growing but still limited. Emily was concerned that without a more directive stance not all of the boys would turn up to these sessions that were critical to their learning for the GCSE course. In addition, the coaches would have had significant problems organising the hiring of the equipment needed for the analysis work and the captains would have had problems trying to book an appropriate room. These sessions highlighted that establishing access to additional facilities and resources is a further important issue to consider at the planning stage of Sport Education unit development.

Although in some respects the boys were seen to take a positive interest in their individual and collective learning (particularly via some of the roles), their commitment to the lessons and to completion of some elements of the unit became a matter of some concern. For example, the boys were notably poor at keeping the league table of results up to date and individual progress reports were completed in a somewhat lethargic manner. The boys were interested in the formal competitions and in their individual progress, but recording this for themselves using the progress report system proved problematic. Encouragingly, they could verbalise progress information when necessary. In relation to collective responsibility, a system was developed whereby, when the captain's progress reports were completed, the team were given the opportunity to comment on how they could progress further as a team. They were asked to decide on a specific element that the team should work on and, similarly, to identify an individual target. The students were very quick to identify what they needed to improve and were enthusiastic in working on identified areas for improvement.

The role of the publicist was also something that diminished as the season continued, mainly due to a reluctance to complete homework set that related to this role. For example, publicists were set the task of designing a poster to promote their team, to be displayed on the Sport Education notice board. Ways in which the commitment and interest could have been sustained and enhanced were identified during the unit. Specifically, stronger links could have been established with information and communication technology and bookings of the IT suite arranged for completion of homework tasks, and with the aim of the Sport Education work being the focus of a weekly bulletin in the school magazine. As discussed in Chapter 5, the cross-curricular dimension of learning could also be extended by providing opportunities for dictaphone recording of commentary, and by establishing formal linkages between verbal and written work produced in the Sport Education season and English lessons.

During observations of the class it became apparent that the coaches were knowledgeable about how to speak and liaise with team members. However, the rest of the team displayed some difficulty respecting comments made by others. Session six in the unit was therefore specifically modified to include a discussion on communication, based on a task completed for JSLA training. The discussion made the need for cooperative communication a focus for the remaining three sessions in the season. It proved a worthy addition to the season as the students clearly started to gain a fuller understanding of their collective responsibility. They recognised that they needed to work together to improve everyone's performance. Further observations indicated they were becoming more patient with one another, were not so intent on receiving the coach's attention immediately and were making greater efforts to try to think their own way through problems.

With two lessons remaining in the unit it was agreed with the observing class teacher that the focus of the last two sessions would be modified in response to desires to refocus attention on GCSE course requirements. Specifically, attention was shifted away from tactical awareness and understanding (with a view on the culminating festival) towards formal assessment. It was recognised that this switch would affect students' scores in the tactical understanding aspect of the Sport Education test, as this area of work would not then have been covered as thoroughly as was desired. However the formal assessment gave Emily the opportunity to visually compare the students' techniques with that seen in baseline assessment tasks.[3]

Formative assessment was ongoing through the unit. The coaches and teacher-researcher completed collaborative formative assessment regularly throughout the season. One coach displayed particularly good observation and analysis skills, intently watching how his team was developing and giving sound feedback and advice quickly after completion of a length. The other coach required more guidance in the coaching process and was asked to observe the other coach at work in order to gain a better understanding of aspects of the role. Using a question and answer technique as he watched the other coach, he was able to develop a better understanding of when and how to complete informal observations and use these to inform the next planned practice/session. The boys and particularly the coaches gained a heightened understanding of the need for regular assessment as an integral element of the learning process (see Chapter 4). Within normal physical education lessons these types of experience are less likely to occur, simply because students would not necessarily be placed in similar situations and relations with one another.

The summative assessment at the end of the season was teacher planned and led, due to the need to complete GCSE assessments. The students contributed suggestions to the grades to be given based on what they knew of each other's technique and observations of other performances. The final decisions, however, necessarily rested with the observing class teacher.

Within the formal competitions that were incorporated in the season, one team dominated in terms of performance. The various team roles were fulfilled reasonably equally but swimming technique was much better amongst the members of one team. This team consequently won all of the races. However, the other team did not seem too embarrassed or de-motivated by this situation. Their own swimming times were improving and they knew that individually and collectively they were progressing. They retained strong motivation to participate in races every week no matter what the outcome and were also supportive of one another in the competitive setting. When one student was struggling with technique other team members made it their responsibility to cheer them on. The weaker performers were not overtly punished or penalised by their peers, but were instead encouraged to feel that they could continue to improve if they kept trying and invested in the practice sessions. Allowing opportunities for additional practices and providing resources (such as drill and technique cards) to support and encourage practice were therefore recognised as important issues to consider in organising a Sport Education unit.

The organisation of the *culminating event* was another instance in which Emily took a lead and more directive role. This was deemed appropriate given the scheduling and location of the event, which was to be held off-site and outside of lesson time and required liaison with the external facility staff. In these circumstances it was considered best that Emily undertook the liaison. Clearly, with older groups or in a next Sport Education season, some more mature students could become involved in this aspect of the work. (One obvious way forward would be for an events committee to be established with the committee members then agreeing upon individual organisational responsibilities for the event.) The use of an external facility also highlighted the need (stressed in Chapter 7) for Sport Education developments to become 'partnership based'. Ideally the external facility staff would be aware that, as part of the Sport Education experience, students from the school would undertake to meet with them to discuss facility needs and procedures for the culminating event.

Beyond the facility booking issue, the Sport Education group had important responsibilities for the smooth running of the event. They were required to apply the correct procedures for implementation of an Olympic start in the sponsored swim, thereby giving the event an important 'authentic feel'. They were also watching students who had said that they would swim properly throughout the swim to see if they completed the stroke correctly in accordance with FINA rules. An experienced teacher and the student referee had the responsibility for overall supervision of the event. Several turn judges were also put in place, not so much to apply their detailed knowledge of the rules but to ensure that all students completed their lengths fully for the purposes of the sponsored event. Finally a desk control officer was in place to collect the results of the participants' achievements, to work out how much sponsorship each needed to collect and to receive any money donated at the event.

Reflection on the season

Overall the season was a successful, productive experience with many positive examples of how the Sport Education design for the unit contributed to improved knowledge and understanding of swimming. One of the most rewarding experiences was watching the coaches living up to the expectations that had been set for them, with notable improvements seen through the season in their abilities and in the skills, knowledge and understanding of their teams. As a beginning teacher Emily found it invigorating to watch the boys improve within their teams and clearly enjoy working together. The impression was that the team mattered to them and that they were more than willing to work hard towards the formal competitions.

Yet, as indicated, there were areas in which difficulties were experienced and where modifications should be considered in future developments. Some of the team members lacked commitment to their role. How to overcome this, ideally through peer pressure rather than direct teacher intervention, is a matter to now pursue. This may be something that could be more effectively addressed in a longer season and perhaps with the introduction of buddy, mentor or role rotation systems. With less time pressure and less of a focus on examination course requirements, it may also be possible to give students a greater role in establishing the content to be covered in various sessions, thereby once again enhancing responsibility, ownership and hopefully motivation for learning.

In relation to what the season achieved, it was notable that it started to tackle the issue of absenteeism. One student in particular for the first time felt guilty about not attending school and recognised that he had made little or no contribution to the team. After the first lesson, none of the boys turned up without kit, which again was a marked change from the normal occurrence. The season demonstrated the way in which in Sport Education all members of the team have to learn to work with one another over an extended period of time. This requires enhanced social skills to cope with an arguably more pressurised environment, with personal performances and contributions very public to the team throughout the season. Generally the boys reacted well to this situation and enjoyed the prominent team concept. Some acknowledged that they felt pressure in performing competitively in front of others, but also commented that this increased their motivation to perform to the best of their ability.

As other teachers have also recognised (see Chapters 10, 11 and 12) absenteeism could cause disruption within the Sport Education setting. For example, the absence of a coach could have a detrimental effect on intended continuity in learning and mean that the progress seen in a session was more limited. However, in a real life sporting situation, teams would have to adapt and take responsibility for their own training or match performance. On some occasions, teams in Sport Education may face equivalent challenges and need to therefore be encouraged to develop strategies for what action will be taken in the event of absenteeism. Teams could be asked to establish a 'reserve' or 'stand-in' for each key role, with the understanding that with appointment as 'reserve' comes a responsibility to develop a basic under-standing of the demands of the role and the input that is required on a weekly basis.

A league table had been established to enable individuals to compare their times over the season and for coaches to see if improvements had been made in particular strokes. During the unit the scope for these types of com-parison was limited as the boys swam different strokes for each of the first four weeks. It was recognised that a modified structure allowing earlier more direct comparison would be a preferable format to adopt. There also seemed a case for additional informal intervention to encourage a greater commit-ment to maintenance of the league table. It may have been useful to remind coaches of the expectation that league results would provide evidence of individual and team improvement through the season.

Conclusion

With the results from the formal test at the end of the unit, a strong recom-mendation could be made for the use of Sport Education over a more trad-itional framework and approach. In the knowledge and understanding test scores the students in the Sport Education group scored higher in all of the test categories, compared to students in the non-Sport Education group. It was acknowledged that in this Sport Education season limited attention was devoted to *tactical* knowledge and understanding and the students' scores were rather low for this category. The Sport Education group had an increased knowledge of tactics compared to the non-Sport Education group, but it was felt that this aspect of their learning could have been extended further. Emily recognised that she could have been more alert to opportun-ities to highlight certain tactics being used during races and that a longer season may also have encouraged (or formally demanded) experimentation with different tactics.

In the light of this study, it was considered that a Sport Education approach can provide an innovative means of fulfilling the requirements of the NCPE in England. Emily was left with the view that the requirements of the acquiring and developing aspect can be easily met with good progressive planning and ongoing support for learning in the team context. This aspect (of developing and acquiring skills) was extended further for the Sport Edu-cation group in comparison to the non-Sport Education group, specifically via the season involving them in learning competitive diving, tumble turns and officials' duties. Meanwhile the phased nature of the season can be used to create demands to apply skills in increasingly demanding (technically and in relation to competitive context) situations. Furthermore, various roles can all be seen to encourage the development of selecting and applying skills, tactics and organisational concepts. In relation to the aspect evaluation and improvement of performance, as well as the involvement in coaching, the experience of officiating enabled refinement of observational skills. Specifically the boys were challenged to closely analyse others' technique to ensure compliance of rules relating, for example, to touch turns and finishes in swimming. Overall, comparing the Sport Education season to the unit of work followed by the non-Sport Education group, the season provided more opportunities for fulfilment of the evaluating and improving aspect of the NCPE. During sessions two, four and seven all of the students were required to judge performances and decide how to improve them by giving coaching points. This opportunity was further extended by individuals taking on a coaching role. For the future Emily also saw that there may be benefits in establishing a more formal commitment for the teams (led by the coaches) to participate in additional analysis sessions. The teams (or an event committee if formed) could be given the responsibility for organising these extra sessions on a rotation basis or, alternatively, organisation of these sessions could in itself become a new role.

While not denying any of this learning potential of Sport Education, at the same time it is important to stress the extent of planning and ongoing monitoring and adaptation that is needed for successful implementation. Particular attention needs to be given to the implications of various roles for the learning opportunities that students in or out of those roles may be missing. The example that came to the fore here was that of personal skill development being in danger of neglect for those students acting as coaches. Overall, however, for all involved this was regarded as a very positive first experience of Sport Education.

Notes

1   Any maintained secondary school in England may apply to be designated as a Specialist School, signalling a commitment to a particular 'identity' and ethos, intended to permeate the school, its curriculum and pedagogical developments, and 'partnership' activities with community groups and other schools. The number of specialist subject areas has been progressively increased to now include technology, languages, sports, arts (visual, performing or media), business and enterprise, engineering, science, and mathematics and computing (DfES, 2003). In all cases the commitment to teaching all curriculum subjects and covering the full National Curriculum remains firmly in place. The specialism is intended to act as a focus and catalyst for improvement in teaching and learning across the breadth of the curriculum. Further information about Specialist Schools can be obtained via the DfES standards site: http://www.standards.dfes.gov.uk/specialistschools/.
2   Excellence in Cities (EiC) is a targeted programme of support for schools in deprived areas of England. It is directed towards the transformation of urban secondary education in these areas where it is deemed that standards have been 'too low for too long'. EiC initiative therefore centres on a programme of strategies focused on teaching and learning, behaviour and attendance, and leadership. Schools work in partnership with their local education authority in delivering the programme. Details can be accessed via the DfES standards site: http://www.standards.dfes.gov.uk/sie/eic/.

3   Baseline assessment tasks were taken in the first session by the observing class
    teacher. Each student had to complete a four length warm-up, two lengths of each
    stroke (one for butterfly), any turns, two dives and a game of water-polo.

References

Department for Education and Skills (DfES) (2003). *A New Specialist System: Trans-forming Secondary Education*, London: DfES.

Department for Education and Skills (DfES)/Department of Culture, Media and Sport (DCMS) (2003). *Learning through PE and Sport: A Guide to the Physical Education, School Sport and Club Links Strategy*, London: DfES Publications.

OFSTED (2002). *Inspection Report: Brookfield High School* (May 2002, Inspection number: 190326), London: OFSTED.

Siedentop, D. (1994). *Sport Education: Quality PE through Positive Sport Experiences*, Champaign, Illinois: Human Kinetics.

14 Sport Education and outdoor and adventurous activities

Dawn Penney and Barbara Wilkie

Introduction

This chapter reports developments in provision of physical education, sport and leadership experiences at a secondary (5–16 years) community school in Hampshire, that is also now a designated Specialist Sports College.[1] Hamble Community School's application for this status reflected its commitment to:

- physical education and sport being at the heart of education, school and wider communities; and therefore
- realising the potential of physical education and sport to play a key role in the development of lifelong skills and interests amongst *all* young people.

The innovative practices that we report here link directly with these commitments. It is important to note that the innovation was not, at the time, labelled as 'Sport Education'. However, it is recognised that many of the principles and characteristics of Sport Education were central to the developments and that the learning opportunities created can justifiably be associated with the model. The diverse learning roles established, the strength of the cross-curricular dimension, the fundamental concerns to incorporate but go beyond a focus on performance, to engage young people who seemed to have little affinity with 'more traditional' (and particularly games) activities in physical education, and to feature experiences that would have direct relevance to students' lives, all speak for themselves in that regard.

In important respects the developments at Hamble also provide insights into new and exciting ways forward for the development of Sport Education in physical education in England. Anyone doubting the scope for this model to be taken forward across the full range of activity areas within the NCPE and, furthermore, to be developed not merely within the curriculum but also in extra-curricular, club or community settings should find much here to remove those doubts. The teachers and students at Hamble Community Sports College and the staff and children at Hamble

River Sailing Club have provided very clear evidence of the scope for Sport Education to be productively developed in outdoor and adventurous activity contexts. Links to the agendas for citizenship and lifelong learning that were discussed in Chapters 6 and 7 are also very apparent here.

Relevance and meaning for young people's lives: a local activity, local identities and real futures

Although every school's location is unique, Hamble Community Sports College still stands out in this respect. It is located on the south coast of England, just a few miles from a river estuary that is the hub of sailing in the Solent. Its local community is inherently a 'sailing community'. Variously many local people:

- enjoy sailing as a family based recreational activity;
- participate in local sailing club competitions;
- pursue higher level performance opportunities in sailing;
- study for the many qualifications that are a requirement for participation and competition (including navigation and safety qualifications);
- follow careers in boat design, boat building, sail-making and other specialist support industries;
- take up the roles of sailing instructors or coaches; or
- are involved in other services designed for the sailing community in its widest sense – including many day and weekend visitors and holiday makers who visit during a year and arrive in their thousands for events such as the Southampton Boat Show, the Cowes Sailing Week and, in recent years, the start or finish of legs of major international sailing events such as the 'BT Global Challenge'.

The list above shows the scope and diversity of roles that people play in sailing and a sailing community. It is the community that many of the young people at Hamble Community Sports College are not only a part of now; it is also where many of their futures lie. In Sport Education terms, in this local context, sailing is undoubtedly an authentic activity, presenting many and varied authentic identities for students.

Sailing, the sailing community and its significance in both leisure and vocational terms have yet to be explored to their full potential within the curriculum at Hamble. The school's application for Sports College status recognised this and the ways in which sailing could provide a focus for developing notions of lifelong and community based learning. The developments that we describe here represent something of a forerunner to ongoing innovation in curriculum and out of hours provision in physical education and sport at Hamble Community Sports College.

Extending learning: out of school hours and in partnership

The learning experiences that we focus on were developed in partnership, by staff from the physical education department at (the then) Hamble Community School,[2] instructors and members of Hamble River Sailing Club, and staff at the local further education ('16+') college. The experiences were provided outside of curriculum time but linked (in an informal manner) with specific curriculum activities organised by the school. These included cross-curricular activity weeks held at the local outdoor activity centre, swimming within physical education, and Duke of Edinburgh's Award courses at key stage 4. What we now refer to as the 'Sport Ed sailing' course happened during sailing club time, on Wednesday evenings and Saturdays.

At a time when there is much talk of a need for the strengthening of school–sports club links (see Chapters 1 and 7), it is important to highlight that in this development it was the students themselves who were that link. They were in Year 10 at Hamble Community School and members of Hamble River Sailing Club. Notably, the Sport Ed sailing course was designed to offer these young people an entry into a host of sailing related opportunities and to give them the motivation and key foundation skills, knowledge and understanding to pursue those opportunities. The course also directly reflected specific *development needs of the club*:

- to attract more young people into the club to work with younger children;
- to skill and qualify young people to be able to sustain its youth sailing development;
- to enhance the performance development pathways available to its youth members; and
- to have boats suitable for young children to use in their early experiences of sailing.

The course was staffed by instructors and other members of the sailing club and staff at the local 16+ college. The partnerships were initiated and coordinated by the then Head of Physical Education at Hamble Community School, who was also able to create further links and extended opportunities for the young people on the course. As we explain below, these included the extension of the fitness and training dimension of the course and the chance for leadership work in sailing to count towards a Duke of Edinburgh's Award.

The course involved sessions held at the sailing club, the school and the technical college. Formally, it spanned six weeks, but ultimately proved to be an ongoing learning experience for many of the students involved. The students involved in the initiative were described by the then Head of Physical Education as 'a different type [of student] . . . not games players . . .

risk-takers with energy … but no outlet for it … not GCSE or sports-people'. They were eight boys and two girls whose existing interest in sailing was recognised as something that could engage them as learners and particularly as prospective leaders.

Clearly, it is important to acknowledge that various characteristics created somewhat unique potential for this development. Location and the resources that the partner organisations brought with them were fundamental and are not available everywhere. But as we discuss later, some of the principles and ideas could easily be taken forward in other outdoor activity settings. It is also important to acknowledge that there were financial issues to be overcome, including costs of transport (for people and boats!), and the purchase of specialist equipment and materials. From the outset it was recognised that the course would be a non-starter if it was costly for the young people themselves. While the area in which Hamble is located may have an image of affluence, the reality is that the area 'has almost full employment but many jobs are low paid' (OFSTED, 2002: 7). An 'Awards for All' grant from Sport England, together with donations of equipment, and the collective contributions from the school, sailing club and technical college, proved crucial in covering the costs arising in this initiative.

The 'Sport Ed' sailing course

As explained, this development was not specifically modelled on Sport Education. It is in retrospect that the compatibility with the model and framework has been recognised. Not all of the features associated with Sport Education were built into the sailing course. Some, however, came through very strongly. The course was designed to:

- go beyond a focus on performance;
- involve students taking on new roles;
- develop new learning;
- locate learning in a team context;
- encourage students to support others' learning; and
- incorporate special events.

All of the students were interested in the opportunities that being a member of the sailing club offered for them to extend their personal sailing capabilities. However, they had also reached a point whereby they needed new challenges to maintain their interest in education. The students were identified 'underachievers'. The Sport Ed sailing course was designed to present a variety of new challenges, linking directly with prospective careers: in racing, in instruction and in boat building. The course specifically provided an introduction to boat handling, construction and basic rigging of boats, water safety and navigation. All of the sessions had a practical emphasis which it was hoped would appeal to these students. After the introduction, the students were encouraged to then go on to a GNVQ Boat Building course that ran on one day per week. In addition, Hamble River Sailing Club offered open sailing for the students at no cost on Wednesday evenings and weekends and opportunities to become more involved in working with younger and less experienced sailors. Thus, there were the prospects of sustained involvement and ongoing learning, which as we explain below were taken up to great effect.

Viewed in 'Sport Education terms' the students were presented with opportunities to take on a wide variety of roles and related responsibilities:

- as *junior sailing instructors* with a key role to play in introducing children to sailing for the first time and new skills and knowledge to therefore develop, relating to safety, conditions and equipment, as well as instruction and coaching;
- as a *team of boat builders* with varying specialist responsibilities within a design and building project to produce new small boats specifically for the club's expanding youth membership;
- as *competitive sailors* in club competitions, with a need to acknowledge the strength and fitness demands of competitive sailing and follow training programmes for that;
- as *helpers in the organisation and running of 'family days' at the club*, at which families are encouraged to come and watch children participating in races, and enjoy the sport and the club as a social activity.

Further, the course can also be firmly associated with many of the pedagogical principles central to Sport Education and discussed in Chapter 1.

Working as a team and towards shared objectives: The boat design and building project positioned the students as a team, working under the guidance and instruction of club members and 16+ college staff. The project was literally intended to go from design drawings through to the launch of a boat. The boat would be wooden and the project would open up an array of specialisms: for carpentry skills, knowledge of choice and use of various resins; sail-making skills; production of boat covers; choice and purchase of ropes; and book-keeping. The plan was to initially produce a prototype boat, and launch day would be an exciting test of the team's success!

The strong commitment of the club instructors and the expertise provided by staff at the local marine tech centre meant that the students had great support and good role models in their project. The marine tech college staff oversaw the boat building and its schedule. Students elected to take on certain responsibilities in the building process and in some instances this was a guided choice with individual learning strengths being matched to task demands. For example, staff recognised that not all of the students would be able to read the plans for building the boats. The boats came as kits and one of the tasks was to check all of the parts. Variously, students then took responsibility for matters such as purchase of resins required and addressing the rigging needed. The Royal Yachting Association (RYA) was involved in marketing the kits and operated a match-funding scheme, so that the school paid for one kit and the RYA provided another for no cost. Following building of the prototype, two boats were therefore built in tandem, to be used for junior sailing at the sailing club.

The boat building project was an example of the way in which Sport Education initiatives can 'snowball'. In this instance, a local television station became involved, tracking the building progress. The boats had to be ready for a feature launch for the BBC 'Big Wave' programme. All of the builders attended the launch, which was filmed with a safety boat in attendance!

Progressively taking greater and a shared responsibility for learning: The boat building project challenged the students to work together, recognise their respective strengths and interests and support each other's development. Meanwhile all practical sailing (and other outdoor and adventurous activities) demands very clear self-responsibility and responsibility for others if it is to be safe. In moving towards becoming junior instructors, students had to extend their personal responsibility and develop the skills and knowledge to take responsibility for others in sailing activities. This type of development needs to be progressive and supported. The students moved from a situation in which they were instructed, to one in which they were 'instructing with instruction', to one in which they were independent in the instruction role. The sailing safety element of the course also necessarily involved survival training, some of which was based at the school swimming pool. Communication skills, group management and organisational skills, as well as knowledge relating to the handling (safely) of boats and equipment with young children, were thus all areas of learning for the students on the course.

From the club's perspective, the growth in their junior membership signalled the success of the initiative. The club's youth membership grew from 5 to 80 members aged between 5 and 17 years over a three year period. The eight (out of the original group of ten) students who retained their involvement became role models for younger children.

Adopting a holistic view of performance: Sport Education endeavours to promote a 'full' understanding of what is involved in the improvement of performance, and particularly extend skills, knowledge and understanding relating to the development of fitness for performance, and to evaluation of performance. Perhaps contrary to common perceptions, sailing demands considerable and very specialist fitness. The sailing course incorporated strength training at the school gym, with additional evening opportunities available for students to make use of the fitness equipment in the gym. Meanwhile, developing evaluation skills was central to their role as instructors. Finally, in incorporating racing events, the course would cover regulations and rules for sailing.

Real relevance and real potential: We have already indicated the direct connections that the course sought to make to roles and career opportunities in sailing and in the local community. The vision was that the course would 'open doors' for the students: to stay on at the club as junior instructors, to progress to gain qualifications as senior instructors, in safety boat handling, in navigation, and/or to take up jobs within a boat building industry that is acknowledged as short of people with carpentry skills in particular, and/or continue to extend their own level of performance in the sport.

Festivity: The family days at the sailing club, featuring youth competitions, with trophies presented and a barbecue alongside the clubhouse, captured the inclusive emphasis that festivals in Sport Education are intended to promote.

Reflections and future directions

Undoubtedly, this was an ambitious initiative but also very rewarding for the students involved, the school and the sailing club. It remains an ongoing development. The *students* involved have the opportunity to progress from junior instructor awards to senior instructors. They also have local opportunities to pursue other courses of study, including an NVQ Boat Building course, navigation and day or coastal skipper courses. The *school* faces the challenge of how to build on the success and, specifically, enhance links to sailing within the curriculum. There is recognition of the need for key stage 3 students to be provided with opportunities to try sailing. Time-tabling of key stage 4 physical education has been adjusted, so that physical education is the last session of the school day and students can access off-site activities such as sailing. The school also recognises the potential to be capitalising on recent national success in sailing in promoting sailing as a competitive sport for young people. Arguably, it is ideally placed to do this. The *club* link remains invaluable and, as this initiative demonstrated, can be clearly mutually beneficial. The club faces the challenge of how to retain its new junior members and support their progress into various roles as adult club members. All involved remain aware of development costs. Once built, the new boats needed transporting. Trailers for use on roads and for launching at the river are some of the additional and essential resources that it is easy to overlook in projects such as this. The school has worked hard with the sailing club to secure donations of second hand trailers and some additional boats, all of which are being used to support the development of the youth squads.

Meanwhile, other outdoor and adventurous activities appear to present further exciting potential for the development of Sport Education. A Duke of Edinburgh's Award expedition can easily be envisaged as a 'culminating event', with particular team members taking on specific responsibilities in the planning phase and during the expedition. With prospective roles such as route planner, budget manager, menu planner and safety officer come prompts once again for Sport Education to be a catalyst for enhanced cross-curricular links (see Chapter 5). Similarly, we can view orienteering as a very attractive potential focus activity for new Sport Education initiatives. Thus, this chapter like many others ends on an optimistic note, celebrating success and recognising considerable scope for further developments.

Notes

1   Any maintained secondary school in England may apply to be designated as a Specialist School, signalling a commitment to a particular 'identity' and ethos, intended to permeate the school, its curriculum and pedagogical developments, and 'partnership' activities with community groups and other schools. The number of specialist subject areas has been progressively increased to now include technology, languages, sports, arts (visual, performing or media), business and enterprise, engineering, science, and mathematics and computing (DfES, 2003). In all cases the commitment to teaching all curriculum subjects and covering the full National Curriculum remains firmly in place. The specialism is intended to act as a focus and catalyst for improvement in teaching and learning across the breadth of the curriculum. Further information about Specialist Schools can be obtained via the DfES standards site: http://www.standards.dfes.gov.uk/specialistschools/.
2   Prior to designation as a Specialist Sports College, the school name was Hamble Community School.

References

Department for Education and Skills (DfES) (2003). *A New Specialist System: Transforming Secondary Education*, London: DFES.
OFSTED (2002). *Inspection Report: Hamble School* (November 2001, Inspection number: 198319), London: OFSTED.

Part 4
Looking to the future

15 Sport Education in teacher education

Gary D. Kinchin, Dawn Penney and Gill Clarke

Introduction

Earlier chapters in this book have provided detailed insights into ways in which Sport Education may be developed and evaluated in schools as a curricular innovation. Many of the units described were taught by experienced teachers who participated in Sport Education professional development activities. Significantly, these activities have not been 'one-off' sessions. Instead, several of the developments described have progressed within a framework of ongoing support for the teachers involved, and a sustained partnership with university based staff. The success of this approach has reaffirmed that maintaining quality programmes of physical education and sustaining innovation 'requires substantial long-term investments, both logistical and human' (Siedentop and Locke, 1997: 26). Further, it has lent support to Armour and Yelling's (2004) recent emphasis that, to be valued and productive, professional development work needs to:

- be school based and directly linked to teachers' own practice;
- be re-orientated to focus upon teachers' professional *learning*; and
- ideally be a collaborative endeavour.

Particularly in our work with Mountbatten School and Language College (see Chapters 10, 11 and 12), we have seen the ways in which very positive 'professional learning' relationships can be established over time. Notably, the partnership with Mountbatten provided the basis from which to extend the Sport Education professional learning community to involve local teachers from neighbouring schools. Given that schools in England continue to effectively be set against one another through 'league tables' of achievements and 'standards', we should celebrate collaboration and, more specifically, teachers' willingness to share professional knowledge and experiences.

This chapter focuses on collaboration and 'partnerships' that in our view are fundamental if the development of Sport Education in physical education is to be more than occasional, temporary and/or of notably varied quality. It addresses the need for linkages to be established between emerging innovative practices in schools and initial (or pre-service) teacher education courses in physical education, and discusses ways in which such linkages can be advanced.

Initial teacher education: the logical, necessary but missing link in the development of Sport Education

In some respects it seems as if it is stating the obvious to say that, 'if we want to change the school curriculum, we must necessarily change the way in which we educate our future teachers' (Laker, 2003: 154). Yet, the irony is that, certainly in England, the approach to reform of curriculum requirements appears to have been one in which teacher education is considered as an afterthought. Our own interests are in changes to the school curriculum, but particularly the curriculum as experienced by students. Thus, pedagogy is our priority and we believe that teacher education has a key role to play in supporting pedagogical innovation and advancement in physical education, including the development of Sport Education in physical education. This is not to imply that training institutions should be regarded as the sole sources of innovative thinking about the curriculum, teaching and learning in physical education or, more specifically, how it may prospectively be reflected in practice in schools. Far from it. Rather, our emphasis is that stronger and notably 'forward looking' partnerships between training institutions and schools are essential if we are to avoid situations in which either beginning teachers see no scope to try out in real teaching and learning contexts new ideas and approaches that they have been introduced to in their training or, equally, feel inadequately prepared to become involved in innovative practices that they see being developed in schools.

The development of Sport Education in physical education in England is a case in point in relation to these interests. We can envisage a pattern of somewhat fragmented and incoherent development continuing. Firstly, there is the prospect of new teachers entering schools that are developing Sport Education in physical education, without having had a comprehensive introduction to Sport Education in their university based training and/or the opportunity to try teaching using a Sport Education approach in their school based training. Secondly, there is also the prospect that, having been introduced to Sport Education in their university based training, new teachers will enter school contexts in which no moves have been made to develop Sport Education and/or other staff know very little about it. Simply stated, what we are talking about here is a need for more 'joined up thinking' and collaboration in efforts to advance teaching and learning in physical education through planned and well structured innovative work in universities and in the schools that they have a training link with. Siedentop and Locke (1997) have articulated a similar vision in stating that physical education teacher training programmes 'must make choices about what they believe good physical education to be and then prepare their novice teachers to deliver that physical education by preparing and socialising them in schools where it is being delivered successfully' (p. 29). We are very aware that not all training institutions are positioned to make such selective choices of school placements for trainee teachers. Productive partnerships that also involve universities and schools in collaborative continuing professional development work are, therefore, all the more important.

A strong case can thus be made for training to be a catalyst for curriculum and pedagogical innovation in schools, and for training institutions to act as providers of ongoing support for that innovation. However, in the case of Sport Education we have relatively few insights into how either role has been developed internationally and might now be taken forward in England. There are only a few published examples of how Sport Education has been used in the preparation of teachers (Collier, 1998) or in higher education/ tertiary teaching contexts more generally (see Bennett, 2000; Bennett and Hastie, 1997). In the USA some providers of initial teacher training have delivered specific practical subject knowledge components using Sport Education (Kinchin, 1999). Kinchin (1999) has drawn particular attention to the merits of using Sport Education in addressing social aspects of learning (including issues of equity) in physical education and the scope to simultaneously introduce training teachers to 'alternative' forms of assessment. In other instances a series of planned experiences directed at Sport Education have been established within training, including practical work, observation of Sport Education in schools and actual teaching of Sport Education under the supervision of a mentor (Collier, 1998).

Edith Cowan University (ECU) in Western Australia is nationally and internationally recognised for its research based development of Sport Education. Teachers involved in the development have participated in Sport Education in Physical Education (SEPEP) workshops. Their trialling of SEPEP has provided key insights into the issues arising for teachers and students involved for the first time in SEPEP. Teachers' professional judgements of its relative merits as an innovation and approach in physical education have featured prominently in reporting and, furthermore, shaped ongoing development work (Alexander and Luckman, 2001; Alexander et al., 1993; Medland et al., 1994; Taggart et al., 1995). The work at ECU has thus been directly linked with teachers' professional development and conducted in the context of sustained partnerships with teachers. Notably, Sport Education has at the same time been embedded into the Physical Education Teacher Education courses at ECU, and not only in a single unit. Elements of Sport Education are introduced and revisited across a number of units and throughout the years of training. In their training, beginning teachers will be members of SEPEP teams that are retained throughout a unit, will participate in the various roles associated with Sport Education, will have allocated responsibilities in the organisation of end of season festivals, will produce team posters for the SEPEP notice board, and so on.

Some will have the opportunity to then work with experienced teachers in teaching SEPEP during their school based training. Opportunities also arise to take Sport Education forward in the context of junior sport development (for example, in a partnership initiative with specific state sports organisations). Thus, Andrew Taggart, Ken Alexander and colleagues at the Sport and Physical Activity Research Centre (SPARC) at ECU have done much to promote the sustained development of Sport Education and in particular establish direct linkages between research, continuing professional development, curriculum innovation in schools, pre-service teacher education and junior sport development. They are the first to admit that such an approach is not easy. As Placek *et al.* (1995) pointed out, the task of 'working with all players in our profession' (p. 259) is likely to be difficult and lengthy.

Within England and Wales both the three and four year routes to Qualified Teacher Status (QTS) and the one year postgraduate (PGCE) route to QTS present opportunities for some of these overseas developments to be adapted and extended to provide beginning teachers with a sound introduction to Sport Education. We acknowledge that many training providers already regard the one year PGCE course as extremely pressured. In this context, it is important that Sport Education is not presented as yet another additional course element. Rather, Sport Education needs to be associated with the extension of the pedagogical frameworks and approaches that are utilised in teaching *existing elements* of the PGCE, and that are a focus during school based experience. Thus, Sport Education may be a prompt for 'doing some things differently' within the PGCE course in both university based and school based training. Needless to say, such change requires thorough discussion with all parties involved. Doubtless, some staff within both universities and schools will be somewhat sceptical about the prospective merits of attempting to teach elements of the PGCE using a Sport Education framework and approach. They may feel that doing so presents an unnecessary complication or even distraction from core and pressing business, and that it is something that 'can wait', to be addressed after QTS has been gained. In our view, however, Sport Education is an important aspect of the physical education curriculum and pedagogy that training teachers should be introduced to. It is likely to be something that they can then assist (and even take a lead) in taking forward in the schools in which they gain employment as newly qualified teachers. The discussion below focuses, therefore, upon the ways in which the PGCE secondary physical education course at the University of Southampton has been developed to incorporate both university and school based experience of Sport Education. The University of Southampton, rather like Edith Cowan University in Western Australia, has sought to advance concurrent initial teacher training and continuing professional development activities focusing on Sport Education. Our belief is that the professional challenge of curriculum and pedagogical innovation can productively be a shared one, involving training, newly qualified and experienced teachers of physical education.

Sport Education at the University of Southampton

The structure of the PGCE course at the University of Southampton and the nature of this predominantly school based route to QTS status does not permit a sustained practical focus on Sport Education. Sport Education has, however, become an embedded element within the PGCE course in secondary physical education and a focus of ongoing research and development in initial teacher training. The course engages training teachers both conceptually and practically with Sport Education. Sport Education has also been adopted in a growing number of partner schools. Training teachers who are placed in these schools will have opportunities to observe and/or to teach Sport Education as part of their placement experience and are also encouraged to share their observations and reflections with peers when they return to the University.

University based provision: initial lecture and practical work

An initial lecture on Sport Education is provided as a lead into practical sessions. The training teachers then have opportunities to partially 'experience the model as a participant' (Collier, 1998: 44). Sample practical sessions are planned to illustrate how some of the features of Sport Education (affiliation, festivity, records and competition) might be operationalised within a variety of school contexts. These sessions are built into the games component of the PGCE course and specifically direct attention to:

- *Planning of units/seasons*: some previously developed units are distributed as examples in addition to further practical and support materials.
- *Management and administration*: the development of teams, the implementation of non-playing roles and responsibilities, point systems and league positions, introducing and holding learners accountable for in-class routines (leading warm-ups, fulfilling roles), deciding upon competition formats are all introduced.
- *Pedagogy*: sessions demonstrate teacher-led and learner-led strategies and offer guidance on ways to progressively shift from one model of teaching to the other (use of task cards, practice formats and outlines).
- *Issues of assessment*: sessions show links with the four aspects of learning within the National Curriculum Physical Education. Other learning which can be assessed (for example, cross-curricular learning, see Chapters 5 and 6) and the use of different assessment strategies such as journal writing (Kinchin, 2000) are addressed.

Training teachers have responded positively to these sessions. They can recognise the defining features of the model and what it is seeking to achieve, and are able to relate them to their own individual sport histories and interests in sport and physical activity as participants, observers and 'consumers'.

It [Sport Education] is more pupil orientated learning so they [students/ pupils] are more in charge of what they are doing in their lesson time. It gives some pupils more of a chance to appear in a team and have that team spirit because some of the less able pupils just won't get the opportunity to appear in a team environment at all. We all know what the benefits of being in a team can be.

(Trainee 1)

It gives pupils the opportunities to learn about themselves, their potential, their capabilities in an enjoyable way. It also provides increased opportunities for group work, teamwork, group cohesion. I think the most important thing is that it [Sport Education] appears enjoyable, as there is the chance to develop a real feeling of belonging in a real sense.

(Trainee 2)

Understandably, some of the training teachers remain somewhat unsure of the practicalities of achieving these outcomes of Sport Education:

I've been hearing all the theory behind this [Sport Education] but I am not quite sure in practice how this might work in a school and how kids will respond.

(Trainee 1)

Given that research has indicated that novice and inexperienced teachers will tend to use more command styles of teaching and are concerned primarily with 'survival' in the lesson and with classroom management (see for example Behets, 1990), it is not surprising that some trainees are sceptical and unsure of a curricular innovation that moves progressively to a more student-led approach. We recognise that adjustment to new pedagogical practices and relationships takes time. This is true in a teacher education context as well as a school context.

University based provision: team-taught sessions

Later within the PGCE course, team-taught lectures on Sport Education are conducted. These lectures are planned and taught in partnership with secondary teachers who are using the model in schools. The rationale, goals and features of Sport Education are revisited and an overview of research into Sport Education is provided. The progressive development of roles and responsibilities of teachers and students across a unit is discussed and teachers share the practicalities and outcomes of their development of Sport Education, to match their particular teaching context. Training teachers again responded positively and appear to gain 'a sense of what is possible and observe how the model provides a framework for individual teachers to shape and create programs that fit with each school's individual needs' (Collier, 1998: 44).

The training teachers have completed questionnaires designed to capture their perceptions of the team-taught sessions. The data arising has enabled some assessment of:

- how training teachers perceive Sport Education to be different from their physical education;
- the benefits they envisage for teachers and students;
- what they see as potential barriers to implementation of Sport Education in schools;
- how likely they are to attempt Sport Education in schools;
- the concerns or gaps in their understanding of Sport Education that they currently have.

Our experiences show that training teachers typically identify the holistic emphasis and authenticity of Sport Education (specifically the features of festivity, leagues and non-playing roles) and the greater student responsibility for learning as characteristics that distinguish Sport Education from their personal physical education experiences. Sport Education is perceived as having a number of attractions, including: teacher as a facilitator; greater student responsibility and ownership in learning; and attention being directed to issues of equity, inclusion and team membership. The routines and organisational structure of Sport Education are also recognised as likely to create greater activity time for students and reduce class management demands for the teacher (see Clarke and Quill, 2003; Kinchin, Quill and Clarke, 2002).

Importantly, the training teachers also commonly make reference to potential barriers to the successful implementation of Sport Education in schools. They recognise the potential for resistance within some physical education departments (sometimes referring to their most recent teaching placements) and the curriculum design and timetabling difficulties that may arise. For example, they query whether it will be possible to accommodate extended units. They also question whether students could manage the responsibility asked of them within Sport Education.

Many claim to see Sport Education as set to feature in their future teaching, but ask for more practical support materials and more opportunities to see Sport Education 'in action'. The training teachers have also identified the following concerns that they might have if asked to teach Sport Education during their school experience, namely:

- the impact upon student achievement;
- the impact upon their class management and control; and
- whether Sport Education could effectively serve the learning needs of more able and talented students.

These concerns highlight the need for teacher education courses to foster and sustain a climate of trust in which pedagogical creativity and experimentation in teaching are seen as entirely appropriate and legitimate activities for training teachers to engage in.

Observing Sport Education in schools

Opportunities to see Sport Education 'for real' in schools are possible for a small number of the training teachers who are fortunate enough to be placed in schools using Sport Education within their curriculum. Ideally, all trainees would have these opportunities that are undoubtedly critical in bridging the 'gap' between the 'rhetoric and reality' of Sport Education. Efforts are therefore ongoing to involve more partner schools in the development of Sport Education through continuing professional development work and through the publication and dissemination of articles about developments in university and school contexts. Encouragingly, several teachers from partner schools have requested that dedicated time be given to Sport Education as a specific aspect of their ongoing professional development. Meanwhile, some of the training teachers have provided descriptions of Sport Education in schools that have shown faith in its prospective merits:

> I was very impressed with how well it was run. The teacher almost sat back and let the pupils get on with it . . . the pupils were on task . . . the kids' motivational levels improved . . . there was very little inactivity and off-task . . . The teacher would guide them to a drill and allow them to go away and set off . . . I just thought that was a very good way of me seeing all the theory behind this working in a school environment . . . the pupils would talk a lot about the drill they were doing . . . the majority of pupils took on board other ideas . . . And with the roles, rather than just turning up and being a player, there is a purpose.
>
> (Trainee 2)

> I did have reservations at first when I was first told about it [Sport Education] . . . and then once I was exposed to more of it I really did buy into the idea. I can now definitely see the benefits. The teacher, I think his role became . . . his presence was more peripheral but that was not a negative thing . . . he was facilitating the learning experience and I think, because the pupils were not constantly being told what to do, the onus was on them . . . after five weeks they [students/pupils] were really into it . . . If everyone has a role you are almost on an even keel and your input is as much valued as the next pupil . . . there is some equality taking place there.
>
> (Trainee 1)

These training teachers were still unsure as to whether Sport Education would meet the needs of the higher ability students from a performance point of view. However, they described other ways in which they had seen such students working in teams, including leading drills, peer coaching, and providing evaluation and support to lesser ability peers. They also described their feelings and concerns before attempting to use Sport Education in schools:

> I am . . . wondering how they [students/pupils] will react. At School X their PE is quite stereotypical in the traditional way so I might find it quite hard to change their [students'/pupils'] opinions.
>
> (Trainee 2)

Even at a very early stage of development, the training teachers saw notable gains arising from the use of sustained teams, in terms of student enjoyment and cooperation in physical education:

> Participation improved throughout the unit of work with pupils earning points for taking part; this could be attributed to them not wanting to let their team down. Also another side issue was that kit was commented on to have had improved . . . Pupils seemed to enjoy the lessons as they had a goal of working towards the festival at the end of the unit of work. I noticed that during the lessons that the higher ability pupils helped the lower ability in trying to improve their skills so to improve the team.
>
> (Trainee 1, written reflection)

> Where Sport Ed. was used, all pupils were receptive to being part of a team, and were motivated by a league points system. Having experienced and observed its delivery in two different schools, I have seen varied levels of success. I think that Sport Ed. is an excellent way of delivering P.E when taught in the correct environment. I hope to use Sport Ed. in a proactive way in my NQT post.
>
> (Trainee 2, written reflection)

Extending Sport Education via continuing professional development activities

During their 12 week extended school based teaching placement, training teachers also have the opportunity to participate in continuing professional development activities, including local professional network meetings. Recently, a number of local physical education network meetings have addressed Sport Education. Having heard of developments in local schools, more teachers are interested in learning about Sport Education, what it is attempting to achieve and the experiences of those using it. Training teachers have been able to contribute to the debates, have heard other teachers speak of their efforts to develop Sport Education, and have also seen teachers teach sample lessons with Year 9 pupils.

Linking Sport Education with university assignments and projects

The PGCE course at the University of Southampton includes a 3,000 word 'Special Study' as a required component for all training teachers seeking Qualified Teacher Status. Most routes into teaching will include an opportunity for an action research or teacher evaluation project. The Special Study is a small piece of classroom based research completed by the training teachers during their extended teaching placement. Some training teachers have elected to complete their assignment with an aspect of Sport Education as the focus of their study. We therefore have emerging examples of small projects investigating roles and responsibilities, the development of team cohesion, affiliation during form tutor time, and linkages with aspects of citizenship.

Developing school based research

Interest in Sport Education at one school within the University of Southampton partnership developed following conversations between university based tutors and the head of a physical education department during visits to observe student teachers. Planning meetings then led to the development of a Sport Education pilot unit to be implemented by three members of the department. Following considerable success with the pilot work, a research agenda has been established which has included collaborative writing for publication (see Kinchin et al., 2003). The school's commitment to Sport Education from the perspective of teaching and learning is evident, with up to four training teachers per year having opportunities to spend time in the department.

The importance of partnership

The transference of Sport Education from the university to the school hinges somewhat upon the receptivity of the physical education department and sensitivity of university staff, and training teachers. Clearly, there is the scope (and in this instance definite plans) to develop school based training sites for Sport Education with sessions taught collaboratively by teachers and teacher educators. This arrangement can only benefit training teachers and strengthen the partnership between university and schools.

Given Sport Education's limited history as a curriculum and instruction model in the context of physical education in England (see Chapter 1 and Almond, 1997), it is likely many teachers involved in initial teacher training will have little if any understanding of Sport Education. Some staff within training institutions are likely to similarly lack comprehensive knowledge of Sport Education and/or have very limited experience of using it in physical education teaching. We recognise, therefore, that the need for continuing professional development is considerable and, furthermore, needs to be sustained over time. Collaborative supportive networks need to be established if the sorts of developments that we have described here are to be strengthened and also become more widespread. We believe that the risks inherent in attempting to build new professional relationships and develop new pedagogical practices are worth taking. Investments that are directed towards extending the pedagogical repertoire of the teachers of tomorrow are surely well worth making. Arguably, it is time to be promoting more 'alternative' visions and pedagogical possibilities in contexts of physical education teacher education (see also Fernandez-Balboa, 2003).

References

Alexander, K. and Luckman, J. (2001). Australian Teachers' Perceptions and Uses of the Sport Education Curriculum Model, *European Physical Education Review*, 7, 3, pp. 243–68.

Alexander, K., Taggart, A. and Medland, A. (1993). Sport Education in Physical Education: Try before You Buy, *ACHPER National Journal*, Summer, pp. 16–23.

Almond, L. (1997). *Physical Education in Schools* (2nd edn), London: Kogan Page.

Armour, K. and Yelling, M. (2004). Continuing Professional Development for Experienced Physical Education Teachers: Towards Effective Provision, *Sport, Education and Society*, 9, 1, pp. 95–114.

Behets, D. (1990). Concerns of Pre-service Physical Education Teachers, *Journal of Teaching in Physical Education*, 10, pp. 66–75.

Bennett, G. (2000). Sport Education as an Alternative for the Basic Instruction Program, *Chronicle of Physical Education in Higher Education*, 11, 3, pp. 3, 9–11.

Bennett, G. and Hastie, P. (1997). The Implementation of the Sport Education Curriculum Model into a Collegiate Physical Activity Course, *Journal of Physical Education, Recreation and Dance*, 68, 1, pp. 39–44.

Clarke, G. and Quill, A. (2003). Researching Sport Education in Action: A Case Study, *European Physical Education Review*, 9, 3, pp. 253–66.

Collier, C. (1998). Sport Education and Preservice Education, *Journal of Physical Education, Recreation and Dance*, 69, 5, pp. 44–5.

Fernandez-Balboa, J. M. (2003). Physical Education in the Digital (Postmodern) Era, in A. Laker (ed.), *The Future of Physical Education: Building a New Pedagogy*, London: Routledge.

Kinchin, G. D. (1999). Implementing Seasons of Sport Education into One PETE Institution: What Do the Participants Tell Us?, Paper presented at the *National Association for Sport and Physical Education Conference on Physical Education: Exemplary Practice in Teacher Education*, Bloomingdale, Illinois, October 1999.

Kinchin, G. D. (2000). Tackling Social Issues in Physical Education Class: What about Journal Writing?, *Strategies*, 13, 5, pp. 22–5.

Kinchin, G. D., Quill, M. and Clarke, G. (2002). Focus on Sport Education in Action, *British Journal of Teaching PE*, 33, 1, pp. 10–12.

Kinchin, G. D., Roderick, S., Wardle, C. and Sprosen, A. (2003). An Interview with Sport Educators, *PE and Sport Today*, 11, pp. 52–4.

Laker, A. (2003). The Future of Physical Education: Is This a 'New Pedagogy'?, in A. Laker (ed.), *The Future of Physical Education: Building a New Pedagogy*, London: Routledge.

Medland, A., Alexander, K., Taggart, A and Thorpe, S. (1994). *Sport Education in Physical Education (SEPEP): Introducing the Findings from the 1994 National SEPEP Trials, Executive Summary*, Perth, Western Australia: Sport and Physical Activity Research Centre, Edith Cowan University.

Placek, J. H., Dodds, P., Doolittle, S. A., Portman, P. A., Ratcliffe, T. A. and Pinkham, K. M. (1995). Teaching Recruits' Physical Education Backgrounds and their Beliefs about Purposes for their Subject Matter, *Journal of Teaching in Physical Education*, 14, pp. 246–61.

Siedentop, D. and Locke, L. (1997). Making a Difference for Physical Education: What Professors and Practitioners Must Build Together, *Journal of Physical Education, Recreation and Dance*, 68, 4, pp. 25–33.

Taggart, A., Browne, T. and Alexander, K. (1995). Three Schools' Approaches to Assessment in Sport Education, *Australian Council for Health, Physical Education and Recreation (ACHPER) Healthy Lifestyles Journal*, 42, 4, pp. 12–15.

16 New relationships, new futures

Dawn Penney and Gill Clarke

Introduction

The research reported in this book and described in preceding chapters has advanced understanding of the potential development of Sport Education in physical education, particularly in England and Wales. It has provided important insights into ways in which research *can* be an integral element of curriculum development at the 'chalk face' in schools. It has shown that university based researchers *can* work alongside and in real partnership with teachers, and that teachers *can* themselves establish an identity and role as researchers. Significantly it has also directly confronted ways in which the 'rhetoric' of curriculum development potential *can* be advanced in practice, with pragmatic issues not merely acknowledged in a superficial manner, but established as critical and ongoing points of reference in development initiatives. Finally, it has given important credibility to the notion that, in looking to the future, we should not only be envisaging practice as informed by policy developments, but also be looking to the scope for *practice-led* policy developments.

This chapter thus focuses upon a number of issues that have been central in the research and curriculum developments that have been reported in this book. The issues are all characterised by a relational focus:

- policy and practice in physical education;
- research and curriculum development;
- teachers and researchers;
- Sport Education and physical education;
- the potential and pragmatics of 'real change' in physical education.

In discussing each issue we draw attention to the advances towards new 'connections' and productive relationships that we contend have been made in and through our collaborative work with teachers developing Sport Education in physical education. Our focus is on moves that we hope will help to counter past tendencies to view each of the issues in dichotomous terms.

The chapter therefore aims to capture notable achievements made in the course of the research and curriculum activities that inspired this book. But at the same time, it seeks to direct attention to issues that undoubtedly need to be a focus for further research and development in physical education. We certainly do not intend to imply that we have found solutions to longstanding points of tension. Rather, we aim to encourage positive engagement with acknowledged tensions, and the generation of more examples of ways of alleviating tensions to the benefit of all involved.

Policy and practice in physical education

Throughout this book and indeed throughout the research undertaken and ongoing with teachers, we have made a conscious effort to make explicit connections to policy developments emanating from central government. We have emphasised compatibility between the prospective development of Sport Education in physical education and current political visions for physical education and sport in schools, and education more broadly. Arguably we have presented a strong case for Sport Education to be adopted as a key means of fulfilling established requirements and advancing stated visions.

We hope, however, that we have not generated images of teachers (and their university based colleagues) as *passive* respondents to policy developments. We have emphasised the ongoing need for critical, informed engagement with contemporary policy developments and, furthermore, claims about Sport Education's potential merits as a curriculum and pedagogical framework. We have adopted and sought to promote a questioning stance in relation to these merits and, similarly, readings of policies. As discussed in Chapter 1, we embarked upon the collaborative research with specific interests for future developments in physical education. With teachers we have explored ways in which Sport Education, when adopted and developed in particular ways, can provide a basis for those interests (particularly in equity and inclusion) being realised in the practices of physical education and experiences of young people. Thus, we contend that the teachers involved have been anything but passive implementers of policy requirements and political visions. Rather, teachers have very clearly established and been pursuing *their* visions for Sport Education and physical education *in their schools'* and *for their students' education and lives beyond school.* Those visions have been informed by and sensitive to government policy initiatives, but they have not been totally defined or fully shaped by external agendas. In saying this we are not implying any inefficiency in 'implementation' or suggesting that there has been deviation from an expected line of response. Rather, we highlight the flaws inherent in talk of 'implementation', that invariably denies exactly the curriculum and pedagogical creativity that we should be celebrating and promoting as innovative and appropriately responsive to individual contexts.

The chapters in Part 3 thus need to be recognised as providing important support for an emphasis of curriculum 'making' as an ongoing process and, furthermore, of teachers as innovative professionals in that process. The developments reported in schools should be held up as positive reference points for other teachers contemplating new curriculum developments in physical education. But arguably, the recognition and prospective 'use' of the developments need to go further. The practices in these schools are surely also of the sort that should be of interest to individuals in positions of influence in relation to future policy development. Thus, our contention is that the sort of sustained collaborative work reported in this book should be seen as a sound foundation for '*practice-led policy*' that utilises the considerable, yet too often marginalised, skills of teachers as innovators in curriculum development.

Research and curriculum development

The relationship between research and curriculum development is one that is much talked about, but all too frequently in terms that reaffirm that we are dealing with two distinct things here. Research is referred to as potentially being undertaken in response to curriculum development, as capable of generating findings that can inform curriculum development and/or as being carried out in parallel with curriculum development. While a close relationship may be portrayed and advocated, commentaries continue to fall short of clearly deconstructing the historical divide between research and curriculum development. There is a subtle yet very significant difference between activities occurring simultaneously and them being reconfigured into a process in which it is impossible to any longer draw a distinction between 'research' and 'curriculum development'. In our ongoing work with teachers we have endeavoured to move towards a situation in which we can claim that this subtle step has been taken. As we discussed in Chapter 2, making this step demands some shifts in thinking about 'research': when it is done, by whom and in what ways. But equally, it demands a rethinking of 'curriculum development' such that it becomes recognised as necessarily 'evidence based'.

The chapters within Part 3 of this book provide descriptions of collaborative research based curriculum development. As such they represent important examples of ways in which research can be *integral to* curriculum developments in schools. Significantly the 'research based curriculum development process' is seen as a *single* process, centring on teaching and learning. Cues for adjustments to the focus and direction of curriculum, pedagogical and research activities are internally generated, from data gathered in the course of everyday professional activities. Teachers are not merely acting as researchers on specified occasions, but rather have reconfigured their professional role to that of 'teacher-researcher'. Before discussing that role, it is worth reflecting that there are important and outstanding limits to the research–curriculum development linkage that we have endeavoured to foster here. Our focus has been upon schools and teaching and learning within them. We have acknowledged but not attempted to engage with the influence of 'other agencies' upon the directions and boundaries for developments within schools. While we are anxious to promote a view of curriculum 'making' as the core business of teachers, we nevertheless acknowledge that this 'making' is within particular conditions and constraints. We therefore recognise a need to be seeking to embed research into the 'curriculum development' that is undertaken in these 'other arenas', not only in schools. In 1994 Hammersley made the observation that the Education Reform Act of 1988:

> certainly throws substantial doubt on the well-foundedness of any optimism researchers may have had about the influence of their work on national policy making in education. It is not just that educational research played little or no role in shaping the Act, but even more that in many respects the legislation goes in opposite directions to those indicated by its findings.
>
> (p. 139)

Nationally and locally, there is a strong case for energies to be directed towards the development of collaborative research based curriculum development processes within government and curriculum agency/authority arenas. The challenge is for the research–curriculum development integration to be established and visible across the many sites and phases of development. We do not delude ourselves that this will be easy to achieve. As others have identified, in some arenas there will be firm interests in retaining precisely the boundaries and divisions (between research and curriculum development, researchers and teachers) that we contend should be de-constructed (see for example Ozga, 2000).

Teachers and researchers

Simply stated, here we are promoting a move from thinking of teaching and research as two distinct roles (and often involving two individuals), to the development of a new professional role and identity, as 'teacher-researcher'. 'Research' as it is typically envisaged by teachers has little appeal for many. The very word 'research' invariably generates perceptions of an additional, demanding activity, requiring notably different skills and knowledge to those that are central to quality teaching and curriculum development at the 'grass roots' level. It may well be seen as likely to detract from teaching and learning time and be an unnecessary complication amidst already very busy professional lives. Questions may also be lingering about the purpose of the proposed research. What and whom exactly is all this for and, specifically, what will be the benefits for the teachers and students involved? Can we really justify the time and energy that are to be invested in the research?

Our view has always been that teachers are right to be posing these questions of research and researchers. As university based researchers, we have much to learn about how to undertake research *with* teachers in the pursuit of improvements in teaching and learning in their schools. As we discussed in Chapter 2, that learning is ongoing. The accounts of research that we have provided in this book confirm that the process has been productive for all involved. Significantly, we have seen how teachers' attitudes towards research and the role of teacher-researcher have become progressively more positive. As with any new professional role, it needs to be recognised as one that *with good support and guidance*, and *dedicated time*, can be successfully taken on. Opportunities to meet with university and school colleagues to discuss issues arising, express concerns and share ideas about how to proceed have been invaluable for teacher-researchers to become confident in their role and take greater ownership of research agendas and activities. This has been the case in the research reported here but also in other school based teacher-research projects (Penney *et al.*, 2003; Penney and Harris, 2003).

While universities may be regarded as having 'research expertise', university based researchers should not be seen as the only possible source of support for teacher-researchers. Having a fellow teacher-researcher to share the dilemmas and raise issues with can be helpful and reassuring. Messages that teacher-research is possible and, furthermore, worthwhile and rewarding have far greater credibility when they come from a teacher-researcher who has 'been there and actually done it'. Hence, we see a need for investment to support the professional growth of teacher-researchers such that they can take on a mentorship role within their schools and wider professional networks and communities. In addition, we suggest that there is a need for greater encouragement and support for teachers to report the findings of the research that they have come to lead and shape. Credibility with professional audiences is again an important consideration, but perhaps more importantly we need to be addressing ethics and equity in research. Specifically we should be ensuring that, whenever possible, teacher-researchers are the key figures in reporting and disseminating research plans, progress, experiences and findings.

Another area in which we see teacher-researchers as the individuals who are best placed to achieve advances is that of involving students more actively and centrally in research in schools. Teachers are the people building learning relationships with students on a daily basis. The challenge is now to embed research roles and responsibilities into those relationships and establish systems to support students taking on the new roles and responsibilities. As we reaffirm below, none of this is easy, nor will it be instantly achieved. But that is not to say that it cannot be done, or should not be attempted. The process of taking the risk, trying new activities and approaches with students and, quite likely, seeing their positive reactions and responses can be highly rewarding. Encouragingly, there are success stories that reaffirm the interest, skills and initiative that students can show and develop as researchers (Fitzgerald, Jobling and Kirk, 2003). Yet, we need to retain a critical awareness and particularly be reflecting upon whose agendas students will pursue and, furthermore, the issues that they might (or not) feel able to pursue as student-researchers, and the sorts of research relationships that they are able to build with peers and teachers. In considering these matters it is crucial that power-relationships are acknowledged in research. As Colley's (2001) work on mentoring has demonstrated, there will be a need to consider not only how we are positioning students, but also how they are positioning themselves.

Sport Education and physical education

From the outset, we have stressed that we were not looking to Sport Education as an alternative to physical education. Rather, we have been exploring it in relation to its potential to strengthen and advance pedagogical practices, student experiences and achievements in physical education. We maintain that stance and, further, our accompanying belief that in and of itself Sport Education guarantees nothing in relation to these desired advancements. The developments that we have discussed in this book give considerable support to an emphasis upon the compatibility of Sport Education and contemporary physical education. They suggest a host of possibilities in relation to the prospective development of Sport Education in physical education and particularly in schools in England. Yet we are then left in a position whereby questions that are being posed in relation to physical education need to similarly be asked of Sport Education. Indeed, we need to ask specifically, amidst the myriad of outcomes that Sport Education may be linked to, which can it justifiably be claiming to address and progress students towards? Which is it best suited to address? With Sport Education as physical education, it is easy to talk of links to multiple outcomes. Yet there is a real need to be clear about precisely what we are aiming to achieve in and through the adoption of Sport Education and to then monitor the extent to which we are succeeding in doing so. Teaching and learning priorities will vary. The point here is not that there is *one* legitimate focus in Sport Education, but rather that *a* clear focus should be established from the outset and be apparent in the ensuing Sport Education units, lessons and assessment tasks that are developed. Siedentop and Tannehill (2000) have suggested that the 'principle' needing to be embedded in physical education curriculum design is that 'less is more' (p. 135). The same could be said of Sport Education. Peter Hastie (2003) recently expressed the view that, 'Because of its flexibility, the future of sport education is particularly bright . . . [it] can fit comfortably as part of a well-rounded physical education curriculum' (Hastie, 2003: 133). We similarly stress that Sport Education needs to be acknowledged as a part of physical education, but also that those involved in its development need to be discussing the specific learning outcomes to be addressed in this part of the curriculum.

There is a strong case for Sport Education to be positioned as a key framework and approach via which to address the social goals of physical education and to thereby achieve the 'synergy between the learning goals and social goals of physical education' that Siedentop and Tannehill (2000: 106) have identified as needed. However, as emphasised previously, learning relating to social goals will only be achieved if it is established as an explicit focus in curriculum planning and teaching.

> Everybody who has spent time in physical education classes or on playgrounds observing children and youth in activity understands that students can and do disadvantage and abuse one another and that groups of students are stereotyped and often ostracised from a fair opportunity to participate. The predictable result is student alienation from physical education as a school subject and, subsequently, from a physically active lifestyle.
>
> (Siedentop and Tannehill, 2000: 107)

Throughout our research and also in writing this book we have drawn attention to the potential role that Sport Education may play in advancing equity and inclusion in physical education. In Sport Education as in any part of physical education, it takes strategic and sensitive actions on the part of both teachers and students to achieve greater equity and inclusion. As Hastie (2003) has observed, we do not yet know enough about this or indeed many other aspects of Sport Education *as experienced by students*.

> We still need to know considerably more about skill development during seasons of sport education . . . we need more understanding about how student coaches operate within their teams . . . student coaches are not the expert instructors that most teachers are. We do, however, need to understand if there are ways in which we can assist peer coaches develop more systematic skills for improving the performances of their team-mates.
>
> We also know nothing about the teaching strategy by peer coaches . . . We also do not know the effects of long-term participation in sport education. We have no longitudinal data about those students who have played in multiple seasons or years in sport education. First, we might ask whether the novelty of the system of taking roles and being on consistent teams wears off after a certain period. More important, however, would be to gauge the extent to which students are beginning to realise those long-terms goals of sport education. Are they indeed participating and behaving in ways that preserve, protect, and enhance sporting cultures, whether it is a local youth sport culture or a national culture? Perhaps the best yardstick would be to measure how many

students decide voluntarily to become involved in sport after-school and outside of school.

(Hastie, 2003: 132)

Thus, there is much more we need to know about Sport Education in physical education. The developments reported in this book have provided some important further insights into the issues identified by Hastie (2003), but the need for sustained research is very apparent.

Hastie's final point also directs us to the need to consider the role of Sport Education in advancing lifelong physical education goals. As we discussed in Chapter 7, as an organisational and pedagogical framework, Sport Education may offer a key means of cementing linkages between the physical education curriculum and participation in physical activity and sport outside of the curriculum. Development work in 'other arenas' (community and club) and 'with (external) partners' undoubtedly presents challenges of a different order to curriculum based initiatives. Yet there seems an urgent need for more people to be venturing into these still largely uncharted waters.

The potential and pragmatics of 'real change' in physical education

Invariably exploration of new initiatives in education reveals that there is by and large always an appealing rhetoric that promises much, while accompanying reports of the realities of schools' and teachers' efforts to take initiatives forward often paint a somewhat different picture. Throughout this book we have been open in stressing the positive potential that we see in Sport Education. But our research and writing has also endeavoured to fully engage with the practicalities of attempting to realise that potential. The flexibility that is associated with Sport Education is certainly important in this regard. It legitimates an approach to development in which discourses of pragmatism are privileged rather than subordinated. The emphasis can justifiably be upon adaptation of Sport Education as it is described in texts, to better suit specific circumstances, teachers, learners and the human and physical resources available. Teachers are justified in using their professional judgement in considering which particular aspects of the considerable potential it is realistic and appropriate to seek to realise in their specific context. With this approach it seems far more likely that teachers will develop a genuine sense of ownership of the initiative and that, therefore, foundations will be established for something more than superficial change in physical education. Yet at the same time we remain very aware that promoting adaptation and emphasising flexibility may result in exactly that: superficial rather than any 'real' change in thinking and pedagogical practices. The sort of change that Sparkes (1991) characterised as 'real' change takes time and requires sustained professional support. These are practical issues that are key to realising the potential of Sport Education in physical education and which require confrontation.

Once again, however, we return to the matters of 'rhetoric and reality'. It is all too easy to talk of developing supportive professional networks or 'learning communities'. The reality is that it is far more difficult to establish structures and relationships that really prove themselves to be supportive in a meaningful sense for those involved at the times when they may be struggling to see a way forward, are desperate to discuss dilemmas that they are experiencing or, conversely, want to share a success story. As Siedentop and Tannehill (2000) have pointed out:

> Learning communities are not gimmicks, nor are they an educational fad. You can't just decide one day that learning communities sound like a good thing and expect to develop one the next week. Learning communities have specific characteristics that take time and effort to develop. Learning communities are bounded environments that persist over time. Members share important common goals, and they cooperate to achieve those goals.
>
> (p. 98)

Discussing and furthermore negotiating those common goals is therefore essential. In this regard it is notable that Flintoff (2003) has stressed that partnerships or alliances that involve sporting agencies or organisations need to retain an *educational* perspective. While seeking this, there is nevertheless a need to acknowledge that establishing a shared vision demands negotiation in which compromises have to be made in order to reach a point of compatibility of perspectives. Sport Education may yet prove key to achieving such compatibility in the context of partnership initiatives between educational and sport organisations.

Finally, a further practical point to make is that it is certainly naïve to expect instant success or total acceptance of proposals for the development of Sport Education in the 'principled' way that we have advocated (see Chapter 1 and Part 2). We see positive potential but not all will share in that vision nor necessarily feel inclined or in a position to pursue it. Teachers may face a very similar situation with their students. Resistance or even open opposition from some needs to be expected, worked through and seen as an entirely legitimate part of the development process (Kinchin and O'Sullivan, 2003). Some will 'come around' and maybe even become unexpected enthusiastic advocates of an initiative that they first seemed sceptical about. Different reactions are entirely understandable when we consider that physical education remains a contested curriculum and pedagogical terrain. Indeed, Laker (2003) recently commented that, internationally, 'Debates are continuing about what should constitute physical education, who should decide the content, how it should be delivered and what elements are important to the well-being of the youth of our nations' (p. 153). The place, purpose and prospective merits of Sport Education in physical education are important considerations in such debates. Fernandez-Balboa (2003) has pointed out that 'new times demand new forms of teaching and learning' (p. 139). We believe that significant advances can be made in teaching and learning in physical education through the development of Sport Education, and that it can be developed in ways that suit 'new times', new teaching and learning needs and expectations. Yet we remain acutely aware of the skills, energy, enthusiasm, commitment and support that are required for successful development that will also be sustainable.

Conclusion

Concluding this chapter and furthermore this book, it is perhaps appropriate to mix optimism with some potentially harsh realities. In the years that it has taken to advance the research that we have reported and to bring commentaries on it together, we have seen what can only be described as inspiring professional advances. These are continuing and not only in the schools that have featured in this book. Interest in Sport Education in physical education is growing rapidly in England. Our hope is that the interest will lead to adoption not merely of attractive new rhetoric, but of the sound pedagogical principles that we stressed in Chapter 1. In addition we hope that the interest will not only be in Sport Education, but also in the kinds of research that we have developed with teachers and described in this book.

References

Colley, H. (2001). Understanding Experiences of Engagement Mentoring for 'Disaffected' Young People and their Student Mentors: Problems of Data Analysis in Qualitative Research, Paper presented at the *British Educational Research Association Conference*, University of Leeds, 13–15 September.

Fernandez-Balboa, J.-M. (2003). Physical Education in the Digital (Postmodern) Era, in A. Laker (ed.), *The Future of Physical Education: Building a New Pedagogy*, London: Routledge.

Fitzgerald, H., Jobling, A. and Kirk, D. (2003). Valuing the Voices of Young Disabled People: Exploring Experiences of Physical Education and Sport, *European Journal of Physical Education*, 8, 2, pp. 141–59.

Flintoff, A. (2003). The School Sport Co-ordinator Programme: Changing the Role of the Physical Education Teacher?, *Sport Education and Society*, 8, 2, pp. 231–50.

Hammersley, M. (1994). Ethnography, Policy Making and Practice in Education, in D. Halpin and B. Troyna (eds), *Researching Education Policy: Ethical and Methodological Issues*, London: Falmer Press.

Hastie, P. (2003). Sport Education, in A. Laker (ed.), *The Future of Physical Education: Building a New Pedagogy*, London: Routledge.

Kinchin, G. D. and O'Sullivan, M. (2003). Incidences of Student Support for and Resistance to a Curricular Innovation in High School Physical Education, *Journal of Teaching in Physical Education*, 22, pp. 245–60.

Laker, A. (2003). The Future of Physical Education: Is This the New Pedagogy?, in A. Laker (ed.), *The Future of Physical Education: Building a New Pedagogy*, London: Routledge.

Ozga, J. (2000). *Policy Research in Educational Settings: Contested Terrain*, Buckingham: Open University Press.

Penney, D. and Harris, J. (2003). BPRS Teachers Researching the Impact of TOP Skill, *British Journal of Teaching Physical Education*, 34, 4, pp. 26–30.

Penney, D., Hill, K. and Evans, P. (2003). Integrating Research and Curriculum Development: Progress through Partnership, *British Journal of Teaching Physical Education*, 34, 2, pp. 39–43.

Siedentop, D. and Tannehill, D. (2000). *Developing Teaching Skills in Physical Education* (4th edn), London: Mayfield Publishing Company.

Sparkes, A. C. (1991). Curriculum Change: On Gaining a Sense of Perspective, in N. Armstrong and A. Sparkes (eds), *Issues in Physical Education*, London: Cassell Education.

Index

literacy: and Sport Education 74–80, 83, 129, 147, 149, 156

mathematics *see* numeracy

National Curriculum: citizenship 17, 19, 39, 81, 84–5, 87; foundation stage 113–15; key stages 6, 15, 16, 55, 56, 57; PSHE 87; revision of 14, 18, 41
National Curriculum: Physical Education 14, 15, 55, 71, 141; activities 9,15, 16, 206; aspects 15, 16, 17, 63, 146, 147, 176, 177; athletic activities 9, 16, 176; games 9, 16, 123; gymnastic activities 9, 16, 165; requirements 15, 16, 17, 101, 11, 112, 176, 182, 203; in Wales 15, 16, 71, 72
netball: in Sport Education 90, 151, 158–9
numeracy: and Sport Education 76–7, 80, 129, 147, 149, 156

opportunity and excellence *see* 'The 14–19 strategy'
outdoor and adventurous activities: in Sport Education 188, 206–13

Personal, Social and Health Education (PSHE): in the National Curriculum 87; in Sport Education 79, 85, 87, 92
Physical Education, School Sport and Club Links (PESSCL) 103–4, 187
Playing for Success 106

research 26–35, 46, 105, 112, 222, 226, 231–4; ethics 30–2
roles *see* Sport Education, roles

School Sport Coordinators 103, 105
Seasons *see* Sport Education, season(s)
Siedentop, D. 3, 5, 6, 8–10, 17–18, 39, 46, 51, 53, 67, 77, 93, 99, 100, 109, 116–17, 217–18, 234–5, 237
Soccer: in Sport Education 51, 61, 83, 98, 149, 152, 160, 162
Special Educational Needs (SEN): in Sport Education 198

Specialist Sports College 103, 188, 204, 206–7
sports day *see* Sport Education, festival
Sport Education: ability 10, 46, 51, 91, 153, 178, 166, 178, 180, 198; absenteeism 150, 168, 179, 202; authenticity 13, 59, 62, 84, 87, 106, 182, 201; boys 10, 50–1, 61, 92, 166, 170–1, 177–8, 190; community-based activities 12, 105, 206, 211–2; characteristics 6,7, 42; competition(s) 7, 8, 52, 125, 130–1, 148, 153, 179, 181, 192, 197, 199, 200, 202, 210; festival 6–8, 78–80, 106, 109, 124, 125, 131, 146–7, 149, 154, 167, 169, 170–1, 178–9, 181, 192, 201, 212, 225; girls 10, 49–51, 62, 92, 166, 170–1, 177–8, 180; extra-curricular activities 103, 105, 106; in primary schools 10, 77, 81, 112, 122–39; responsibilities in 7, 10–12, 52, 81, 88–90, 94, 102, 106, 114, 117, 134, 150–1, 169, 180, 182, 187, 193–4, 198, 201, 210–11, 221; roles 7, 10, 47, 49–50, 64, 74, 76–81, 89–90, 106–7, 118–19, 125, 128, 131–2, 135, 139, 145–6, 148, 150–2, 155, 166, 169, 171, 178, 180, 187, 193–7, 199, 202, 204, 206, 210, 221; routines 116, 177; season(s) 6, 8, 11, 46, 81, 93, 125, 145, 147–8, 166, 168, 175, 179, 187–8, 190–2, 194–6, 202–4, 221; teacher education 217–28; teams 6, 10, 47–9, 63–4, 77–81, 90, 92, 94, 100–1, 106, 109, 116–18, 124, 127–8, 131–2, 135, 145, 148–9, 151, 155, 160–4, 166, 168–9, 171, 173–4, 178, 180, 193, 196
Sport for Peace 12, 51, 52
Standard Assessment Tests (SATs) 42
Step into Sport 85, 104
swimming: in Sport Education 187–205

teachers as researchers 23, 26–8, 31–2, 231–4
TPSR (Teaching of Personal and Social Responsibility) 11–12